The History of
PIONEER
LEXINGTON
1779-1806

| 112 | 111 | 110 | 109 | | 108 | 107 | 106 | 105 | | 104 | 103 | 102 | 101 | 100 | 99 | 98 |

SEVENTH STREET

| 83 | 84 | 85 | 86 | | 87 | 88 | 89 | 90 | | 91 | 92 | 93 | 94 | 95 | 96 | 97 |

SIXTH STREET

| 68 | 69 | 70 | 71 | | 72 | 73 | 74 | 75 | | 76 | 77 | 78 | 79 | 80 | 81 | 82 |

FIFTH STREET

| 67 | 66 | 65 | 64 | | 63 | 62 | 61 | 60 | | 59 | 58 | 57 | 56 | 55 | 54 | 53 |

19 X 45 POLES

FOURTH STREET

| 39 | 38 | 37 | 36 | | 35 | 34 | 33 | 32 | | 31 | 30 | 29 | 28 | 27 | 26 | 25 | 24 |

17½ X 45 POLES   17½ X 45 POLES

THIRD STREET

| 1 | 2 | 3 | 4 | | 5 | 6 | 7 | 8 |

17½ X 40 POLES

| 9 |
| 15 |
| 47 |

| 10 |
| 40 |
| 46 |

| 11 |
| 41 |
| 45 |

SECOND STREET

| A | B | C | D | | E | F | G | H |

17½ X 40 POLES

MULBERRY STREET

| 12 |
| 44 |

CROSS STREET

| 13 |
| 21 | 22 | 23 |
| 43 |

15 X 45 POLES

WALNUT STREET   BACK STREET

| 14 |
| 42 |

SHORT STREET

STREET

GRAVE YARD   23 22 21 20   19 18 17 16   15 14 13 12 11

10 9 8 7 6   PUBLIC SQUARE   1 2 3 4 5

MAIN STREET

LOCUST STREET   24 25 26 27 28   29 30 31 32 33 34   SPRING STREET 35 36 37 38 39

40 41 42 43 44   45 46 47 48 49 50   MILL STREET   51 52 53 54 55

COMMONS OR WATER STREET

87 86 85 84 83   LOWER STREET 82 81 80 79 77   76 75 74 73 72

71 70 69 68 67   66 65 64 63 62 61   60 59 58 57 56

| 16 | 17 | 18 | 19 | 20 | 50 | 51 |

19½ X 36 POLES

HIGH STREET

S 45° E ~ 115 POLES

| W | V | U | T | S | R | | Q | P | O | N | M | L | K | J |

11⅗ X 51 POLES

N 45° E ~ 54 POLES

S 45° E ~ 170 POLES

THE TOWN BOUNDS OF LEXINGTON ~ 1791

The History of
PIONEER
LEXINGTON
1779-1806

CHARLES R. STAPLES

Foreword by
Thomas D. Clark

THE UNIVERSITY PRESS OF KENTUCKY

Publication of this volume was made possible in part by grants from
The Thomas D. Clark Foundation,
the Lexington-Fayette County Historic Commission, and
the Lexington Historical Publishing Corporation.

Frontispiece: The Town Bounds of Lexington, 1791

Scholarly publisher for the Commonwealth,
serving Bellarmine College, Berea College, Centre
College of Kentucky, Eastern Kentucky University,
The Filson Club, Georgetown College, Kentucky
Historical Society, Kentucky State University,
Morehead State University, Murray State University,
Northern Kentucky University, Transylvania University,
University of Kentucky, University of Louisville,
and Western Kentucky University.

Editorial and Sales Offices: The University Press of Kentucky
663 South Limestone Street, Lexington, Kentucky 40508-4008

Library of Congress Cataloging-in-Publication Data
Staples, Charles R. (Charles Richard), 1875-
  The history of pioneer Lexington, 1779-1806 / Charles R.
Staples ; foreword by Thomas D. Clark.
      p.   cm.
  Includes index.
  ISBN 0-8131-1913-8 (cloth : alk. paper)
  1. Lexington (Ky.)—History. 2. Frontier and pioneer life—
Kentucky—Lexington. 3. Lexington (Ky.)—Social life and customs.
I. Title
F459.L6S83   1996
976.9'47—dc20   96-19041

This book is printed on acid-free recycled paper meeting
the requirements of the American National Standard
for Permanence of Paper for Printed Library Materials.

Manufactured in the United States of America

CONTENTS

Illustrations follow page 46

FOREWORD

This history of pioneer Lexington, Kentucky, is the result of years of research by Charles Richard Staples. The book is, in fact, the offspring of a long and devoted love affair between a man and his town. Throughout his life the author cherished his Lexington birth, and through his research he vicariously experienced the seminal years when the first settlers felled the trees and cut back the cane to clear their way through the Bluegrass wilderness. No less than the initial explorers of the site of the original fort and cabins, Staples loved even the name of Lexington, inspired by the opening battle of the War for Independence.

The circular Lexington fort was located on the bank of the Town Fork of the sprawling Elkhorn Creek system. Built as a haven of safety from Indian attacks, the stockade was never tested by a major assault. Lexington's fort period was brief, and few other towns on the western frontier emerged as rapidly from primitive beginnings. The span of time from the construction of the fort and of Robert Patterson's one room log cabin to the laying out of town lots and streets was remarkably short. This low-lying spot along a stream prone to flooding was to become a vital focal point for the western movement in America. Lexington's pioneer history differed little from that of other western urban places, except that the fort was located in the middle of a highly fertile and productive agrarian-pastoral eden. It probably was a miracle of history as well as geography that Lexington thrived as completely as it did so far from a river in the age when flatboat trade was at its height. One explanation for the town's survival was surely contained in the numerous advertisements for pack horse trains and for sturdy boatmen who could endure grueling journeys downstream to New Orleans.

In the history of Kentucky, however, Lexington was vitally important in the fields of population concentration, commerce, and social development. When the Virginia General Assembly was petitioned in 1779 for a charter and a grant of land on which to build a town, it is doubtful if any member of that body had any concept of conditions in the western country. The Assembly approved a grant of 640 acres—a square mile—plus seventy more acres.

Lexington's political organization began in late January 1780. As the original endpapers to Staples's book indicate, the site was laid out in a precise geometrical pattern of eighty-seven "in-lots" along a commons on Water Street, and 112 "out-lots" within a dissecting grid of streets. The town, however, was located along a directional diagonal. A mayor–town council form of government ruled the town, and within this municipal plan the Fayette County Courthouse and square became the key central spot. The Fayette County government had become functional before the town of Lexington was organized. In time the courthouse saw the rise of a remarkably able assembly of lawyers who not only played leading roles in legal affairs, but also were to become major political leaders in the future Commonwealth.

Up front in the panorama of the rise of Lexington was a veritable galaxy of personalities, ranging from editor John Bradford, entrepreneur John Morrison, pioneer settler Robert Patterson, and lawyer-politician Henry Clay to the town vagrant and drunkard, John Shaw the "Well Digger." After 1787 the town was home to the first newspaper published south of Pittsburgh and the first printing plant capable of producing slender books and the Acts of the Kentucky General Assembly. Here Samuel Ayres practiced the trade of silversmith, Luke Usher operated a brewery, and Jacob Boshart ran a blue dying shop. Periodically two or three of the main merchants published rather extensive lists of merchandise that had just arrived from Philadelphia or Baltimore. During the decade of the 1790s, merchants advertised an amazing assortment of merchandise, and tradesmen offered a multiplicity of services. These so intrigued Charles Staples that he spoke of them as if they were still operating along Main Street.

So immersed did Charlie Staples become in his search for facts that he developed vicarious speaking acquaintances with most of Lexington's early personalities. At times during conversations his contemporary listeners were confused as to whether he spoke of someone then living in the town or someone who had lived there more than a century and a half earlier. He spoke of Robert Patterson, John Bradford, Alexander McConnell, Henry Clay, and Levi Todd as if he had just stopped and chatted with them at Main and Mill Streets. He knew well the locations of their businesses and offices, where in the out-lot grid they lived, and who was suing whom over a bad debt or an overlapping land claim. It almost seemed as though Staples had been on hand at Postlethwait's Tavern to greet the foreign travelers who came by stage coach down the Limestone-Lexington Road.

Charles R. Staples earned his livelihood as a safety inspector for the Southern Railway System, an occupation far removed from his calling toward historical research. The job did afford him considerable leisure time to search through ancient court records and newspaper files. Although he had no formal background in the study of history or in the arts of research and writing, he had a native instinct for fact finding and the documentary importance of data. Staples was almost as much a presence in the Fayette County Courthouse, the Lexington City Hall, and the public library as were the people paid to work in those places, and he was much better informed than many of them. It is difficult to imagine a page of the *Kentucky Gazette* he did not peruse, or a long forgotten bundle of court papers he did not dust off, untie, and read in his search for nuggets of information about the early town and its citizens. Few members of the Fayette bar were as familiar with the contents of the court order books, deeds, and wills as was Staples. He had a natural genius for ferreting out and collecting pertinent bits of local historical data. Above all, Staples had an elephantine memory; he was literally a walking source of encyclopedic information about his town.

Perhaps it is not uncharitable to suggest that he lacked complete competence to write a book of a finished scholarly character. His focus was purely upon facts, not style. To Staples, recording the founding and progress of frontier Lexington was a factual end within itself. He knew nothing of scholarly frontier theories, and he would have viewed them largely as intellectual bubbles. Though making no claim to literary form and polish, the author developed an astonishingly clear narrative detailing events, personalities, town government, the operation of mercantile establishments, and institutional developments. Running throughout *The History of Pioneer Lexington* is a keen sense of the rapidity with which Lexington emerged from the pioneer chrysalis stage into a rapidly maturing center of commerce, culture, and professional services. The town

early became the eye of the social and economic centrifu-
gal forces that were energized by an inflow of population
during the latter two decades of the eighteenth century.

The Lexington of the past, as in the present, existed
paradoxically within the tight bonds of a self-satisfied in-
ertia and provincialism, yet it achieved a near state of so-
phisticated universality. From early years it was a point of
visitation for that endless procession of foreign visitors who
came on the "grand tour" to view the western country. From
the outset Lexington gave considerable promise of becoming a center of cultural and intellectual refinement, but it
could never really stifle the deterrent forces of provincial-
ity and religious bigotry.

No other document depositories in Kentucky contain
more reflective records of the Commonwealth's nagging
land disputes than do those lodged in the Fayette County
Courthouse. Staples listed the names of the Fayette County
Bar, a substantial list that is still less impressive than are
the records of the members' litigious squabbles. This phase
of Lexington history makes intriguing reading. Throughout his book the author reflects the effects land, litigation,
and the immediate natural environment had on the rise of
the magnet town of Lexington.

Almost at the final moment when Staples had completed his history, a cleaning woman misplaced it. For a
time it seemed that all of the author's labors had ended in
disaster. A diligent search, including the Lexington city
dump, finally restored the manuscript uninjured. Staples
first considered *The Little Town of Lexington* as title, but
a sober reconsideration resulted in *The History of Pioneer
Lexington, 1779-1806*. Even after the manuscript was
completed, the author found new material that could be
inserted almost as interstices in the text. Staples finally
reached the stage when adding any more material would
have increased the cost of production beyond his financial
resources. Although the title page bears the imprint
Transylvania Press, the book was privately printed in a limited edition. At the time of its publication it received some
local notice, but little if any from the usual sources of historical review. The main value of Charles Staples's book
lies in its generous inclusions of documentary data. Well
beyond this, the compilation of this rich body of basic docu-

mentary materials relieves the fragile sources from the wear
and tear of frequent use.

In final analysis, the contents of *The History of Pioneer Lexington* steer current readers with dependable accuracy and comprehensiveness along the circuitous path
of pioneering on a virgin frontier. Frequently the book reveals a sense of the dynamics of a civilization making the
adaptations and compromises that settling a raw frontier
required. Staples worked so long and so assiduously at re-
searching and writing this book that he developed an intimate acquaintance with most of the leading personalities
who in one way or another helped shape the course of history for the rising town of Lexington. He scarcely differ-
entiated the long deceased pioneers from the people walking the streets of Lexington in 1950. In his conversations
in the meetings of the Book Thieves (a small discussion
group of Kentucky bibliophiles), he spoke as though one
could stroll down Main Street, stop in John Bradford's
Kentucky Gazette office to learn the news, go by J.
Maccoun and Tilford's store to see what new merchandise
had come down from Maysville by pack horse train, and
then stop in Postlethwait's Tavern for a glass of imported
Madeira wine. Staples has left a rich description of how it
was in those far-off days when there was vibrant expect-
ancy for a town that had broken out of a cane brake to
boast of its success as part of the great western movement
at the transition from the eighteenth to the nineteenth
century.

—THOMAS D. CLARK

To SAMUEL M. WILSON, President,
and the Members of the CAKES AND ALE CLUB

PREFACE

Born during a time of unusual interest, the Little Town of Lexington early developed a well established community life amid the privations of the frontier, and became the first metropolis of the Western Country. Many of those who have written of this period have stressed the Indian depredations and devoted very little space to the lives and occupations of the settlers after they had removed from the stockades and did something besides "fight Indians and talk Politics".

This effort will attempt to show the social and economic life of the Town of Lexington, during the first quarter of a century after the building of the block house in April 1779, with the military and political campaigns omitted.

It is regrettable that this was not done long ago; for with the passing of the years, and the neglect of opportunity, many interesting events that should have been preserved cannot be told "with any degree of accuracy as history, but mentioned only as tradition." Much has perished, yet much remains, in the files of the Kentucky Gazette in the Lexington Public Library; records in the vaults of the Fayette County and Circuit Courts; a few copies of the Fayette County tax books, found in the vaults of the Kentucky State Historical Society at Frankfort; the journals of travelers passing through the Blue Grass, and also, the valuable interviews with pioneers found in the Draper MSS collection in the Wisconsin State Historical Society.

It is necessarily a source book with no pretentions to literary merit; the importance of the subject matter being the only claim on the reader's attention. All the author can hope to do is to present a fair and truthful record of the many facts illustrative of the pioneer period of Lexington.

It at least has the merit of being the first history of Lexington written by a native.

This work is not exhaustive and no doubt many records will be found that will throw additional light upon the pioneer period, but it is hoped that it will furnish some idea of an inland frontier village "in the good old days before steamboats and railroads annihilated time and space," and when, with the exception of New Orleans, the Town of Lexington was the largest town west of the Allegheny mountains.

The author is indebted to many kind friends for information and location of source materials. To the continual prodding administered in large doses by that group of pleasant companions, whose families have facetiously dubbed them "The Book Thieves," Dr. Claude W. Trapp, Dr. John S. Chambers, Major Samuel M. Wilson, Dr. T. D. Clark, Mr. J. Winston Coleman, Mr. Wm. H. Townsend and Dr. Frank L. McVey due acknowledgments are made. Mrs. C. W. Trapp and Mr. C. Frank Dunn graciously read the manuscript and corrected many errors of rhetoric. Miss Ludie J. Kinkead and Mrs. Margaret Bridwell of the Filson Club, Mrs. Jouett Taylor Cannon of the Kentucky State Historical Society, and the staff of the Lexington Public Library have patiently assisted with many worthwhile suggestions.

CHAS. R. STAPLES.

646 Central Ave.,
Lexington, Kentucky.

BY WAY OF INTRODUCTION

THE Pioneers sleep in their narrow graves, many unmarked, their names almost forgotten, while their privations and adventures, steeped in the fiction of family tradition, have been handed down to us as facts. To these pioneers, Kentucky was the "promised land" and on the Point Pleasant campaign in October 1774, "Kentucky" had been a subject as exciting as the war itself.[1] The extravagant reports of the early surveyors and hunters were more than borne out by the first views of the dense woodlands of locust, black walnut, hickory, sugar maples, buckeyes and blue ash.

Confirmation of the report of the new "land of Canaan" started a living stream of emigrants over the mountains and down the Ohio. Many emigrants stopped in the Blue Grass, but many more, finding the desirable acreages occupied, swept on to the Spanish territory beyond the Mississippi. In three campaigns of atrocities and barbarities the Indian hunters vainly tried to stem this flood of settlers, but the apprenticeship served in Dunmore's War enabled the pioneers to combat the savages, whose best efforts only delayed the settlement of Kentucky for a few years, and then the hunting ground of the Indians was occupied, often with only a Dechard rifle, an ax and a hoe as a title. The settlement of this country was made under difficulties, amid dangers and hardships, and "for many years after the first settlements, it was almost a daily struggle between the whites and the savages for the possession of the Blue Grass."

The Settlers worked and hunted in squads, armed with rifles for their protection. For an individual to stray away alone from the forts, or blockhouses, was almost certain death, and "those within the walls of the stockades lay down to sleep at night with grave

---

1 Autobiography of Daniel Trabue.

uncertainty as to whether they would awake in this world or the next.[1]

The story of the hardships in crossing the mountains has been told until it is now an old story, but it still is enchanting reading, because there has been no other such migration in history. It started with small groups of hunters and surveyors; and then followed by an endless line of pioneers with their families and a few household necessities, fighting their way along the trail that was later to be called "The Wilderness Road."[2]

The primitive Kentuckians all lived the same kind of life, as with free land and equal opportunities for wealth, all social distinctions were levelled.[3] The cabins were all of logs with ends notched so they would fit close when the walls were "raised", and the chinks between the logs were daubed with clay, while the chimney was built outside the cabin, sometimes of small stones in clay, but at first, mostly of clay and small sticks. Because the Indians were often able to pull down these chimneys and enter the cabin through the fireplace, it later became the custom to build them inside the walls.

The pioneers represented every stratum of society, the hunter, the farmer, the mechanic, the land grabber and "many sons of Virginia aristocracy already in debt and ruined by the economic upheaval of the Revolution, disposed of their estates in the Tidewater country and sought their fortunes in this undeveloped country." Lord Carmathen complained to John Adams that British merchants were losing debts owed by Virginians by the migration of the debtors to Kentucky.[4]

After clearing the ground and building their cabins, the men worked their crops and hunted, while the women milked the cows, cooked, prepared flax,

---

1 Perrin's—History Fayette County, page 60.
2 Barker's—Life of Stephen Austin, page 8.
3 Cotterell's—Pioneer Kentucky.
4 Callander of Virginia State Papers, Vol. 4, p. 595.

spun and made garments of linen or linsey. When corn was to be had, they ground it in the hand mills. The tables dishes were of pewter and the spoons usually made from bones. The wooden vessels, the noggin, and the piggin, and the trencher, were all hand-made. The man who could fashion these articles was much in demand. Tin cups were the first articles imported into the Blue Grass. The noggin went out of use when the pioneers learned to make trenchers. The dripper was a notched board on which pewter plates were placed to be dried after washing.[1] The cups were carefully treasured until gourds could be raised, "and often the knife carried by the hunter was the only one available for family use." The famous Kentucky hunting shirt was made of linsey or dressed skins. It was not a coat in any sense, but a kind of loose tunic that slipped over the head, with close fitting sleeves, and sometimes it was slit at the neck and laced together with buckskin thongs. Some of these shirts were made with a broad cape or collar, which were sometimes decorated at the sleeve ends and seams with a leather fringe. This garment hung loosely from the shoulders without any effort to shape it to the body, and was confined at the waist with a broad belt.[2]

The breeches were made of deer skins, frequently with fur on the inside for warmth. They were usually tied below the knee to keep them from dragging and interfering with the wearer's movements. Both men and women wore moccasins made of deer skins with the hair turned inside, and in winter they were stuffed with buffalo hair or moss, and sometimes grass, to keep out the cold. Men and boys wore coonskins for head-gear.[3] The furnishings of the cabins were all of the same home-made simplicity. At first the floors were of packed dirt, and later, slabs of wood, called puncheon, held down by wooden pegs, replaced the dirt. Beds

---

1 Interview of Jane Stevenson in Draper MSS. 11CC 247, Madison, Wisc.
2 Warwick's—Early American Costumes, page 292.
3 Hall's—Annals of the West.

were forks of limbs driven into earthen floor with
cross poles to support the cords, on which brush and
corn stalks were laid. One pioneer says; "I was five
years at Lexington before I saw a table or a bedstead".[1]
Tables were made of hackberry, split and the heart
taken out, so that it could be planed with an adz and
then set on four legs. An iron pot, a kettle and a
frying pan were often the only cooking utensils and
the stove was the open fire place. The fire was never
allowed to go out. Tradition tells of a fire that was
carried over the Virginia mountains in an iron pot,
from camp to camp until Lexington was reached, where
it was installed in a fire place in a cabin. Here it
smouldered or blazed for many years as occasion required. When a fire did go out, it was necessary to
send a pine chunk to a neighboring cabin to secure a
new start. The food was served on a wooden slab
around which the family and visitors grouped on stools
as only a few of the rich had cane-bottom chairs. Many
prominent citizens prided themselves upon their ability
to supply their household needs by using a few hand
tools.

Corn pone and game meats, later substituted by
hog meat, was the usual bill of fare. Gardens soon
produced a variety of fresh vegetables. "Tea and
Coffee were reserved for the sick and were considered
as a mark of effeminacy if taken by people in good
health".[2]

The efforts of the Indians to drive out the settlers
failed rapidly, and after the Battle of the Blue Licks,
August 19, 1782, Central Kentucky was not again visited
by any large body of Indians. Prowlers, however, in
small groups kept up their depredations until 1794.
So far as available records disclose, John Wymore was
the only citizen of Lexington who was killed by the
Indians within the bounds of the town, although David
Hunter and Robert (or Charles) Knox were killed

---

1 Interview with Asa Farrar, Draper MSS. 13CC1.
2 Cotterell's—Pioneer Kentucky, page 246.

between McConnell's station and Lexington. These last two were residents of McConnell's Station.[1] John Wymore and his family arrived in Lexington in the fall of 1779. He carried in his hunting bag the first pig brought to Lexington. "In the spring of 1781, he with James Wason and Henry McDonald were hauling timber from a hill, (now the site of Central Christian Church at Walnut and Short streets), when an alarm of "Indians" was given. These men retreated towards the fort, but when they reached what is now Upper and Short streets, Wymore was shot by an Indian. McDonald took refuge behind a wild cherry tree growing where the Court House now stands and shot the Indian as he stooped over to scalp Wymore. The alarm reached the fort and headed by James Masterson, a brother-in-law of Wymore's, relief came immediately. As the settlers charged out of the gate of the stockade, Indians concealed in the cane fired a volley, but without causing any damage. Masterson ran to Wymore and seeing the Indian trying to raise himself, jerked the Indian's tomahawk from his belt and struck him on the head and then scalped him. This scalp was hung on a pole, so the wind would blow it about and mortify the Indians." The dead Indian's head was cut off and placed in the cherry tree. The cane was so thick Wymore and McDonald could not be shot at until they got into the open woods near the fort. After this the settlers cleared the cane away around the fort for seventy to eighty yards."[2] This attack came a few days before the assault on Bryan's station. David Mitchell, an old man, was injured about this time, but recovered.

Twice the citizens of Lexington went into the fort, for fear of the Indians, one report being that there were 300 Indians at Great Crossing in Scott County.[3] These Indian alarms were almost constant during good weather, and the pioneers were always expecting an attack. While James Masterson, Joseph Turner and

1 Interview with Jane Stevenson, Draper MSS. 13CC138.
2 Interview with Martin Wymore—Draper MSS. 11CC128-133.
3 Interview with Asa Farrar, Draper MSS, 13CC1.

John Wymore, Jun., were out hunting news reached Lexington of the defeat of Cornwallis. Those in the fort expressed their joy by gathering combustible materials and kindling a great bonfire. In the meantime, the hunters returning, came in view of the fort and discovering the conflagration gave up all for lost. They supposed the fort had been taken and that it was burning. Without venturing closer to ascertain the correctness of their impressions, they hastened down to John Morrison's station on Hickman creek only to learn Morrison was in Lexington engaged in the celebration.[1] Continued Indian ravages caused many pioneers to become discouraged and believing the land could never be settled, some who had entered claims for land were glad to get their money back by selling it for low prices. The presence of an enormous amount of game sustained the settlers until crops could mature. "Buffalos would pass the station of Lexington every day and sometimes all day long. Virginians and land jobbers used to come out and spend the winter at the station and go back in the spring before Indian raids would begin. There were fifteen Virginians in a cabin in the fort and a buffalo was driven up with the cows and other cattle, and some of the settlers got this buffalo up before the cabin occupied by the Virginians and waived a red handkerchief trying to get it to jump in among them."

With the close of the Revolutionary War the emigrants increased more rapidly.

---

[1] Interview with Martin Wymore, Draper MSS. 11CC128.

LAYING OFF THE LOTS.

IN November 1780 the Virginia Assembly divided Kentucky County by the establishment of the counties of Fayette, Lincoln and Jefferson, and Lexington became the "capital" of Fayette county which then included all of Kentucky north and east of the Kentucky River. "But Lexington was not built in a day. Many dreary days and months passed between the building of the stockade and the last Indian raids", and, although the first blockhouse was erected in the spring of 1779, by March 8, 1785 only fifty five cabins had been built outside the walls of the fort.[1]

Just when the site of the Town of Lexington received its name has been a subject of much discussion. The version generally accepted is that early in June 1775 a party of hunters from Harrodsburg camped around a spring[2] and talking with enthusiasm of the beautiful country through which they had passed fell to discussing a settlement and a name. One suggested "York," another "Lancaster," but these were dropped for "Lexington," as the discussion had turned to the strange story reaching them through the wilderness, of how the British Army had been repulsed in a little Massachusetts village. This story of the "christening" of Lexington was discussed at some length in the Kentucky Observer and Reporter, published by William W. Worley, in Lexington, July 29, 1809. The article is not signed but on account of the eulogy to John Maxwell, it is probable the article was inspired by an interview with the old pioneer. Another version of the same story says Major (John) Morrison and some companions had a camp in 1775. The news of the battle of Lexington came while they were there and the spot was named Lexington.[3] This party was composed of John Maxwell, Hugh Shannon, Levi Todd,

---

1 Trustees Book, Town of Lexington.
2 Diary of James Nourse.
3 Interview with Waller Bullock, Draper MSS. 11CC180.

John McCrackin, Isaac Greer, James Dunkin, William McConnell. They assisted McConnell to build a rude cabin on their camping ground as a foundation for a land title. Here they planted some corn and snap beans. This site was afterwards in turn McConnell's station, Royal Spring and Mill, the Headley distillery and is now in part covered by the yards of the Louisville and Nashville Railroad. Several members of this party made the long journey through the Wilderness and participated in the struggle for independence.

The actual day on which the first block house was built in Lexington has also been a much discussed subject, but evidently it was between April 15th and April 19th, 1779, when the first tree for the blockhouse was cut down by a party of pioneers from Harrodsburg.[1] The Draper collection of Kentucky Historical Manuscripts in the Wisconsin Historical Society, at Madison, Wis., has many of the John D. Shane interviews with the pioneers of Kentucky. Among these is one that was obtained from Josiah Collins in Bath County, during May 1841, which contains the names of the party from Harrodsburg who were the actual founders of the town of Lexington; Josiah Collins, Robert Patterson, Francis McConnell, William McConnell, Samuel Johnson, William Davis, George Gray, David Mitchell, William Mitchell, John Morrison, William McCrackin, Samuel Mays, James McIlvane, John Story, James Wason, Jacob Light, Elisha Bethy, Roswell Stevens, Nicholas Brabstone, James McBride, Elisha Collins, William Hayden, Benjamin Hayden, David Vance and James January. Josiah Collins claims that he cut down the first tree, which was a burr oak, about two feet across at the butt, which stood near the spring and this log was used on the lower side of the block house. They also cleared about thirty acres and planted corn.[2] Collins served under Captain James Harrod at Harrodsburg during 1778 and seems to have been in the

---

[1] Van Cleve—The American Pioneer, page 343.
[2] Interview with Josiah Collins, Draper MSS. 12CC65.

company of Captain John Holder in Madison County, near Boonesborough in June 1779.

In its early days Lexington was like many other frontier villages; it was first a blockhouse, and then a stockade in which the settlers lived and kept their stock at night, and then a few cabins began to appear near the walls of the fort. The deposition of John Niblack says "the early settlers in Lexington worked all the lots together without regard to ownership".[1]

The site of the Town of Lexington first appears in written record when Lord Dunmore, Governor of Virginia, issued a military warrant dated April 19, 1774, to James Buford, a sergeant in the Virginia Militia, who had served during the French and Indian War, for 200 acres, a tract which included a considerable portion of the present business section of Lexington. This tract was surveyed on August 5, 1775, by Colonel John Floyd—"near the head of middle fork of Elkhorn and adjoining the tract of John Maxwell." This survey was transferred by Buford to James Cowden and by the latter to Charles Cummings, who sold it to John Floyd.[2] The latter sold it to Colonel John Todd and from this tract seventy acres was given by Todd to the trustees of Lexington. Additional acreage was afterwards transferred to the Trustees by Mrs. Mary Todd Russell, daughter and sole heir of Colonel John Todd, who fell on the battlefield at the Blue Licks, August 19, 1782.[3] Another portion of the town site was obtained from John Maxwell, whose survey included the area bounded generally by South Broadway, East Maxwell and High Streets. William Pendleton had a survey which extended northeastwardly towards Second and Deweese streets. A portion of the town area was obtained out of the survey of Francis McConnell, which lay to the north and west of Main and Jefferson. Four hundred acres of this tract

1 Lindsay's Heirs vs. Trustees Town of Lexington, Complete Record Book "D", page 585, Fayette Circuit Court.
2 Samuel M. Wilson—First Land Court of Kentucky.
3 Fayette County Clerk's office—Deed Book "W", page 259.

had been located by Robert Patterson for Judge John Coburn in 1776, and a part of this survey was afterwards conveyed to James Parry. Robert Patterson conveyed a portion of his lands which lay west of Lower (now Patterson) Street, which extended southward to the present yards of the Southern Railway Company.

The actual boundaries of these surveys can be only approximated because of the confusion found in the indifferent descriptions of the surveys, but from all of these was secured the seven hundred and ten acres contained in the town boundary. The Act of the Virginia Assembly recites; "six hundred and forty acres have been laid out by the settlers, and seventy acres contiguous to same have been purchased by them, being a part of a survey made for John Floyd".[1] Robert Patterson in a deposition says; "the lines of the town were first 640 acres and extended further to the north and northeast than to the south. Was very little or no land south of the branch."

The political organization of Lexington began on January 25, 1780 when the settlers signed the "citizen's compact." The conditions of this agreement, in brief, were;—the town was to be laid off in so many "in lots" of one-half acre each, and so many "out lots" of five acres each. Every man over twenty one years of age, who had been a resident of Lexington for six months, or those who had raised a crop of corn for the ensuing year, and also, widows, were entitled to one "in lot" and one "out lot." It was also agreed that each "in lot" should be cleared of standing timber by June 1st. The drawing for lots which had been held during the previous year was to be null and void, and all given equal chances under the new drawing. By reason of some crops already standing on some of the out lots, and a threatened Indian raid, it was agreed, further not to interfere with any crops on such lands.

---

[1] Henning's Statutes, Vol. 11, page 100.

A penalty of 500 pounds was agreed upon for any violation of this agreement. This document was signed by

Robert Patterson,
William Elliott,
William Davis,
Samuel Johnson,
James Lindsay,
James Guy,
(James) Morrow,
Hugh Shannon,
Alexander McNair,
William Martin,
Jacob Wimer (Wymore)
Charles Seaman,
John Wumor (Wymore)
John W. Clark,
James Farrow,
Elisha Colans (Collins),
Joseph Turner,
Mathew Caldwell,
Hugh Thompson,
James January,
Wm. McDonald,
Alexander McConnell[1]

Chr. Johnston,
John Stevenson,
Robert Thompson,
William Niblack,
(mutilated) Wimor,
Thomas Stevenson,
John Niblack,
(Michael) Warnock,
Hugh McNair,
John Wimor (Wymore)
Samuel Martin,
John Stevenson,
Arthur Lindsay,
William Shannon,
James McNitt,
James Wason,
Isaac McBride,
William Hedon (Haydon)
John Newell,
David Vance,
John Foreon (Froman)
Cyrus Colans (Collins).

The trustees' book under date of March 26, 1781 shows;

"The inhabitants of the Town of Lexington, met to choose trustees for the said town, when the following persons were chosen, to wit: Levi Todd, Robert Patterson, David Mitchell, Henry McDonald, Michael Warnock."

These trustees served until early in the year 1782 when the same record shows under date of March 16, 1782, (page 7) a new set of trustees had been selected by the townsmen; William Steele, William McConnell, Andrew Steele, Samuel Kelly, William Henderson, William Mitchell and John Todd. In neither entry

1 Complete Record Book "F", page 545—Fayette Circuit Court.

does the record show the total number of votes cast, nor the number received by the individual candidates.

A Plat of the in lots is to be found on page No. 2, of the Trustees' book, dated March 26, 1781, but the original owners made so many exchanges that the trustees entered a revised list of the lot owners, which is shown on page No. 13 of same book. This list shows the owners and lot numbers as follows:

No. 6 Francis McDonald
7 Benjamin Haydon
8 James January
9 James Wason
10 Samuel Johnson
11 Ephriam January
12 Levi Todd
13 John Morrison
14 (David) Vantz
15 John Clark
16 Josiah Collins
17 Mathew Walker
18 James McConnell
19
20
21 Widow McDonald
22 Valentine Dickinson
23 Martin Dickinson
24 John Martin
25 Chris. Kirtner
26 William Anderson
27 James Mitchell
28 Samuel January
29 Robert Stanhope
30 John Wymer, Jr. (Wymore)
31 Jane Todd
32 William Howard
33
34 Robert Parker
35 Robert Todd
36 Patrick Owens
37 James Morrow
38 Benjamin Netherland

39 heirs of John Todd, Dec.
40 David Blanchard
41 (where the
42 garrison
43 stands)
44 Christopher Greenup
45
46 Alexander McConnell
47 Widow Kirtner
48 Timothy Peyton
49 John Sharp
50 George Shepperd
51 Caleb Masterson
52 John Niblack
53 John Mekins
54 Charles Williams
55
56
57 Humphrey Marshall
58 Amos Batterton
59 John Carty
60 Michael Warnock
61 Francis McConnell
62 Samuel Kelly
63 Elisha Collins
64 Archibald Dickinson
65
66 Peter January
67 John Brooks
68 John Williams
69 William McConnell
70 Thomas Marshall
71 James McDonald

72 William Haydon
73
74 Hugh Thompson
75 William Martin
76 Hugh Martin
77 John McDaniel
78 Andrew Steele
79 William McConnell

80 William Steele
81
82 John Torrence
83 Mathew Patterson
84 William Galloway
85 Adam Zumwalt
86 Jacob Zumwalt
87 Stoffel Zumwalt

The plat of the in lots shows that Mulberry (now Limestone) street was the east, or "upper end" of Lexington, Locust (now Tucker) the west or "lower end," Short street the northern and High street the southern boundaries. This last named was to be three poles wide, Main street five poles wide and "The Commons" ten poles. This street included Vine and Water streets and the branch between, so often mentioned as "the Town Fork of Elkhorn." The "public square" extended from Upper to Mill (sometimes called Middle) streets. Four hundred feet of ground between lots 19 and 20 extending from Main to Short streets, was set aside for a graveyard, and was later deeded by the Trustees to the Baptist congregation for a building lot. One half of this lot had been offered to the Presbyterians on which to build a church and school house, but the offer was declined.

On December 20, 1781, the trustees held a meeting at Higbee's Tavern on the southwest corner of High and Mulberry and approved the plat of the town. Until this was done there were only a few cabins built near the blockhouse, and, "an unfinished church and school house."

There was a total of 87 in lots, being five to each block, with the exception of the block between Mill and Upper streets, and the block west of Spring street. Each of these contained six lots. The out lots extended from Short to Seventh street, and from High to Maxwell. Mulberry and Main Cross (now Broadway) streets extended the full length of the in lots and the out lots. Maxwell extended only from Main Cross to Mulberry.

The out lots were drawn for at the same time as the in lots. Each of these contained five acres and the list of those drawing these lots is given on page 5 of the Trustees' book:

James Masterson	A	John McDonald	20
William McDonald	B	Joseph Lindsay	21
Henry McDonald	C	Jane Thompson	22
Samuel McMillen	D	John Todd	23
David Mitchell	E	James Lindsay	24
Thornton Farrow	F	Alexander McConnell	25
Nicholas Brabston	G	Hugh Thompson	26
James McBride	H	James Morrow	27
Wm. Henderson	I	Robert Thompson	28
Samuel Martin	J	Hugh McDonald	29
John Torrence	K	James McGinty	30
Wm. Martin, Sr.	L	John Martin	31
John Clark	M	Samuel Johnson	32
William Niblack	N	James January	33
Francis McDonald	O	James Wason	34
Francis McConnell	Q	William Haydon	35
Daniel McClain	R	Josiah Collins	36
Robert Stanhope	S	Mathew Walker	37
John Wymore	2	James McConnell	38
Hugh Martin	3	John McDonald	39
David Vance	4	Michael Warnock	40
William Mitchell	5	William Martin	41
Timothy Peyton	6	James McConnell	42
Elisha Collins	7	Alexander McConnell	43
John Morrison	8	William McConnell	44
Stephen Collins	9	For a clergyman	45
Levi Todd	10	John Williams	46
Ephriam January	11	Peter January	47
Alexander McClain	12	Joseph Walker	48
Samuel Kelly	13	John Niblack	49
Caleb Masterson	14	Charles Seaman	50
Joseph Turner	16	Francis McDermaid	51
William McConnell	19		

At a meeting of the Trustees of the Town, held on March 8, 1785, a list was entered in the Minute Book showing the lots on which no cabins had been erected. Reference to this plat shows no cabins had been built on Main street between Upper and Mulberry; only two

on Main street between Main Cross and Spring street;
none on Main street west of Spring; none between
Upper and Mulberry on the south side of "The Commons"; none on High street between Upper and Mill,
and only one between Mill and Spring streets. No
cabin had been built on High street west of Spring,
excepting the house of Robert Patterson.

The fact that these lots had not been built upon
was due in part to a lack of qualified builders, and also
to a lack of competent housekeepers, since the remarkable ease with which widows found a second husband
shows the females were much in the minority. A contributing cause was the military campaigns named in
various depositions. James Haydon says: "I served as
a spy under Robert Patterson, William McConnell and
William Steele at Lexington. Joined George Rogers
Clark in 1781 and was detailed to hunt. Killed, cleaned
and dressed 4,000 pounds of buffalo meat in one month.'
John Niblack says: "I settled at Lexington in 1779
and knew James Morrow there. We were both on the
expedition under General Clark against the Shawnees in
1782. Joseph Lindsay was the contractor who furnished the lead and powder." Robert Patterson says:
"In July or about the first of August I was ordered
from Lexington with the Lexington Militia to co-
operate with the "Charles" galley on the Ohio. We
camped at Big Riffle, two miles above Big Bone Creek
mouth."[1]

These expeditions took the younger men away
from Lexington during the good building weather and
was a contributing cause why more lots had not been
built upon. James Masterson, who arrived in Lexington
in the spring of 1780, built the first hewn log cabin.[2]
He was one of the first to bring into the Blue Grass,
any considerable number of slaves.

[1] Morgan, et. al. vs. Parker, Complete Record Book "E", page
352—Fayette Circuit Court.
[2] Interview with Martin Wymore, Draper MSS. 11CC128.

There was a great waste of timber in clearing this land. With no open country in or around Lexington, every acre had to be cleared of standing timber or cane, before a cabin could be built or crops planted. As late as 1785 the Trustees were still trying to get the stumps of trees removed from the streets.

THE STOCKADE.

THE block house mentioned in statement of Josiah Collins was erected near what is now the southwest corner of Main and Mill streets; the selection of this spot was probably determined by the proximity to the spring. "When Lexington was first opened as a county seat, there was but one spring and altho' forty or fifty persons only used to attend, the townsmen had to go and bring up all the water they would need before these persons would come, for the spring would be muddied then so as to be unfit for use. The seeps, however, gradually opened, and new springs broke out all along (north side of branch). They also dug that one in further and more, and it got stronger as they went further into the bank."[1]

The stockade, which has been mentioned by so many historians as "the fort at Lexington," was built on the south side of Main street, and about thirty feet west of the blockhouse referred to by Josiah Collins. The capture of Martin's station, followed by the sacking of Hinkston's or Ruddle's, in June 1780, alarmed the citizens for the safety of the little Town of Lexington. Colonel John Todd wrote the Governor of Virginia;

"Lexington, 15 April 1781.

"May it please your excellency;

"The inhabitants of Fayette County have been so harrassed this spring by the Indians, that I was for some time apprehensive that this whole country would be evacuated, as panics of that kind have proved very catching. The fate of the neighboring garrisons at Licking last year was fresh in their minds. The only plan that I could devise to prevent it, and sufficiently secure the provisions laid up at Bryant's and this place, was to build a new fort upon a very advantageous situation at this place, and make it

---

1 Interview with Wymore, Draper MSS. 11CC128.

proof against swivels and small artillery, which
so terrify our people. I laid off the fort upon
the simplest plan of a quadrangle, and divided
the work among four of the most pushing men,
with a bastion to each, authorizing them to employ workers from this and the neighboring sta-
tions, and assuring them of their pay myself.
On the faith of such assurance, considerable sums
of money had been spent and advanced to the
workmen, so that the work in about 20 days has
been nearly completed, in a workman like manner. The gate is nearly finished and the magazine contracted for. The whole expense
amounts to £11,341.10s. I believe four times
the expense never before made for the public a
work equal to this."

In another letter Colonel Todds refers to "in
emulation among the overseers, and rewards in liquor
to the men proved powerful incentives to industry.
Being a charge of uncommon nature I thought proper
to present it to your excellency and the council, being
better judges of the necessity and the expediency of
the work than the auditors, who are probably unacquainted with the circumstances of this country. By
either of the delegates your excellency may have an
opportunity of transmitting the money."

The almost daily fluctuations of Virginia currency
make it impossible to determine the value of the amount
named when converted into hard money but it was a
considerable sum of money for those days.

Amongst the Clark MSS, in the Virginia State
Archives at Richmond, Virginia is found the account
rendered by Colonel John Todd, giving the names of
the "four most pushing men" and the groups of laborers serving under them:

"Expense in building fort at Lexington, April
    13, 1781—
The Commonwealth of Virginia to John Morrison
on account of expenditures for work done at
the New Fort, Dr

March &
April
1781

John Morrison
David Mitchell
Levi Todd
William Haydon
Benjamin Haydon
James McGinty
John Todd
William Niblack
Benjamin Briggs
John Williams
Samuel McMillen
Charles Seaman
Caleb Masterson
John Clark
John Nut (or Nitt)

Joseph Turner and Team

Robert Patterson acct. of work at new fort—
David Vance
Francis McDurmid
Francis McDurmid senr.
John Torrence
Henry McDonald
Robert Stanhope
Archibald Dickinson
Stephen Collins
John Wymer (Wymore)
Nicholas Brabston
James Haydon
John Stevenson
James Masterson
James Wason
Patrick Owens
Francis Patterson

Horse Highere (sic)
Wm. Haydon, team
Wm. Robertson 1 horse
John Wymer 1 horse

Jas. Wason 1 horse
Wm McConnell 1 do
Peter January 1 do

Wm. McConnells acct of work N fort
Michael Warnock
Francis McDonald
John Napier
Ratcliff Boone
James Boone
James Morrow
John Fitzgerald
William Shannon
John Casey
James Welch
James Hayden (x)
Francis Harper
Josiah Collins
James McConnell

Samuel January and Team

Wm. Martin acct. work on the New Fort
Samuel Martin
William Martin
John Martin
John McDonald
Hugh McDonald
James McDonald
Daniel McClain
Levi Todd
Alexander McClain
John Clark (x)
Hugh Martin
Caleb Masterson (x)
Hugh Thompson
Wm. McDurmid & son
Robert Stanhope (x)
John Todd (x)
William McConnell (*)
Peter January (*)
Samuel January & team (*)

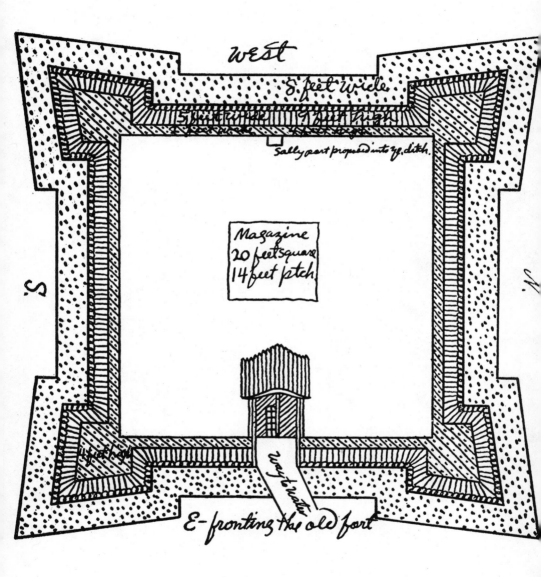

WEST

8 feet wide

Sally port proposed into ye ditch.

Magazine
20 feet square
14 feet pitch.

S.

N.

way to water

14 feet gate

E - fronting the old fort

To 4 over lookers Morrison, Patterson,
McConnell & Martin
Gate Expenses
Wood work
McBride, Torrence and McConnell
for iron 80D smith work 100D
Magazine Expense
to 3 men 2 days cutting timber
to 2 men 3 days riving & cutting
4 square flooring a 200D
to Team for Hauling timber 10D
Liquor given to the men at sundry times
21 quarts a 100D
John Little for Drum
The above acc examined and approved
Jn Todd
April 15th, 1781

The Clark papers containing these accounts were
also published by the Illinois Historical Collection[1]
with some slight difference in the names. Those
marked (x) are not found in photostat of the original
MSS., while those marked (*) are in the original but
not in the Collection named.

The sketch of the fort accompanying Colonel
Todd's letter shows

"80 feet square in the clear. Walls 7 feet thick
of rammed dirt enclosed in good timber, 9 feet
high, from 4 feet upwards 5 feet thick, and proof
against small arms. Ditch 8 feet wide and
between 4 and 5 feet deep. In center is the
magazine 20 feet square with 14 foot pitch. East
gate fronted old fort. Sally port on west side
into ditch."[2]

From this description we learn there was a shelf
upon which riflemen could stand while defending the
fort, which was protected by the high pickets against
any shots that might be fired from the hill south of
the branch. The lots around the fort were cleared of

---

[1] Illinois Historical Collection, Vol. VIII., pp. 521-3, (Vol. 3, Va. Series).
[2] Draper MSS—11S202 Wis. Historical Society.

standing timber for 70 to 80 yards, to afford sweep for rifle fire from the fort. One corner of this stockade extended nearly to the north side of Main Street.

The attack of the British and Indians on Bryan's Station August 14 to 16th 1782, alarmed the Lexington people and a "new fort" was built near the northwest corner of Broadway and High. "They set to and built a large fort, very strong and surrounded with a ditch on the outside, up where Keiser's lot (afterwards) was, right opposite to Caldwell's on the hill. In this fort there was never but one house built, which was occupied by old Mr. January then 105 years old, and lady, who were too frail to move in haste, in case of alarm. This fort was intended to be cannon proof."[1]

The stockade on Main street evidently stood until July, 1787, at which time the trustees' book shows that part of lot No. 43 was issued to John Bradford, which according to the plat of the in lots, had been one of the lots occupied by this fort. The families began moving out of the fort into individual cabins in March 1784.[2]

The completion of the fort gave the settlers a feeling of security and assured the permanent existence of the settlement. The "Articles of Agreement between the Citizens of Lexington," which had been signed by forty seven settlers January 25, 1780, was the only authority under which the affairs of the town were conducted, and the settlers determined to have legal authority. A petition addressed to the Speaker of the Virginia Assembly—to establish the Town of Lexington, dated April 14, 1782, was circulated and signed by the following settlers;

William Davis	James McDonald
Benjamin Haydon	Daniel McClain
Joseph Lindsay	B. Netherland
John Maxwell	Patrick Owens
James Morrow	Charles Seaman
Francis McConnell	John Todd, Jr.

[1] Interview with Wymore—Draper MSS. 11CC128.
[2] Interview with Jane Stevenson—Draper MSS. 11CC251.

A.

Tates Creek R.

Captain Wilson

Hickman R.

Springle

Buckeye R.

Satorwhite
C. House

Bryants R.

Craigs R.

Russels R.

Irvine

Hackneys

Scots

Johnstons Mill R.

Echols + Brown

Frankfort R.

Lastburn R.

2011 Acres
Robt. Todd, S. F.
March 24th, 1791

Joseph Turner
David Williams
James Dawson
James January
Hugh Martin
David Mitchell
James McBride
Henry McDonald
James McGintey
Samuel McMillan
William Niblack
Robert Patterson
Robert Stanhope
Levi Todd
David Vance

John Williams
William Elliot
Peter January
Samuel Martin
John Morrison
William McConnell
Hugh McDonald
Alexander McClain
John Napier
John Nitt (Nutt)
Aaron Pickens
Robert Thompson
John Torrence
Michael Warnock
John Wymore.

In response to this appeal the Virginia Assembly passed an act[1] recognizing the Town of Lexington, and then the trustees issued deeds for the lots already drawn by the settlers, and to those new comers who could qualify. To prevent an exodus when rumors of Indian raids were in circulation, the trustees passed a rule "that any person removing from the Town, when it was deemed necessary to reside in the fort, shall forfeit all rights in the said Town."

The Act establishing the town named the trustees who were to serve to the end of the year, and after that, they were chosen by popular vote at election held the last of each year or the beginning of the new year.[2]

The minute book of the trustees' meetings shows frequent orders requiring the settlers to clear Main street of stumps, and finally in 1785 this appears to have been accomplished as far west as the graveyard now occupied by the First Baptist Church property. This same book also shows that cabins were built outside the stockade more rapidly after this year. The fire hazard became so great that the trustees declined to permit any more chimneys to be built of mud and sticks. This same year they built a bridge across the

1 Henning's Statutes, Vol. 11, page 100.
2 See Kentucky Gazette, April 30, 1791; December 10, 1801.

town fork of Elkhorn at Main Cross street. Other
bridges were built on Main street across Mill street
and on Main street across Spring street. The next
year a bridge was built over the town fork on Mulberry street. The trustees also issued very stringent
orders prohibiting boys from fishing off any of these
bridges. Mill street was opened south of High street,
by Thomas Bradley, in 1788 and John Cocke built
what is claimed to be the first water mill in Kentucky
this same year, at the lower end of Lexington using
the waters of Town Fork.

The winter of 1779 and 1780 was very hard on
the pioneers. Very little food stuffs had been produced
locally, and the great crowding in of new comers oc-
casioned a scarcity of provisions in the country. "Many
families never tasted bread until a crop of corn matured
and was fit to be ground into meal. Their dependence
was entirely on game, of which the buffalo was the
principal source[1]. Many families used the breasts of
turkey for bread." Snow and ice covered the ground
without a thaw from November to the succeeding
March. The people were in great distress and many
in the wilderness were frost-bitten. Some died and
some ate of the dead cattle and horses. Many of the
people had to go to the Falls of the Ohio for corn to
plant[2]. David Mitchell's deposition tells how he was
employed to kill game for the use of those living in the
stockade.[3]

Conditions rapidly changed after several corn
crops had reduced the ground so wheat could be raised.
All crops were reported as good and as game
was still plentiful, the settlers began to live easier.
Gardening and farming rewarded their efforts, and the
bountiful crops made them appreciate the characteri-
zation of the early surveyors that this region was a
second paradise. "The deep vegetable mould had

---

1 Bradford's Notes—No. 8, Oct. 13, 1826.
2 Journal of Daniel Trabue—Colonial Men and Times, page 56.
3 Land Trials, "A", page 277—Fayette Circuit Court.

been accumulating for centuries, making it a hot bed
of fertility."

In 1783 and 1784 it is estimated 12,000 new inhabitants arrived in Kentucky. This increase created a
demand for additional courts. In 1785 the Virginia
Assembly "granted the prayer of sundry citizens" and
Bourbon county was formed out of part of Fayette.
In 1788 Fayette County gave up parts of its area when
Woodford County was organized. After Kentucky
became a state in 1792 Clark county was formed out
of parts of Fayette and Bourbon. In 1798 Jessamine
was organized out of the southern portion of Fayette
and the latter then arrived at its present dimensions.

THE FRONTIER VILLAGE.

THE growth of the Town of Lexington was necessarily very slow during the first few years. An early pioneer relates—"there were four cabins and a blockhouse in Lexington in the fall of 1779 when my father got there."[1] With succeeding years and an increase in the number of cabins, mercantile establishments began to appear. William McConnell had a tan yard, the first in the new country, on Hunt's row (now Water Street). There is a tradition that he was one of the footmen who responded to the call for assistance at the time of the attack on Bryan's station. Not being able to enter the besieged stockade, he had turned back towards Lexington, when the Indians overtook him and killed him. He was buried beside the road.[2] John Nutt started what is thought to have been the first powder Mill at McConnell's station, one mile below Lexington.[3]

The year 1784 found Lexington with thirty cabins scattered around the outside of the stockade. Main street had been extended westward from the fort towards the cemetery, but was still obstructed with the roots and stumps of trees. A log school house stood near the west side of the present court house and "there was an unfinished church near the fort." The area of land included in the town limits amounted to 710 acres, as named in the act of the Virginia Assembly incorporating the town of Lexington. It was a typical frontier village excepting the lack of stores and trading places.

The early stores of Lexington were evidently of a very transitory character. Peddlers arrived with small stocks of goods on pack horses and would open their wares in any room available, usually the front room of some cabin on Main street. When his supply was disposed of the trader would return to Philadelphia

---

[1] Interview with Jane Stevenson, Draper MSS. 11CC247.
[2] Interview with Martin Wymore, Draper MSS. 11CC128.
[3] *Ibid.*

or Baltimore for a fresh stock of goods, taking with him, furs or produce he had accepted in exchange for his goods.[1] When he returned to Lexington he would try to get his former location, but failing would accept accommodations in any room not occupied. When this stock was gone, he would again make a trip to "the eastern settlements"[2], and repeat this procedure. During his absence some other trader would arrive in town and open his stock on the same stand. In the busier seasons, stands on Main street were at a premium and should a prospective trader be a few days late he had to be satisfied with some location on one of the side streets, and frequently had to go outside the center of the village[3].

The first storekeeper who was a resident of the town was Peter January. "January had the only store there. You could have put it all in one wagon. If there had been much buying, 2 or 3 families wo'd have bo't it out. But it was so hard to get the goods there and they cost so much at first, that there were but few purchasers."[4] There is a tradition that Peter January arrived in this wilderness as Pierre Janviere, but anglicized his name for the benefit of the pioneers who were unable to pronounce it. He is reported to have built the first brick house in Lexington, which he called "Mount Hope," on north Mill street at what is now the corner of New Street. This brick house has been a much debated subject.[5] The subject as to who opened the first regular store in Lexington also has been much discussed. Several Kentucky historians have asserted that the first store was opened in the spring of 1784 by James Wilkinson, who claimed to be the active partner of a commercial company of Philadelphia. This store was opened in March 1784 but James Wilkinson became prominent in Western affairs and devoted very little space to his life and affairs in

1 Advertisements in Kentucky Gazette, November 17, 1789.
2 *Ibid*, December 15, 1787.
3 *Ibid.*, April 12, 1788, January 9, 1796.
4 Interview with J. Kemper—Draper MSS. 12CC130.
5 Unpublished diary of General James Taylor.

Lexington in his three volume memoirs, "My Own
Times." "In a short time we find his agents covering
the country, buying and selling produce and controlling
the supply of salt."[1]

Wilkinson and Armstrong had served during the
Revolutionary War on the staff of General Gates. They
arrived in the Blue Grass with considerable prestige on
account of the first named having been the courier to
carry the inventory of prisoners and war supplies sur-
rendered by General John Burgoyne, after the Battle
of Saratoga, to the Continental Congress.[2] He was
present when General Charles Lee was captured, but
effected his own escape. Considerable doubt has arisen
in recent years as to Wilkinson's connection with any
commercial organization, although he seems to have
acted for a time as the agent of Barclay, Moyland and
Company. Whether he was a partner has never been
determined. The partnership with Armstrong was
dissolved in September 1789.[3]

The story of the transportation of the merchandise
comprising the stock of the Wilkinson store has only
recently been found, adding another chapter to the
beginning of Lexington's mercantile endeavors. In
the suit of James Wilkinson vs. Humphrey Marshall,
which is recorded in Complete Record Book "B" of
the Supreme Court of Kentucky, Robert Clement testified on September 1, 1790—"I left Philadelphia in
October 1783 in the employ of James Wilkinson and
proceeded to Pittsburg accompanied by Captains Dun
and Armstrong - enroute for the District of Kentucky.
On the voyage to the Falls of the Ohio, the said Armstrong landed at Limestone (now Maysville) by reason
of ice in the Ohio river. We took protection by going
up a creek called Destruction creek and lay there
until the beginning of March, when Alexander McClane
and others came to our relief. McClane and Dun took
most of the goods to Lexington by pack horses."

1 Political Beginnings of Kentucky—Brown, page 91.
2 Letters of Richard Henry Lee, Vol. 1, page 343.
3 Proof of the Corruption of General Wilkinson—Clark.

Alexander McClane testified in same suit; "In month of February 1784 he was employed by James Wilkinson to go with some pack horses to the Ohio river to pack up to Lexington some goods which said Wilkinson had cast away below the Miami (River). Said Wilkinson, Robert Johnson and others went (from Lexington) and we struck the Ohio river above the mouth of the Big Miami and then walked down the river to place where said goods were under Captain Dun. Deponent came to Lexington accompanied by Captain Dun, a negro slave of James Wilkinson and ——Alexander who assisted in bringing the goods." Caleb Shipp testified "Was with James Wilkinson and Robert Johnson on the trip from Lexington——. Account of the heavy snows we were seven days going from Lexington to the river." Robert Johnson testified—"In latter part of February 1784 he rode from Elkhorn to the Ohio river and proceeded down the river until opposite the great Miami where James Wilkinson and Alex. McClane left the party for Destruction creek where James Wilkinson had some goods which had been sunk in the river and we recovered the goods and sent them to Lexington. James Wilkinson was left on the Ohio with some goods which he floated down the river in a canoe to Louisville."[1]

The store opened by James Wilkinson evidently did not consume much of his personal attention, as he stated during one of his several Courts Martial, "I left all such matters to my clerks." One of these was Dr. Hugh Shiel, who died in Lexington in 1785, his widow afterwards marrying Judge Harry Innes. In addition to Dr. Sheil, Wilkinson's clerks were Robert Clements and —— Haley, while his final accounts were wound up by Gabriel Maupin, the last clerk.[2]

"The store of James Wilkinson must have been of great interest and benefit to the pioneers of the Town

1 Wilkinson vs. Marshall, pages 51-83-96 Supreme Court Complete Record Book "B", Kentucky Court of Appeals.
2 Wilkinson's—"My Own Times", page 227, also see Kentucky Historical Society Register Vol. 24, page 259.

of Lexington, as it supplied them with articles not produced locally, and, in addition, enabled them to exchange skins, furs and country made produce for powder, lead, wines, buttons, coffee and other items not to be found this side of the Mountains."

Many of the traders who came to Lexington secured their supplies from Baltimore or Philadelphia, and carried these cargoes on wagons to Pittsburg, there loading them on boats floated to Limestone (now Maysville) landing and then by pack horse over Smith's road to Lexington. The average time consumed in making this journey was forty days, and the ordinary cost of carriage for one ton amounted to $65. Taking the class of goods thus transported, the cost of carriage was equal to 33 per cent of the value of the transported article.[1] For many years Ginseng was the only Kentucky product that paid a good return on the expense of shipping to the eastern seaboard.

The year of 1784 also witnessed the arrival of other merchants in Lexington, when Alexander and James Parker from Carlisle, Pennsylvania, opened their store, as did George Gordon and his partner, John Coburn; also Robert Barr, who is always shown on the tax books as "lameman". He arrived in Lexington from Philadelphia and opened his store on Main street at a point now called No. 264 West Main street. He died on 8th September 1821, aged 72 years. He was succeeded by his sons, Thomas and Robert, and later, by his son-in-law Dr. Elisha Warfield, who lived above the store and is reported to have maintained a very beautiful garden from the rear of his home to the banks of the Town Fork. John Coburn evidently did not confine his energies to a mercantile career, since the records at Harrodsburg show he was admitted to practice law on March 9, 1785.[2] Among other arrivals this year was Ned. Darnaby, who gives us a not very attractive picture of Lexington. "There was not then

1 McDougal, MSS., Lexington Public Library.
2 Order Book No. 1, page 48, Mercer County Clerk's office.

a shingle roof in Lexington. The court house was an
open log building with a board roof."[1]

The stocks carried by these stores were very limited
and at first confined to necessities, and were exchanged
for such hard money as was in circulation, but mostly
for furs, bear skins and farm produce, such as butter,
tallow, cheese, eggs, chickens, cured meats, linen woven
cloths, hemp and tobacco.[2] "There was never any
money in the country, 'till Wayne's army come out
and he bo't all the horses up and we had a fine lot of
them in Kentucky then; the good for cavalry, the poor
for pack horses; $40. was the highest price for a pack
horse."[3]

The earliest money in circulation in pioneer Lexington seems to have been Virginia paper, with stray
lots of Continental currency. The legal tender qualities of Virginia money were much reduced by various
acts of the Assembly of that State. The trade established by James Wilkinson with the Spanish Governor
at New Orleans brought many Spanish dollars into
Central Kentucky, in addition to British and hard
coins from other European kingdoms. In fact, there
was such a variety the local merchants had a scale of
values for the different coins which they kept before
them all the time and used in making their trades.
"There was scarcely a country on the civilized globe
whose coins were not represented in Kentucky. The
Louis of France, Rix dollars of Holland, Ducats from
Austria, Fredericks of Prussia, Crusadores of Portugal,
Lires of Italy and Rupees of India, all were to be
found in this wilderness. The Spanish dollar, or Piaster,
was also 'piece of eight' because it was readily cut
into eight pieces for use as small change. Blacksmiths
became very sharp and frequently cut five quarters instead of four, and ten bits instead of eight. In event

1 Interview with Ned. Darnaby, Draper MSS., 11CC165.
2 See Advertisements in Kentucky Gazette 1787 to 1796.
3 Interview with J. Kemper, Draper MSS. 12CC130.

of disputes, the values of all such coins were determined by weighing them.[1]

Much of these coins was used by the local merchants to adjust their accounts for supplies purchased in the East, which further reduced the amount in circulation. This scarcity of hard money caused articles of value to be used as a medium of exchange. Hemp and tobacco became acceptable in exchange for supplies, when the Virginia Assembly passed an act allowing hemp at thirty shilling and tobacco at twenty-five shillings per hundred weight, to be received for Taxes.[2] This tobacco was delivered by the growers to licensed warehouses located at various points along the Kentucky River; at mouth of Boone's creek, mouth of Hickman, mouth of Jessamine and at General Charles Scott's landing in Woodford county. At these points the tobacco was examined by inspectors, who issued receipts to cover the grade and mount. These receipts were readily accepted by our merchants in exchange for goods, as their advertisements in the Kentucky Gazette announce. Tobacco did not become the important crop until the New Orleans markets were opened to James Wilkinson. Impossibility of reaching the markets over the mountains kept the cultivation on a small scale, principally for local consumption, but with protection afforded for the down-the-river trip and the easy method of carriage caused many others to begin raising the "kitefoot."

Hemp was mentioned for the first time in an advertisement in the Kentucky Gazette issued on May 3, 1788, when Robert Barr announced he had hemp seed for sale. It early became a staple crop and found a ready sale when it was made receivable for taxes.[3]

In the absence of banks, hard money was hoarded as a matter of safety. The strong box of Judge Fielding

---

1 Thos. Ashe—"Travels in America", page 190—also see Durrett's MSS "Early Banking in Kentucky".
2 Henning's Statutes, Vol. 10, page 205.
3 Henning's Statutes, Vol. XI., page 30.

L. Turner was inventoried by his executors in August 1844 and showed the following variety; Eagles $2,785; Sovereigns $207; Franks $18; Old American gold $112; Doubloons $328; six pieces of old gold $27; and Carolina Gold $307.[1]

The beaver skin seems to have been the unit of value in trading amongst Lexington merchants. So many deer, or fox, or raccoon skins equalled one beaver skin. It was the "large" money of the pioneers, and had a value of about $4. An indictment in Fayette Circuit Court, the Commonwealth of Kentucky vs. J—— J—— "for theft of nine beaver skins to the value of about $36," may be an indication of the fair value which was accorded such commodity. Bear skins were never referred to as furs, and buffalo hides were classed the same as cow or horse hides. In addition to the skins of animals, many of the stores advertised they would accept certificates of land grants, and military land warrants in exchange for Merchandise.[2]

The lack of close markets caused surplus corn and rye crops to be distilled into whiskey, and nearly every farmer had his still house and mash tubs. Considerable indignation arose amongst our farmers when the federal government put a tax of $1.00 per year on each still. Whiskey was the one crop that could be exported to an advantage. "A horse could carry whiskey that took 24 bushels of rye to make, but could carry only four bushels of the raw product."

When purchasing supplies needed in his household, a farmer would deliver furs, farm produce, whiskey and frequently the cloths woven by the females of his home, and select his goods. Any differences were adjusted by taking powder and lead, or hand made nails.

The Kentucky Gazette advertisements from 1789 to 1796 give us an idea as to the wide variety of articles produced by the pioneers. The merchants offered to accept in trade whiskey, country made sugar, linsey, pork in sides, bacon, hams, tobacco, hemp,

1 Fayette County Will Book "Q", page 144.
2 Advertisements in Kentucky Gazette—1789 to 1798.

ginseng, butter, lard, eggs, wool blankets, country made linens and sides of leather. In many of the advertisements of "land for sale," the offer was made to accept in exchange, young negroes, or young horses.

It is worthy of notice that, in a country where every man, woman and child was compelled to ride as much as did our early settlers, no advertisements for the accommodations of horses appear in the files of the Gazette until 1800. The settlers frequently advertised they "would board and lodge a few genteel boarders", but nothing was ever said about riding animals until after the beginning of the new century.

The first hotel in Lexington, of which record can be found, was started by James Bray, when he opened the "house of entertainment" on Main street, between Main Cross (now Broadway) and Spring streets, in 1784. Captain Thomas Young had a tavern on Upper street facing the court house in 1786, and for many years maintained a reputation for hospitality. Henry Marshall, who came to Lexington from Cumberland County, Pennsylvania, had a tavern in 1788 at a point now No. 324 West Main street. The "Sheaf of Wheat" was opened by Robert Megowan in a two story log building on Main street, now 140 West Main, and in 1789 Stephen Collins began the operation of a hotel in a much larger building on the location that had been used by Henry Marshall. This must have been the best stand in Lexington, since it was next door to the market house, which was used as a state house during the legislative sessions of 1792. Coleman's tavern is first advertised in the Kentucky Gazette in the issue dated May 31, 1797, in which he advertised he was prepared to furnish "an excellent room for shows." John McNair opened the "Sign of the Buffalo" on Main street opposite the court house, which was operated by his widow after his death. John Higbee had his tavern on the southwest corner of High and Mulberry (now Limestone), which was the favorite place for the trustees of the Town of Lexington to hold their monthly meetings. The same proprietor also had a hotel at South Elkhorn, and later a saw mill and water mill. Christopher Keiser opened the "Indian Queen", on the northwest corner of High and Main Cross streets, which was frequently used by lawyers when taking depositions of witnesses from the country. The "Sign of the Cross Keys" was located on the southwest corner of Spring and Main streets, next door to Baron Steuben, the mulatto shoemaker. The Irishman, Luke Usher, after selling out his umbrella plant, erected a brewery on the southwest corner of Vine and Spring streets, which was converted into Lexington's first theatre with a pit. From 1806 to 1816 he controlled the only theatre in Lexington, along with one in Frankfort and another in Louisville. He conducted a hotel, called "Don't Give Up the Ship," on Short street three doors west of Limestone. It was destroyed by fire January 30, 1819, along with the jail and several residences. After this blow Mr. Usher became steward for Transylvania University, and died during May, 1827. Satterwhite's "Eagle Tavern" which was on Short street facing the court house, passed into the hands of Cuthbert Banks in 1803. The latter also operated "Olympian Springs" for a number of years. Patterson Bain had a tavern on Short street on north west side of Broadway. Love & Brent's tavern was located on the north-east corner of Main and Upper, where it faced the court house and had a wide reputation for clean beds and good fare.[1] Captain John Postlethwait, who arrived in Lexington in 1790 from Carlisle, Pennsylvania, opened "Postlethwait's Tavern" during the Spring of 1797, at corner of Main and Mulberry streets. This building had been occupied by Adam Steele and was sold by him in March 1797.[2] This hotel was operated by Joseph Wilson from 1803 to 1807 and then returned to management of John Postlethwait, who after several years conveyed it to Sanford Keen. He was followed by John Brennan and then by John G. Chiles. It

[1] Unpublished diary of General James Taylor.
[2] Burnt Record Book No. 4., page 262—Fayette County Court.

began to be called "Phoenix Hotel" in 1826. This
location has been occupied by a hotel probably longer
than any other similar location in Kentucky. John
Downing operated an Inn on the south side of Main
street, between Upper and Limestone, called "Traveler's Hall," which had been started by Robert Bradley
on Cheapside. It was removed to the Main street
location in 1796, where Downing operated it until 1808.[1]

---

[1] Deposition Wm. Leavy, in Martin vs. Buford, Complete
Record Book "C", Fayette Circuit Court.

EARLY DAYS OF THE SETTLEMENT.

THE close of the year 1784 found Lexington with several stores, which provided a ready market for supplies produced by the farmers. Smith's road, from Limestone to Lexington, by way of the Lower Blue Licks, became a much travelled road and a favorite with emigrants arriving in the Blue Grass. Statehood was talked about and the separation from Virginia much debated. An election was held in Lexington for delegates to represent the county at a convention to be held in Danville, and it resulted in the selection of Levi Todd, Caleb Wallace, Humphrey Marshall, John Fowler and William Ward. No record has been found to indicate the number of votes received by the successful candidates. The convention met at Danville on December 27 of that year.

Among the arrivals in Lexington early in 1785 was Edward West, a Virginian, who was the first watch-maker to settle in Lexington. In later years, he invented a number of useful mechanical devices, among which were a pistol, a nail-cutting machine, and a steamboat. "Ned West had the first steamboat ever invented and ran it across a mill pond in the neighborhood of Lexington. He and my brother John, being from the same part of the country, were very intimate. They sought a great while for perpetual motion. They made some wooden types. The first I saw or knew of them was from a handbill, which was stuck up in Paris, as I came out from Virginia back. Had a son, now in Europe, a celebrated portrait painter. Had his steam boat about 1790."[1]

The Kentucky Gazette makes no mention in its issues of this event, nor of many of the other interesting happenings in Lexington's early history. Evidently, what every one knew was not news. The Gazette had been running for several years at the time of this

---

[1] Fielding Bradford interview, Draper MSS. 13CC211. —see also Perrin's History of Fayette County, page 379.

experiment, yet the editor ignored the event to publish
some Acts of Congress and items lifted from Baltimore
papers regarding the political happenings in European
capitals. The publication of "Bradford's Notes" in
later years supplied some of this deficiency. Mr. West
died September 1, 1827.

The frequent transcribing of the Trustees' minute
book has left no record of the meetings held during
the year of 1784. The Trustees apparently held their
first meeting in the year of 1785 on May 11 and the
record shows they issued and signed deeds for in-lots
to Evan Francis, Simon West, Casper Carsner and
Percival Butler. The numbers of these lots does not
appear in the record. On page 16 of this minute book,
under date of August 9, 1785, the Trustees' books give
us a record of the first claim made against the Town
of Lexington when we find this entry: "Ordered, that
Robert Patterson, Esquire, be authorized to enter a
Caveat against the claim of John Bradford to the said
town, and that he draw on Mr. Robert Parker, Clerk,
and Treasurer of said Trustee's money for that purpose, and he is further authorized to contract
with one or more attorneys to appear and defend said
suit". Bradford lost the suit and was required to pay
the costs. The next meeting recorded in this minute
book is dated October 12, 1785, and shows that the
trustees signed deeds to in-lots to David Mitchell,
Christian Spears, and a lot also to Wilkinson, Armstrong, Dun and Company, but the clerk failed to indicate the numbers or location of any of these lots.

James Monroe, afterwards President, visited Lexington in October, 1785, and after staying a fortnight,
departed for Virginia over the Wilderness Road.[1]
Other visitors of that year have left records of their
impressions, one saying: "Passed through Lexington
in 1785 to Kentucky River. But a few scattered cabins
here and there in Lexington when I passed through."[2]
Another arrival indicates there was some talk of trans-

[1] Wilkinson vs. Marshall—Complete Record Book "B", Supreme
  Court of Kentucky.
[2] Tillery interview—Draper MSS. 11CC274-275.

ferring Lexington to Bryan's station which failed; "In spring of 1785 Rogers came out and took possession (of Bryan's station). In 1780 he had swapped his piece of land in Virginia with Colonel Preston, for this 3,000 acres of Military claim, Rogers running all risks. They wanted to bring the town here but Rogers didn't want it."[1]

The records of the Fayette County Court were destroyed when the office of Levi Todd, then clerk, was burned on the night of January 31, 1803, and thus were lost many records that would throw light upon pioneer Lexington. The Circuit Court Clerk's office has but few papers dated prior to 1796, but from the time John Bradford started the Kentucky Gazette, with his "pi-ed" type on August 11, 1787, we begin to find a more definite record of the stores and their locations.

From the wording of the early advertisements, we learn that some of these stores had been in business for quite a period before the Gazette became the pioneer press of Kentucky, as they refer to "our old stand," and it is from these advertisements we learn also of the stocks of goods carried by the proprietors and the commodities they offered to accept in exchange.

John Bradford came to Kentucky as a deputy surveyor in the fall of 1779,[2] having been born in Prince William county, Virginia, in 1749, a son of Daniel Bradford. In 1771 he married Elizabeth James, who bore him five sons and four daughters. He served in the army during the campaign against the Chillicothe Indians and was appointed deputy surveyor for Kentucky by George May and assigned to the district north of the Kentucky river, where he surveyed many large tracts of land, including one of 6,000 acres in the name of John and Daniel Bradford. He owned considerable acreage on Cane Run in Fayette and Scott counties.

1 Darnaby interview—Draper MSS. 11CC164.
2 Manson vs. Craig—Complete Record Book "E", page 338—Fayette Circuit Court.

When the second convention to discuss independence from Virginia met at Danville in 1785, he learned that there had been a committee, consisting of James Wilkinson, Christopher Greenup and John Coburn, appointed to use their endeavors to induce a printer to settle in Kentucky. Bradford informed this committee that if they would give him the assurance of the public patronage, when the business would be so profitable as to induce other printers to come into Kentucky, he would establish such a paper as soon as the press and an office could be procured. The citizens of Lexington already had given Mr. Bradford sufficient encouragement to keep him from starting his paper in Danville, when the trustees, at a meeting held in July 1786, ordered, "that the use of a public lot be granted John Bradford, free, on condition that he establish a printing press in Lexington; the lot to be free to him as long as the press is in town."

The first office of the Gazette was a log cabin at Main and Main Cross streets, as we learn from the date line of the second issue. In an early issue the editor says: "the editor presents his readers with the Kentucke Gazette 'executed' on paper equal to any western newspaper. The following will be taken for subscriptions: Corn, wheat, country made linen, sugar, whiskey, ash flooring and cured bacon." But he does not mention in his newspaper the aid of the palsied hands of Thomas Parvin, his typesetter. "Parvin had lived at Constant's station in Clark county and was in the fields working with two children when the station was attacked by Indians. Parvin had the palsey very bad; hands trembled so I didn't see how he could set the type. Thomas Parvin was poor and had a good many children. He was a weakly little man and was a school teacher at Strode's (station) for some time. He had lived on Wolf creek, not far from Clintonville."[1] Fielding Bradford says; Thomas Parvin was the first person who worked in the office (of the

1 Interview with Fielding Bradford, Draper MSS. 13CC211.

Gazette) that had served a regular apprenticeship to
the business. He had learned with William Bradford,
of Philadelphia. He taught school in Lexington after
he quit the printing business, and finally moved to
Bourbon county. Type was brought down from Pittsburg, August 1787, paper started. Bought it of John
Scull. I was in Pittsburg 3 months, Spring 1787 from
March to June 1."[1]

There is no known copy preserved of the first
issue of the Gazette with the date of August 11, 1787,
and the valuable files of this paper now owned by the
Lexington Public Library begin with the second
issue dated August 18, 1787. The only advertisement
in the second issue is that of Jacob Myers, who advertised a paper mill "on Dix River above the grist
mill." His death is announced in the Gazette of
June 1, 1827.

The Gazette spelled "Kentucky" in its title line,
ending with e, instead of y, until the issue of March
7, 1789, when the e was dropped and the y substituted.

The date line of the second issue reads; "published
at the corner of Main and Main Cross streets," and
this was continued until the issue of March 8, 1788,
when the date line reads, "published on Main street."
On July 11, 1789, the date line again was changed to
read "Main and Main Cross" street and remained thus
until October 8, 1791, when removal was made to a
location on Main street, where it remained until April
13, 1793, when the Gazette announced removal to
"Cross street." On December 27, 1794, the Gazette
raised its subscription price from fifteen shillings to
twenty one shillings per annum, and began as a semi-
weekly, and removed back to Main street at the same
time. On November 24, 1800, the Gazette changed the
subscription price to $2.00 per annum, and still re-
tained "Main street" at its head. "Being the only
newspaper within 500 miles, it must have occupied a
position of unusual interest. It was carried to the outside settlements by post riders employed by John

1 Interview with Fielding Bradford, Draper MSS. 13CC211.

Bradford, and these were the first efforts to establish
a Post Office service in Kentucky. Living through
the entire romantic period of Kentucky's history, it
brought fame and fortune to its editor, who received
many honors from the citizens of Lexington."[1] He was
early elected a trustee for the town of Lexington and
served many years as chairman of the board. He was
elected a member of the Kentucky Legislature in 1802,
and was chairman of the board of Trustees of Transylvania University. At the time of his death, March
2, 1830, he was serving as sheriff of Fayette County.
One fact not generally quoted in the history of his
career was his attempt to secure a state office, when
the Gazette announced his candidacy for the office of Lieutenant Governor in the issue dated June
9, 1812. In the Gazette dated August 11, 1812 the
complete election returns were published for this office,
as follows;

Richard Hickman	23,444
Young Ewing	7,489
James Crutcher	3,611
John Bradford	3,180

Early in the year of 1825 John Bradford began
the publication of his "Notes," which gave an excellent
description of the early struggle to eliminate the
Indians from the Blue Grass and the other beginnings
of Kentucky's history. These "Notes" did not appear
in consecutive issues of the paper, as No. 24 only appeared on March 2, 1827. They are a wonderful source
material and many of the writers upon the history of
pioneer Kentucky, have quoted liberally from them.

In May, 1785 the election was held to select delegates to attend the convention at Danville, and resulted in the choice of Robert Todd, James Trotter,
Levi Todd and Caleb Wallace as the representatives
from Fayette County.

A description of Lexington about this time is
found in one of the books on early travels in America;
"A Historical, Geographical and Commercial View of

[1] The Pioneer Press of Kentucky—Filson Club No. 3.

the United States," by William Winterbotham, published in London in 1799, by M. D. Simmons:

"Lexington stands at the headquarters of the Elkhorn river and is reckoned the capital of Kentucky. Here courts are held and business regularly conducted. In 1785 it contained about 100 houses and several stores with a good assortment of dry goods. It has increased greatly since."

The third issue of the Gazette contains the advertisement of Robert Barr, which gives some idea of the contents of a frontier general store:

ROBERT BARR.

Has just received a fresh assortment of groceries and dy stuffs, and opened the remaining part of his dry goods, and now are for sale, likewise two Philadelphia made stills, two mill saws, four Dechard rifle guns, a number of cows and calves, with the following medicines: Glauber salts, bark rhubarb, jallap, tarter emetic, cream tartar, Ippececuana, magnesia, camphir, flower sulpher, quicksilver ointment. British oyl, Turlington's balsam, Anderson's pills, Hooper's female pills, Essence of peppermint, licorice balls, etc., also two surveyor's compass and chains, together with a case of platting instruments at 8 pds. each compass.

As I propose quitting trade as soon as this cargo of merchandise is vended, shall in future sell on the lowest terms to expedite the same. Superfine broadcloths with other fine goods will be sold on lower terms than this district can in future be supplied.[1]

The following week, Thomas January advertised an assortment of second-, third-class and coarse cloths, coatings and corduroy, shallouns, callimancoes, moreens and poplin, Irish linen, Beaver and wool hats, knives and forks, needles and pins, copper sauce pans, wool and cotton cards, pen and Cutteau knives, pew-

---

[1] Kentucky Gazette—September 1, 1787.

ter, fine- and coarse-tooth combs, saddlery ware, 8d, 10d, 12d and 20d nails, alum, copperas and brimstone, tea, coffee, pepper and loaf sugar, wine, Jamaica spirits, assorted China and queensware.[1]

The Town Trustees this year were Robert Patterson, William McConnell, William Steele, Robert Todd and John Parker, while Humphrey Marshall and John Fowler were selected as delegates to the convention held at Danville. The trustees' minute book for the meeting held in September, 1787, shows Thomas Young was formally deeded in-lot No. 1, which had been awarded him on October 12, 1785. Parts of this lot are now occupied by the Transylvania Printing Company and the First National Bank and Trust Company buildings. Uriah Garton, who came to Lexington from Orange county, Virginia, received a deed to a lot whose number is not shown, and Nicholas Brabston received a deed to in-lot No. 64, now 250 West Vine street.

An interesting bit of information concerning this county is to be found in two tax books for the county for the year of 1787, which are now a part of the archives of the Kentucky State Historical Society, at Frankfort. The two books, which had been compiled by Richard Young and Thomas Lewis, were all that could be found for this county. These two books evidently represent two-thirds of the county, as Young's district included that part of the county lying between Tate's Creek road and the Harrodsburg pike, and of course included also, that part of the present county of Jessamine between these two pikes. This book shows:

Whites—16 years to 21 years	433
Blacks—over 16 years	569
Blacks—under 16 years	539
Horses	2,095
Cattle	6,669
Carriages	14
Stallions	14

1 Kentucky Gazette—September 8, 1787.

The carriages named in this report were listed as belonging to John Crittenden, four; James Dupuy, two; Daniel Trabue, two; John Watkins, two; and Edmund Woolridge, one.

In the tax book compiled by Thomas Lewis, which embraced the territory west and north of the district covered by Young, we find:

Male whites—16 to 21 years	75
Blacks—above 16 years	216
Blacks—under 16 years	264
Horses—Mules	2,065
Cattle	4,114
Carriages	2
Ordinaries	3

As incomplete as these books are, they give us some idea of the taxable property that had been accumulated by our pioneers within a very few years after the first settlement in this county. It is supposed the tax book for the district of Fayette County, not covered by the two above given, has been destroyed.

EVENTS OF 1787.

EARLY in the year of 1787 William Morton, called "Lord" Morton, opened a general trading store on the southwest corner of Main and Upper streets, in which he carried drugs as a side line. Later, he operated a tanyard on the corner of Main and Lower (now Patterson) streets. In drawing for the out-lots he was awarded the property on North Limestone, from Fifth to Sixth streets, now a part of Duncan Park. His widow died July 25, 1830, aged 76 years.

In June, 1787, James Wilkinson took a cargo of hams, flour and tobacco from central Kentucky, which he loaded on flat boats on the Kentucky river, and floated down the Ohio, and the Mississippi rivers to New Orleans, where they were sold at a considerable advance over Kentucky prices for the same commodities.[1] This journey was the opening scene in the most remarkable epoch in the history of Kentucky. Starting a personal and political conflict, it divided the state into two camps and developed a vindictive animosity that found expression in a series of violent defamatory newspaper articles and pamphlets, charging Kentucky officials and leaders with "The Spanish Conspiracy." The controversy lasted for many years, and was by no means entirely confined to the limits of Kentucky.

The Kentucky Gazette, dated August 18, 1787 advertises: "The partnership of Whitesides and Company, having been dissolved, all persons owing the firm will please call and settle at once.

John Parker."

On August 25, 1787, Baker Ewing announces he had been selected to close out the stock of goods belonging to Semple-Wynkoop and Company, on account of dissolution of partnership. This firm had headquarters in Danville, with connections in the other settlements

1 Wilkinson's—"My Own Times", Vol. 2, p. 112-116.

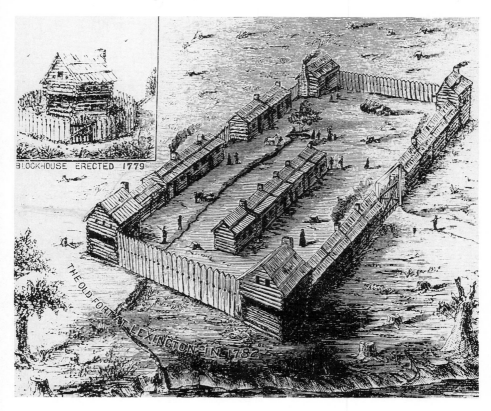

BLOCKHOUSE ERECTED 1779

THE OLD FORT AT LEXINGTON IN 1782

An artist's conception of the blockhouse and fort, the first permanent settlement in Lexington, from George W. Ranck's *History of Lexington,* published in 1872. Courtesy of Special Collections and Archives, King Libraries, University of Kentucky. *Below,* a view of a pioneer woman drawing water from the Bryan's Station spring just before the 1782 Indian attack, taken from the mural by Ann Rice O'Hanlon in the foyer of Memorial Hall at the University of Kentucky, painted as a Public Works of Art Project in 1934 (photo by M. Rezny).

Portrait of Robert Patterson, soldier, political leader, and a founder of Lexington (courtesy of Transylvania University). *Below,* log cabin built by Patterson probably before 1780, moved to Patterson's property between High and Maxwell, Patterson and Merino streets about 1783, and moved to the Transylvania University campus in 1939.

Stone chimney of the Abraham Bowman cabin, built near South Elkhorn Creek on Bowman's Mill Road (photo from 1942 courtesy of Clay Lancaster).

The Adam Rankin house, built circa 1784 at 215 West High Street for the first minister of the First Presbyterian Church and moved in 1971 to 317 South Mill Street (courtesy of the University of Kentucky).

NUMB. II.]   THE   [AUG: 178?

KENTUCKE GAZETTE

SATURDAY, AUGUST 18, 1787.

THE PRINTER OF THE KENTUC-KE GAZETTE TO THE PUBLIC.

AFTER having expended much in procuring the materials and conveying them from Philadelphia, I have ventured to open a Printing Office in the Town of Lexington in the Diftrict of Kentucke. Notwithstanding thefe expences and that of procuring farther fupplies of paper for my bufinefs, and of fupporting neceffary hands, I fhall content myfelf at prefent with the profpect of fmall gains. I confider this country as being yet in an infant ftate, harraffed by the moft favage enemies, having no profitable trade and being drained of money by its prefent intercourfe with the Eaftern parts of America. However the exertions made by a great number of Gentlemen in favour of the prefs convinces me that a Spirit prevails among my countrymen fuperior to their prefent circumftances. Iam fatisfied that every poffible encouragement will be given to my prefent undertaking.

It is impoffible to recount all the advantages that the public will recieve from the publication of a GAZETTE in this Diftrict. Firft, it will give a quick and general information concerning the intentions and behaviour of our neighbouring enemies and put us upon our guard againft their future violence. Secondly, it will communicate a timely intimation of the proceedings of our Legiflature, and prevent us from undergoing various evils by being unacquainted with the laws of our country, fome of which have been in force fometime before they reached the diftrict. Thirdly, it will call our attention to the tranfactions of Congrefs, and fhew us the policy which predominates in our great American Confederacy. It will teach us when we are to prepare for foreign wars; when we are to admire the fuccefsful Hero, the generous Patriot, and the wife Statefman; or to treat with abhorence the betrayor of his Country. Fourthly, it will carry our attention to the ancient world, and gratify our curiofity with refpect to diftant nations who flourifh in the arts of arms or peace. It

will lay open all the Republic of letters to our view and furnifh us with all neceffary inftructions to avoid the danger or fecure the bleffings which may wait on our rifing community. Fifthly, it will afford us an eafy method of underftanding one another and coming to a better agreement in the execution of every defign which may be neceffary for the common good. It will bring the latent fparks of Genius to light, and give the world a refpectable opinion of the people who have come fo many leagues to cultivate a deferted land. When others fee what we have done and what we are ftill able to do; they will come and ftrengthen our hands and be pleafed to partake of our future bleffings.

Indeed it was upon a promife of patronage from the Convention in 1785, that induced me firft to attempt what I have now accomplifhed. I therefore reft fatisfied, that all my Countrymen will be fenfible of my claim to their notice as the firft adventurer in abufinefs wheih has been chiefly inftrumental in bringing mankind from a ftate of blindnefs and flavery to their prefent advancement in knowledge and freedom.

JOHN BRADFORD.

To THE PRINTER OF THE Kentucke GAZETTE

AS I expect your paper will be employed at firft in difcuffing political fubjects, and as I fuppofe that of a feparation from the ftate of Virginia to be the moft interefting at prefent; I hope our politicians will be pleafed through your prefs to give us their fentiments on both fides of the queftion; and I hope they will write, and wefhall read, with that coolnefs and impartiality, which becomes men who have the real intereft of this Country at heart; and that in the end we

may hit upon that policy which will beft fecure life liberty and property to us and our pofterity.

As the moft of us are farmers and unfkilled in policy (altho' we are anxious to do for the beft) we are able to give but a random guefs at the propriety of a feparation—we can fee difficulties on both fides, and would wifh to avoid the worft.

I beg leave therefore to propofe a few querries to the Gentlemen on both fides of the queftion; and will begin with afking thofe who think a feparation neceffary

1ft. By what probable means can a new State fupport Government, defend itfelf from the favages, and pay its quota of the foederal and ftate debt, without a free trade of the river Miffifippi?

Secondly. What probable profpects can a new State have of obtaining a trade down the Miffifippi; and what prfits can we derive from fuch a trade?

Thirdly. will not a feparation leffen our importance in the opinion of the favages, and caufe them to fall on us with greater vigour?

Fourthly. What are the great evils we fuffer for want of a new government; and how could a new ftate remedy thofe evils?

And I would ask thofe who are againft a feparation

Firft. How fhall we defend ourfelves againft the favages under the prefent laws; and how fhall we get paid for doing it?

A page from the second edition of John Bradford's newspaper, published August 18, 1787. "Kentucke" was changed to "Kentucky" in the March 7, 1789, issue.

John Bradford, pioneer publisher (from William Henry Perrin, *The Pioneer Press of Kentucky,* 1888). Courtesy of Special Collections and Archives, King Libraries, University of Kentucky. Bradford lived in the house, built by Thomas Hart in the 1790s, at the corner of Second and Mill streets (*below*) from 1806 to his death in 1830 (photo courtesy of the University of Kentucky). The house was destroyed in 1955.

Hurricane Hall, part of which predates 1800, located on the Georgetown Pike in Fayette County (photo from the late 1800s, courtesy of Mrs. T. M. Watkins Jr.). *Below,* the rear of Hurricane Hall, which remained in the same family for six generations (photo from 1952 courtesy of Clay Lancaster).

Left, Lexington statesman Henry Clay. Portrait, by Matthew H. Jouett, hanging in Ashland, Clay's home (courtesy of the Henry Clay Memorial Foundation; photo courtesy of Clyde T. Burke). *Right,* the Reverend James Moore, first president of Transylvania University and first rector of Christ Church Episcopal. Portrait, by Matthew H. Jouett, hangs in Old Morrison Hall at Transylvania University. *Below,* Masterson's Station, where the first Methodist Church Conference west of the Alleghenies was held in 1790, now the site of Masterson Station Park (photo from the late 1800s courtesy of Clyde T. Burke).

The third Fayette County Court-house, built in 1806 and razed for the present structure in 1883 (photo courtesy of Transylvania University).

The Walnut Hill Church, erected in 1801 a few miles southeast of Lexington, is the oldest Presbyterian Church in Kentucky (photo by M. Rezny).

of central Kentucky. On September 1, 1787, the
Gazette advertises:

> "Teagarden and McCullough at their old
> stand in Lexington, have a general assortment
> of dry goods, groceries, hardware and queens-
> ware, etc., which they will dispose of for cash
> or furs."

> "John Allison, wheelright, had a bay horse
> to stray from his lot. Reward will be paid
> for return."

> Thomas January announced he had "just
> received a fresh assortment at his store oppo-
> site the court house, one door above A. & J.
> Parker."

> "George Teagarden, at the home of John
> Clark, has coffee, Boho tea, chocolate, linen
> stuffs, Mullcavodoes, sugar, pepperall spices,
> nutmegs, blue dy, ginger, indigo, copperas,
> rosin, rasons, rice, china and queensware, glass
> tumblers, west India rum, writing paper, cot-
> ton cards, eight penny nails, etc."

These are examples of the earliest efforts of the
Lexington merchants and show the wide range of the
commodities carried in stock, nearly all of which had
to be sold with considerable addition to cover the cost
of carriage from eastern seaports.

In the issue of the Gazette for September 22, 1787,
a notice takes on a different tone:

> "A company of armed gentlemen will meet
> at Bray's Tavern and will arrange to accom-
> pany those who desire to join the new settle-
> ment to be established on the Licking River."

Fielding Bradford says; "In the summer of 1787
there was only a path where Main street now is, (up
to) about where Masonic Hall and Short street (now
Short and Walnut). Gimson weeds grew so thick
there you couldn't have seen a hog on either side 10
feet from the path."[1]

---

[1] Bradford interview, Draper MSS. 13CC211.

The Trustees' minute book dated July 20, 1787, shows that John Bradford had granted to him, "two poles front of lot No. 43, running back six poles, adjoining lot No. 44," which may represent the period the fort was demolished, as these two lots are shown on the original plat of the town, "where the garrison stands." These lots are now represented by the numbers 314-320 West Main street.

Alexander and James Parker advertised in the Gazette dated September 29, 1787, they would be unable to extend any further credit, alongside a very interesting letter over the signature of John Sevier, Governor of the State of Franklin, extending invitation to settlers and giving terms upon which lands could be secured "at the Muscle Shoals." In an adjoining column are to be found the cards of Mr. Rawleigh Chinn and Henry Lee, both of whom had lost horses, and of Joseph Robinson, who had opened a tanyard at Ruddle's Mill.

On November 24, 1787, the Gazette, for the first time, mentions the name of a merchant who afterwards became one of the best known traders, and who took a leading part in every charitable endeavor, when Mr. Samuel Ayers[1] "advises the public he is located at the corner of High and Main Cross streets, and has for sale stills of all sizes, copper and brass wash kettles, teakettles, frying pans, augurs, tureens, tinware, two foot rules, also, men's and women's saddles, bridle bits, spurs, saddle irons, etc." His name is perpetuated by the alleyway immediately west of the Lafayette Hotel, at which point he established his residence in 1794, and where he resided for many years. His store remained at High and Cross streets for three years, in 1790 being removed to the southeast corner of Main and Mill streets. He died in Danville, Ky., September 20, 1824.

On December 15, 1787, the Gazette contains an advertisement that "James Wilkinson" will purchase

[1] See also deposition, page 577, Complete Record Book D, Fayette Circuit Court.

and ship tobacco, tallow, butter, cured hams, lard, brisketts of beef, etc., which are to be delivered at the mouth of Hickman creek, Dick's river, and at General Scott's landing, all on the Kentucky River:

"These articles being intended for a foreign market it is necessary that they be handled in the manner not only to do the seller credit, but to recommend our commodities to foreign markets, and make them desirous of engaging in commerce in return with the Western Countries."

Peter January, with his son Thomas, started the manufacturing of hemp and bagging on the west side of Mill street, between Second and New streets.[1]

Mr. Robert Barr repeats his former advertisement and adds: "A small quantity of pork will be accepted in exchange." In this same issue we find announcement that Harry Innes and Horatio Turpin are authorized agents to purchase goods advertised as wanted by J. Wilkinson, and that the "Inspectors for these goods will be William Lewis, in Fayette County; Richard Barbour, John Curd, Captain Robert Mosby and John Warren of Mercer county, who will receive same." On December 22, 1787, the Gazette repeats the advertisement of Alexander and James Parker, offering merchandise and dry goods "at their store opposite Bray's tavern." Thus, we learn for the first time the location of this store.

An interruption to the business life of Lexington occurred this year, when Colonel Robert Patterson led an expedition from Lexington against the Cherokees, who were committing depredations on Paint Lick creek, and drove them from the district.[2]

One dread our citizens had at this time was the inadequate protection afforded against fire, which, in a community where every building was constructed of wood, was a cause of constant anxiety. The

[1] McCullough MSS. Lexington Public Library.
[2] Marshall's History of Kentucky.

Gazette makes frequent mention of the hazards of improperly built chimneys and in the issue dated December 22, 1787, we find: "Samuel Cooper takes this method to return his sincere thanks to the citizens of Lexington for their timely assistance in saving his house from being consumed by fire; earnestly recommending to every citizen their attendance on similar occasions with their buckets filled with water from their own houses, as it was by that expedient alone his house was saved."

EVENTS OF 1788.

A T the beginning of the year of 1788 the little town of Lexington was passing through a time of unusual interest, and was a well established frontier village gradually developing a healthy community life. "Not all the pictures of the town are attractive and several of the visitors, accustomed to correctly established society in the east and in Europe, complained of many difficult roads and poor accommodations, but the time of the visit, and the character of the traveler must be considered." One traveler, however, has left a record of the favorable impression Lexington of that year made upon her:

"On 1st of December 1787 we arrived at Lexington. We stayed at my brother's 'till the 4th of December. Lexington is a clean little town with a court house and jail, and some pretty good buildings in it, chiefly logs."

The diary of this fair visitor under date of January 1, 1788, says:

"The society in this place is very agreeable and I flatter myself I shall see many happy days in this country."[1]

Lexington probably lost a warm admirer when this emigrant decided to settle in Woodford county, where she spent her remaining days.

On January 5, 1788, the Gazette publishes the first of notices that were to appear for many years, when the following advertisement was displayed:

"Thomas January announces he intends returning to the settlements in the spring and would all that owe him please call and settle."

Just what results were obtained from this appeal we were not able to learn, but the advertisement appeared in succeeding issues of the Gazette until the 18th of May. In the same issue Moses Moore advertises he has for sale, at the mouth of Hickman creek, a

---

[1] Journal of Mrs. Mary Deweese—Penn. Mag. of History, Vol. 28, p. 197.

considerable quantity of merchandise, which he will exchange for farm products. Gordon and Coburn, also, announce they will be unable to longer continue credit and "will all that owe them please call and settle." Robert Barr announces he will purchase pork at 12 shillings 6 pence per hundredweight.

The minute book of the trustees shows they again renewed their efforts to get the streets in good condition for use by travelers, and on March 7, 1788, (page 23) we find this order: "Resolved—that all streets be opened and cleared of stumps by August 1st." At this same meeting Samuel Blair and John Coburn were appointed a committee to build a bridge over Elkhorn at Cross street, and another committee (not named) was appointed to locate a brick yard for Jacob Springle, which a subsequent entry shows was located on east Seventh street. Mrs. Springle died in Lexington during February 1846, aged 74 years. "She was a resident for 60 years and as a child had been a prisoner of the Indians."[1]

The prices charged for provisions by the Lexington merchants this year, as shown by the advertisements in the Gazette, were; Beef, 2 cents per pound; Buffalo, 1 1-2 cents per pound; Turkeys, 15 cents each; Potatoes, 50 cents per bushel; Flour, $5.00 per barrel, and Whiskey, 50 cents per gallon.

On March 7, 1788, the minute book of the town trustees shows in-lots Nos. 74 and 75 were deeded to George Gordon and John Coburn, now 416-420 West Vine street, and in-lot No. 32 to Hugh McIlvaine, a lot that was afterwards the site of the Lexington gas works, on West Main street. This same year also introduced to Lexington two men, both of whom afterwards were leaders in various commercial enterprises; William Leavy, a native of Ireland, arrived in Lexington from Carlisle, Pennsylvania, and opened a store at a point now represented by the number 342 West Main street. In 1793 he bought out the stock and store of Christopher Greenup, afterwards Governor of

---

[1] Diary of Rev. W. M. Pratt, February 10, 1846.

Kentucky, who had been a merchant at the southwest corner of Main and Mill streets. James Weir, another native of Ireland arrived in Lexington, and after opening a general merchandise store, started a bagging factory and rope walk. In a few years he opened a cotton mill on his farm at South Elkhorn.[1]

The Gazette for April 12, 1788, announced Teagarden and McCullough, at their store on Main street, "three doors below the court house, where Mr. Clarke lately kept," had for sale "camblets, durants, moreens. shallouns, fustians, jeans, corduroys, plush, half ticks, silk, cotton, linnen, Kenting handkerchiefs, black and white gauze, apron lawn, striped and Irish linnen, worsted, thread and cotton stockings, testaments, spelling books, writing paper, Watt's psalms, Hymns, large and small looking glasses, china and queensware, bridles and saddle parts, shoe and knee buckles, pen and cutteau knives, ivory and horn combs, spices, drop shot, castings, indigo, fig blue and rosin, chocolate, muscavado sugar, nutmegs, cloves, cinnamon and ginger, copperas and brimstone."

On May 17, 1788, the Gazette advertised;

"Robert Parker, at the corner of Main and Cross streets, has for sale, cotton, sugar, linen, buttons, brocaded Tiffany, skeleton and cap wiring, gartering and hardware, and many other articles too tedious to mention."

Alexander and James Parker's advertisement appears in the issue of June 7, 1788, announcing they have received a new shipment of deep and light blue broadcloths, brown and light colored ditto, Indian and bed blankets, garters and stay laces, and Hugh McIlvaine says he is now opening his store, one door above (east) of A. & J. Parker's store, with "rose and striped blankets, feathered velvets, marsailles quilting, twist thread, wool hats and sewing needles, also darning and knitting needles."

The tax book for the year of 1788, covering that portion of the town and county west of the Harrods-

1 Perrin's History of Fayette County.

burg pike (then called Curd's road), and extending
to the Versailles Pike (then called Scott's Road), including to the corner of High and Main Cross streets
in the town of Lexington, shows the following results:

Tithables	1,424
Slaves	621
Horses	2,466
Carriages	10
Ordinaries	1
Billiard tables	1

Christopher Keiser is given as the proprietor of
the billiard table, and also he paid the tax on the
ordinary. William Malden is listed as paying the tax
on one carriage.

In the Gazette, under date of April 19, 1788, announcement is made:

"In the election in Fayette County last
Saturday for delegates to the convention,
which is to form the Constitution for the government of the Commonwealth of Kentucky,
resulted in the following state of the polls;

General Wilkinson	742
Caleb T. Wallace	613
Col. T. Marshall	493
John Allen	415
Col. Wm. Ward	392"

A well known Kentucky crop was mentioned in the
Gazette dated May 3rd, 1788, when Robert Barr advertised he had hemp seed for sale. On same date
the Gazette announces the result of the election held
in Mercer county:

Samuel McDowell	275
John Brown	240
Harry Inness	213
John Jouett	196
Christopher Greenup	135

The first regular and formal celebration of Independence Day in Lexington took place July 4, 1788,
with a dinner at the tavern of Thomas Young, at

which fourteen toasts were drunk, accompanied by a discharge of rifles.

The first auctioneer's "cry" appears in the issue of the Gazette for August 2, 1788, when John Warren advertises "merchandise, necessary, durable, useful and ornamental" to be exposed for sale near the court house. Edward West announces he has opened a shop on High Street, "where watchmaking and clockmaking will be done in the neatest and shortest manner," also, that he had watch crystals for sale. On August 23, 1788, announcement is made by Edward Payne and Thomas Lewis: "All those indebted to the subscribers when they kept their store in Lexington are requested to meet us at Thomas Young's tavern September 9th, for adjustments."

This is the first and only time the name of this firm appears in a written record and well illustrates the meagreness of information about some of our early commercial enterprises.

On September 6, 1788, James Wilkinson advertises he has received a quantity of salt, which he desires to exchange for tobacco. In same issue appears a newcomer with the announcement that "John Gowdy, on Main street, nearly opposite Collin's tavern, and one door above A. & J. Parker's, has received a large assortment of dry goods, files, saws, awls, blades, Jews harps, chisels, pipes, etc." Wilkinson and associates seem to have had almost a monopoly of the salt supply in central Kentucky, which they retailed to other portions, as is shown in the pleading of his suit against Daniel Brodhead.[1]

"Wilkinson's pleasing personality, his sharp intellect and perfect poise, and an immaculate appearance added to an ingratiating manner soon made him the leader of a certain group in Kentucky politics, and one who, more than any other man, or group of men, was to influence the course of western events for many years afterwards."[2] Regardless of his complicity with

1 Fayette County Court Order Book, No. 1, page 304.
2 Littell's—Political Transactions.

the alleged "Spanish Conspiracy," he was clear-headed enough to see the advantages of an outlet for Kentucky's products, something that was entirely lacking at the time of his arrival in the Blue Grass. Realizing that New Orleans was the most easily available market —with a minimum of transportation costs—he secured 35,000 pounds of Kentucky's products, which he floated down the Ohio and Mississippi rivers to New Orleans, and after disposing of it took a sailing vessel to Charleston, S. C., whence he returned to Kentucky in the latter part of 1788.[1] He sent another shipment from Kentucky August 8, 1788, and he himself was in New Orleans again in 1789. He states his barges for the second trip cost him 1,000 guineas, with carrying capacity of 40, 60 or 80 hogsheads of tobacco. His expeditions and the difficulties attending the disposal of his cargoes are well explained in the letter of Daniel Clark, which is reproduced in "The Annals of the West," by J. H. Perkins, printed at Cincinnati in 1864. On page 309 he says: "Up to the middle of 1788 all those who ventured on the Mississippi had their property seized by the first commanding officer they met. At this time, however, the King of Spain had ordered the Spanish Governor to purchase more tobacco for the manufacturers at home than the Louisiana growers could produce, and the arrival of the first shipment of Kentucky grown tobacco was at a fortunate moment. This tobacco brought at New Orleans $9.50 per hundredweight, and had cost only $2 in Kentucky. This immense profit made the business attractive. Considerable quantities of flour were also purchased. General Wilkinson returned by sea to Charleston, after appointing Daniel Clarke, Sen., his agent and upon his arrival in Kentucky, bought up all the produce he could collect, which he shipped and disposed of as he had the first shipment, and for some time all the trade from the Ohio was carried on in his name. A line from him was always sufficient to ensure the owner of the boat every privilege he could desire."

1 Wilkinson's "My Own Times", Vol. 2, p. 113.

The very boldness of the enterprise of Wilkinson
appealed to the adventurous Kentuckians, especially
when its successful achievement established a market
for their surplus supplies and produce. The money to
pay the farmers for their produce was sent up from New
Orleans, packed in small kegs on pack horses, as is
shown in the deposition of John Ballinger. After giving some of the details of his overland trip, he says:
"I arrived at Frankfort and delivered the money to
General Wilkinson in the presence of many persons
who were expecting it. They were Lincoln county
farmers and were much disappointed because the entire
shipment of money had not been sent from New
Orleans."[1] During the court martial of General Wilkinson, Elisha Winter testified that he was a resident
of Lexington during the years of 1788, 1789 and 1790,
and that General Wilkinson was then engaged in commerce in both Kentucky and New Orleans. In 1791
the General made a shipment of ten boats of tobacco
to New Orleans, one of which sunk enroute. Mr.
Winter testified that he became a citizen of New
Orleans in 1791. He stated also that he knew in
Lexington Major Swann, the investigating officer, before the trial of the General, as he had visited Mr.
Winter in Kentucky and secured the evidence.[2] While
a resident of Lexington General Wilkinson resided on
West Main street, near Jefferson, and later removed
to Frankfort. He also lived near Versailles, as is
shown in the Stevenson statement. "Wilkinson lived
opposite Mrs. Dupuy near Versailles. Kept a coach
and four with 2 riders seated on the horses, Black. He
sold out to Humphrey Marshall and lived a year or
2 with John Fowler."[3]

The month of September of 1788 brought the
beginning of an industry to Lexington that afterwards
reached considerable proportions and is still a feature
of our economic life. "Early in this month John

---

1 Wilkinson's "My Own Times," Vol. 2, p. 199.
2 Letter of Captain Isaac Guion.
3 Stevenson interview, Draper MSS. 11CC247.

Halley, John Wilkerson and some others, started a
drove of cattle for Virginia. They were fired upon
by some Indians."[1]   No record has been found to
show whether this adventure was successful or not,
but the enterprise of the participants deserves com-
mendation.

On September 5, 1788, Thomas Marshall, "late
Surveyor of Fayette county" closed his office and advertised that "All persons who have plats and certificates in the office are desired to apply for them." On
November 12, 1788, the Town Trustees met and signed
deeds to Robert Barr, for in-lots No. 45 and 46,—now
264-266 west Main street, and in the issue of the
Gazette dated November 14th, John Moore "late of
Ireland, advises he is living with John Little, the
wheelright, where he will make wheel irons equal to
the best."

This year also represents Lexington's first effort
to secure a secret order, when the Lexington Lodge of
Freemasons was organized. A dispensation of the
Grand Lodge of Virginia, on a petition presented by
General Green Clay, was received and Lexington Lodge,
known as No. 25 of Virginia, was organized of date
November 17, 1788, with Richard Clough Anderson
and Green Clay as officers. No record has been found
giving a list of the Charter members. It carried this
number until October, 1800, when the Kentucky Grand
Lodge was organized and Lexington Lodge then became No. 1, of Kentucky.

Another activity of Lexington during the fall of
this year was the organization of the first uniformed
militia company west of the Allegheny mountains. The
muster roll of this company shows: Captain James
Wilkinson, Lieutenant James Hughes, Ensign Archibald Brown, Privates George Gordon, Innes Brent,
Thomas January, Robert Williams, William Morton,
Joseph Byers, John Postlethwait, David Humphries,

---

[1] Wm. Sudduth interview—Filson Club Quarterly, January,
     1928, p. 53.

James Wilson, David Leitch, George Anderson, Robert Holmes, Andrew Holmes, William Levy, George Teagarden, Patrick McCullough, Israel Wright, Gabriel Maupin, David Kirkpatrick, John Hawkins, Samuel McMillan, John Gowdy, and Cornelius Beatty.[1]

Probably organized with some political motive in the background, the Lexington Light Infantry was actively engaged in every call for troops made upon Lexington until the War Between the States in 1861-1865. The members then divided according to their political beliefs, and "The Old Infantry" became only a memory. About the year of 1800 their uniform consisted of a blue coat, with cuffs, breast and collar faced in red, and ornamented with bell buttons. The pantaloons were of blue cloth, the hat black, with left side turned up and held in place by red plume. For a while their favorite parade ground was the level field west of High and Broadway, near Keiser's "Indian Queen" tavern. Later, they used the level ground at Maxwell's spring, where were held most of the political rallies, muster days, and other celebrations so dear to the pioneer Kentuckian. Following James Wilkinson the captains were: James Hughes and Samuel Weisiger, 1791; Cornelius Beatty, 1793; John Postlethwaite, 1797; Thomas Bodley, 1803; and N. S. Hart, 1811-12. This company supplied many trained officers for the War of 1812, the Mexican War, and the War of 1861-1865.[2] The muster roll of the original company is interesting, since it contains the name of nearly every merchant in Lexington for that year.

A typical story of a pioneer, and of the hardships endured by the early settlers of Lexington, is an interview with an arrival in Lexington, late this year. "Asa Farrar left Bennington, Vermont, 8th October 1788 and arrived in Lexington, Ky., 19th December, 1788. When we got to Maysville, we found one cabin and we were two days getting up the hill; taking a

1 Draper MSS. 2MM38—Wisconsin State Historical Society.
2 Perrin's History Fayette County, p. 444.

little of the plunder at a time. We found a horse mill
and tavern and some cabins at Washington. One house
at Blue Licks, and some cabins at Paris. There was
not over 100 men in Lexington (at this time). As many
of them as we could get were employed two days in
clearing out the road from Brennan's (now Phoenix
Hotel), as far as what we called Vanpelt's Lane (now
Rose street); in clearing out to where the race ground
was. There was one burr-oak so large we couldn't
get a saw long enough to run through. Had to cut
on each side to let the saw in. Have no doubt the
tree was four feet over. Forest of Burr oak and black
walnuts. This road lead out to Levi Todd's, where
was the clerk's office; 3 miles out of town. The part
I speak of that we cleared these two days was on
what is now Main street. A hurricane had filled the
passway and they were now clearing it out. There
was a trace in this direction to Boonesborough; and
the road was at this time opened up to that place.
Levi Todd afterwards moved to town. After the road
was opened 4 or 5 years (it was after 1796 for I was
at the clerk's office out there in February 1796 to get
my license to marry) the office was burned. The
place was where Wickliffe's house now is. Twas
believed the office was set on fire to destroy land
claims. Those who could get oral testimony were
enabled in that way again to establish their claims.
The young men in Kentucky were offered an in- and
out-lot in Cincinnati for going to help build Fort
Washington. McClellan, McMillan and Paxton were
of the company. I was not, but was down there frequently."[1] Mr. Farrar was present at the signing of
treaty between General Anthony Wayne and the
Indians at Greenville, Ohio, in August 1795. He became a substantial land owner and left numerous
descendants.

[1] Interview with Asa Farrar, Draper MSS. 13CC1.

EVENTS OF 1789.

WITH the beginning of the year 1789, we find from the pages of the Gazette that the Lexington stores began to advertise more and undertook by that means to let the public know the variety of merchandise carried by them. But, with this increased activity the Gazette is strangely silent regarding the election for the electors of President and Vice President of the United States. Apparently no attention was given this election in the Town of Lexington.

"Wilkinson's expedition of Kentucky products to New Orleans this spring, consisted of twenty-five large boats, some of which carried three pounders and all of them swivel guns. These boats were manned by one hundred and fifty hands."

This year also witnessed a large immigration into Kentucky, and Lexington received its share. New names began to appear as storekeepers, and the Trustees' minute book shows many lots issued to persons not previously appearing in any record. Judge Symmes says "The amazing immigration into Kentucky had stripped all the country around Limestone of every kind of provision in such manner that nothing can be bought at that neighborhood under three times the Lexington price for the same article."[1]

On March 5, 1789, James Bray, Lexington's first tavern keeper, announces he has retired from the tavern, and "will all those who owe him please settle with Mr. Andrew Holmes." This same spring also witnessed the establishing of a new town in Bourbon county, when "Hopewell" (now Paris) was made the county seat.

A bit of gossip from Central Kentucky of this period is found in the letter of John Wilmott to his brother-in-law, Benjamin Talbott, at Baltimore, Maryland, dated January 24, 1789:

---

[1] Letter John Cleves Symmes to Jonathan Drayton, page 56.

"The roads being very bad we was obliged to
leave half our goods at the river (Limestone).
We have a trade with the Spannards which is
a great help for the country. They receive our
tobacco and give money or goods for it. A
number of men have gone to the Spannards
and got passports from the Governor to trade
as much as they please. Corn here is from 6
shillings to 10 per barrel, pork, 15 shillings
per hundred pounds, beef 16, sheep, 20 shillings per head. We was sixty days from
Oningsis Mill on the Monnegahle to Limestone. Brother Robert and John Cockey
Owings were along."[1]

In the Gazette for March 5, 1789, Hugh McIlvaine
advertised a long list of merchandise "just received,
amongst which were; Broad cloths, rose and stripped
blankets, feathers, velvets, cashmirs, stockings, men
and women's gloves, gartering, brass wares, pen knives,
files, saws, rasps, hinges, spurs, plane irons, weeding
hoes, shoe and knee buckles, tumblers, decanters,
pewter dishes, spelling books, testaments, Watt's
psalms and other books on divinity, also, a long list
of drugs."

Benjamin Beall and Company opened a store next
door to Robert Barr where they announced they would
dispose of dry goods, hardware, etc., in exchange for
cash or ginseng. On May 25, 1789, the minute book
of the Trustees shows they signed a deed to John
Parker for in-lot No. 25, now 564-566 west Main
street, and on the same date the Gazette announced
Wilson and Parker had opened a store nearly opposite
the court house "with miscellaneous assortment of
merchandise." David Humphrey advises he lives near
the court house at "The Sign of the Buffalo," where he
repairs clocks and watches and also makes devices
for marking hats, rings, etc. He was the artisan who
devised and made the first seal of the Commonwealth
of Kentucky, for which he received 12 pounds. He

---

[1] Maryland Historical Magazine, Vol. 6, page 352.

also executed the plates showing surveys used by James Hughes in his "Hughes' Reports," the first publication of the various decisions by Kentucky's Supreme Court.

William Morton advertised that he "is now in the house lately occupied by John Duncan, opposite Young's Tavern, with a complete line of dry goods."

On July 4, 1789, the Trustees of the Town of Lexington held a meeting and appointed a committee consisting of Moses Patterson and Alexander Adams "to wall up the spring on Lower Street."

The Gazette for August 29, 1789, announces an association has been formed "against the use of imported wines, rums, brandies, silk, laces, gauze and broadcloth." At a meeting held the following year at Danville, an "effort was made to purchase machinery in order to make this country independent of foreign productions."

This year the tax lists for Lexington and Fayette county were prepared by Andrew McCalla, Bartlett Collins, Robert Johnson, Thomas Lewis and James Trotter. By reason of the irregular manner of reporting and some pages missing, the total figures as to the white population cannot be told with accuracy, but the figures remaining show this county had 2,522 slaves, 9,607 horses, 56 stallions and nine ordinaries.

On September 26, 1789, Nicholas Wood, the baker, advertises he desires to purchase some cheap flour, and that "he makes travelers bisquits." On November 28, Alexander and James Parker advise "they have opened a store where we now live," and W. Butler "taylor" says he is open for business opposite Keiser's tavern on High street. Charles White, "late of New York," announces he intends carrying on the coppersmith's business, to-wit; "Stills, brew and die kettles, repairs all kinds of copper and tinware, locks, and keys, and will buy old copper, lead, pewter and brass."

It was in the fall of this year that Dr. Peter Trisler brought into Fayette county a number of Moravian families from Western Pennsylvania. Many of these settled in the part of Fayette county that was afterwards made into Jessamine county.[1] They were largely composed of artisans and fruit growers and promptly became an important factor in the development of the south end of Fayette county. Several of these families remained in Lexington, where their descendants still can be found.

Green Clay was master of the Masonic Lodge for this year. He had been active in securing authority to organize this lodge and the honor conferred upon him was well deserved.

[1] Young's History of Jessamine County.

EVENTS OF 1790.

WITH the opening of the year 1790 we find a number of changes taking place among the merchants of the Town of Lexington. Many new names appear among the advertisers in the Kentucky Gazette, all of whom proudly claimed a great variety in their stocks of merchandise and "just the items needed" in a growing frontier village.

Robert Patterson, James Parker, Robert Barr, Robert Parker, Samuel Blair, John Coburn and Samuel McMillen were elected trustees of the town for that year, and their first efforts were directed towards correcting errors in titles of some of the in-lots. A number of lot holders were required to deed back to the trustees lots they had received by mistake, and were promptly granted other lots.

In the issue of the Kentucky Gazette dated January 23, 1790, Major Peyton Short and Company advertise "they will open a general assortment of fresh goods on February first, which they desire to sell for cash, and will make advances to all those who have consigned their tobacco to Wilkinson and Short." On the same date, Mr. Samuel Ayers advertises:

SAMUEL AYERS
silversmith and jeweler,
announces he has
lately opened a shop on Main street, opposite to Mr. Collin's tavern and Ladies and Gentlemen, who honor him with their custom may depend on having their commands complied with on the most reasonable terms and shortest notice.

On February 6, 1790 announcement is made in the Gazette that "all those who owe Benjamin Beall and Company, will please call and settle with William Kennedy, who is authorized to close all accounts and receive any money due the firm." On March 6, 1790, Andrew Holmes and Company advertise a general

assortment of merchandise "suitable to the present
and approaching season, which will be sold for cash
or country produce. A few firkins of butter are
wanted." Daniel Weible, the cabinet maker, resides
at Strode's station, where he is prepared to execute
the wishes of his customers promptly. John Smith
and Andrew Steiger, announce "they have opened
and established a butcher shop where Mr. A. Stiger,
Jr. 'lately from Baltimore Town', will kill and dress
all kinds of meats of superior quality and neatest
fashions." This partnership lasted only until April
25, when differences caused a separation, with Steiger
and son continuing at the old stand. On March 25,
1790, Charles Vancouver advertised he had "a considerable quantity of Iron mongery, buckles, buttons,
round glass, queensware, men and women's shoes, hats,
Norwich camblets, callimancoes, India chintzes, muslins, silks, callicoes, and an assortment of British
mounted tools." He was the elder brother of Admiral
George Vancouver, of the British Navy, for whom
Vancouver island and sound were named. Charles
Vancouver attempted to start a settlement on the Big
Sandy River and, after securing the services of a large
number of settlers, had to abandon the idea on account
of continual Indian depredations. He returned to his
home in Sussex, England, from which point he wrote
many letters trying to collect monies due him in these
United States. He was one of the victims of James
Wilkinson's financial pyramid and, like many others,
paid dearly in money and trouble for this association.

On April 12, 1790, the Gazette announces Cornelius
Beatty and Company "have opened a store in Lexington, where they have a general assortment of dry goods
and groceries suitable to the season, which they will
sell for cash, beeswax, bear skins, deer skins, or furs."
Mr. Robert Barr advertises he is offering twenty-five
shillings per hundredweight for hemp delivered at
Frankfort, and twenty-three shillings for deliveries in
Lexington. Payments will be made in merchandise
or cash. Christopher Greenup advertises May 3, 1790,

for "stonemasons, carpenters, quarriers, wood cutters and other laborers, to work at Salt Creek Iron Works." Located in what is now Bath county, these iron works absorbed the surplus labor of Lexington for many years.

In May of this year John Bradford, realizing the unprotected condition of the town of Lexington, undertook to organize the first regular fire company and after considerable effort succeeded in perfecting his "Union Company," which was followed later by others, called "The Kentuckians," "The Lion Company" and "The Resolution." Considerable rivalry developed among these companies, in the promptness with which they responded to fire alarms, and their agility in working the pumps to fill their leather buckets. The "Union" company gave several balls, at which admission was charged, and by this means secured funds with which to purchase supplies needed by them.

On June 7, 1790, Teagarden and McCullough advertise they "will depart for the eastern settlements, on the 15th and will be absent several months, leaving Archibald Huston in charge, who will adjust accounts of all who owe them."

At the meeting of the town trustees, held the night of July 3, 1790, at Higbee's tavern, attended only by Samuel McMillen, Samuel Blair, Robert Parker and James Parker, it was voted:

"Resolved, Two lots having been sold of what is called the town commons to the great prejudice of the inhabitants in general, for which reason we are under the necessity of purchasing them back again. Resolved, That the unappropriated ground lying eastward of the town be sold for the purpose of refunding the purchase money of said two lots, and for digging a canal to carry the branch straight through the town; also, to have a row of lively locusts planted on each side of said canal."

On July 19, 1790, William Morton advertises he has opened a tanyard with James McConnell in charge, and at same time, John Hamilton begins making rope of all kinds, at Francis Dill's, "two miles below Lexington." In this month the convention held at Danville, which was the ninth attempt to secure statehood, voted to accept the terms of the mother State of Virginia, and fixed June 1, 1792, for the independence of Kentucky.

McCabe's directory of Lexington, which was published in 1838, says "In this year (1790) an old lead mine was opened west of Lexington, which had every indication of having been worked before and abandoned."[1]

In the fall of this year, Colonel James Trotter commanded the volunteers from Lexington, and joined General Harmar in an expedition against the Miami Indians. During the month of November, George Eads and James Keyes brought the first coal into Lexington. It had been mined on Sturgeon's creek in Lee county, and was floated in three barges down the Kentucky River to Cleveland's ferry, then hauled into Lexington. The results were not up to their expectations, and it was three years before the experiment was repeated.

On November 16, 1790, Jacob Todhunter announced he had erected a tanyard near John Parker's mill, below South Elkhorn. William Leavy advised he was acting agent for Andrew Holmes and Company and would buy steers, lard, and fat horses.

Richard Monks, a weaver, is mentioned in the county court order books, when two apprentices are placed under his charge. He died in Lexington May 21, 1828, at which time the Gazette says, "He was the first practical weaver to settle in Lexington, having emigrated from Europe."

The Gazette closed the year with complaint about the severity of the weather, and also refers to "the

---

[1] See also, Perrin's History Fayette County, page 220.

eagerness of the citizens to obtain black profile likenesses taken by the Physiognatrace." In this same
issue reference is found to the petition being circulated
to the National Congress, "for permission to fight the
Indians in their own way." This effort was afterwards successful and resulted in a Board of War for
the State of Kentucky, acting independently of the
National Army.

EVENTS OF 1791.

THE year 1791 started with a severe spell of weather and also a shortage of news "from the Eastern Mails. The local Board of War for the district of Kentucky was appointed with discretionary powers to provide for the prosecution of the war. The election of trustees for the town of Lexington for this year resulted in the choice of John Bradford, chairman: Henry Parker, clerk; Samuel McMillen, surveyor. The other members were John Coburn, Peyton Short and James Parker.

On February 12, 1791, Byers and Kirkpatrick announce they have a new assortment of dry goods, groceries and hardware, at the store on Main street, "next door to Mr. Barr." Duncan and Holmes advise they have received a very large assortment of merchandise which "they will sell for cash, public securities, furs and bear skins."

A new note enters into Lexington's affairs when announcement is made that a market house will be built for the benefit of the citizens. On March 19, 1791, the Gazette advertised:

To be let,
on the 28th day of March to
the lowest bidder,
The building of the Brick
work of a market house in

LEXINGTON,

fifty by twenty five feet to stand on
sixteen pillars each three feet square,
twelve feet high, to have one story
above, eleven feet between joists, with
two brick chimneys, a plan of which
may be seen at the printing office, or
at Higbee's Tavern, where the
Trustees of the town will meet on the
above day.

In behalf of the Town,
J. Coburn.

On the same date, the Town Trustees entered an order banning all wooden chimneys to residences. They also had another survey made of the town, which showed there were 2,011 acres within the town limits. These boundaries remained unchanged until 1906. Peter Higbee was elected clerk of the market house, and also collector of the town taxes. The militia report for this year shows there was a total of 1,944 privates, with 184 officers, in the two regiments in Fayette county, including the town of Lexington.

The trustees state they have completed signing the deeds "announced at the previous meeting," among which we find a deed to out-lot No. 35, given to William Morton. The lot was on east side of Limestone, from Fifth to Sixth streets, comprising part of Duncan Park. The trustees also voted to fix the tax rate for the present year at 3 shillings for each tithable, and one pence tax on each 51 shillings real and personal property.

On April 9, 1791, W. & H. Parker advertise for an apprentice tanner, and Frederick Seignor, "taylor," says "he has moved from the house where he formerly lived to John Clark's at corner of Main and Cross streets." Jonas Davenport advertises for an apprentice to learn "the tanning business at the mouth of Hickman creek," promising good board and careful instruction. The Gazette also announces the Federal Congress[1] had voted to admit Kentucky as a state on June 1, 1792, and makes no other comment. Joseph Byers, Basil Duke and Robert Megowan are voted deeds for in-lots by the town trustees. Megowan's lot was on Short street just west of Limestone, while the lot given Basil Duke was on the northeast corner of Short and Market streets.

The troops from Lexington who had served in the campaign from Fort Washington against the Indian towns on the Wabash returned to Lexington during the month of June. The names of only a few Lexing-

---

[1] The Act of Congress was signed February 4, 1791, by President George Washington.

tonians of this expedition have been preserved and
these were; Benjamin Gibbs, John Arnold, John
Peoples, Richard Bartlett, Joseph Jones, Samuel Patterson, John E. King, William McMillan, James Brown,
James McDowell and Thomas Allen.

In the issue of the Gazette dated May 28, 1791, some
interesting figures were published, but the source of
the information was not disclosed:

Census.

Free white in Fayette County, over 16	3,517
Free white in Fayette County, under 16	4,081
Free white females including heads of families	7,028
Slaves	3,752

Notley Conn was master of Lexington Lodge of
Masons for part of this year, and later filled the same
position for Paris, Ky., Lodge No. 4. During the last
half of this year Judge Edmund Bullock was the
Master of Lexington Lodge.

The agitation against wooden chimneys continued
with the Trustees repeating their former order abolish-
ing them, and on the same date Francis Dill advertises he has "Salt for sale for cash, bacon, whiskey,
country sugar and linen, at the house between Robert
Barr's and the store of Byers and Kirkpatrick." At
the meeting held June 27, 1791, the trustees voted:
"Resolved, That market house to be built on Public
ground between the lots of Henry Marshall and
Stephen Collins, near center of the block and facing
on Main street." This building was completed early
in 1792 and was the building used as a State House
when the first Legislature convened after Statehood.[1]

Thomas Lewis, who prepared the tax books for
the district between the Maysville Pike and the Winchester Pike, reported a total of 333 blacks above 16
years of age, 91 blacks between 12 and 16 years, 1,853
horses, eight stallions, one ordinary, and one billiard
table, which was owned by Christopher Keiser. The
district of Andrew McCalla, which included the area

1 Unpublished Diary of General James Taylor.

from Winchester Pike to the Tate's Creek Pike, reported a total of 616 blacks over 21 years, 733 blacks aged 12 to 16 years, 3,164 horses and two stallions. Dr. Thomas Lloyd paid on five horses, the "Widow" Gilmore on 12 horses and James Hosley, "taylor", on two horses.

Some dissatisfaction arose over the location of the market house as selected by the trustees, and on July 2, 1791, they voted to hold an election and give the voters of the town an opportunity to select the site. "Election to be held next Monday at the court house." This poll resulted in the first selection of the Board of Trustees being confirmed, and the market house was built on south side of Main street between Mill and Broadway. The Trustees met and signed a deed to in-lot No. 32 to Lewis Castleman, which lot was on Main street, between Spring and Lower (now Patterson) streets. The Gazette also announced a sale of the effects of Archibald Berry, deceased carpenter, which was held by John Bradford, Esquire. Hugh McIlvaine advertised he was making a shipment of tobacco to New Orleans, in the interest of James Wilkinson, which amounted to a total of 120 hogsheads, using five flat boats and forty men.[1]

An interesting letter on local conditions has been found, dated October 3, 1791 and written by Lieutenant Robert Willmot to his brother-in-law Benjamin Talbott, at Baltimore, describing the conditions in Kentucky: "I made 400 bushels of corn off 35 acres. All provisions are plenty. Immagrants to this place are very great. People export a great deal from this place down the Ohio and a deal to the Army."[2]

On October 8, 1791, Elliott and Williams advertise goods to be exchanged for cattle on foot, and Daniel Weissiger says he will purchase land office and treasury warrants for cash. The Trustees met on October 12, "ordered all fences on Short street to be taken down" and authorized "Mr. Stout" to see that

---

[1] Innes, MSS., Vol. 2, page 53.
[2] Maryland Historical Society Magazine, Vol. 6, page 355.

this order was obeyed. They also ordered the fencing around the stray-pen to be repaired and Mr. Stout also had that job. The site of this lot is now in part occupied by the Leader building.

On December 24, 1791, John Duncan advertises he has received a catalogue of the following named books, at his store on Main street:

Rudiman's Rudiments,	Whittenhall's grammer,
Eutropus,	Philadelphia Latin Grammar,
Clark's Ovid,	Davidson's Virgil,
Cicero's Orations,	Xenophon,
Homer,	Ainsworth's Latin diction,
Guthrie's Geography,	Gibson's Surveying,
Sheridan's Dictionary,	Scott's Dictionary,
Pearcy's Dictionary,	Wilson's Sacramental
Arminian Magazines,	Meditation,
Prayer Books,	Watt's Psalms & Hymns,
Dilworth's Spelling Book	Preacher's Lives,
Buchanan's Domestic	Death of Abel,
Medicines	Writing Papers,
Travels of True	Slates and Pencils.
Godliness,	

Also, groceries and dry goods, "most suitable to the present and approaching season, and many others too numerous to enumerate here. All of the above goods to be sold for cash on reasonable terms, public securities, furs, bear skins and Rye will be taken in exchange. The subscriber returns his thanks to those who have favored him with their custom and hopes to merit a continuence as it shall ever be his study to please."

On December 26, 1791, the trustees met and appointed Benjamin Bradford, clerk and treasurer of the board, vice Henry Parker, resigned. On the same date, John Cocke advertises he desires "to purchase some good flour." According to the Gazette, the weather became very inclement, with snow and ice on the roads and very cold weather. The editor complained of difficulty in hearing from the eastern settlements, and lamented the "total lack of news," so he filled the columns of the Gazette with several items regarding happenings in European cabinets.

This same month an election was held to choose delegates to represent Fayette County during the ninth and last convention, which was to form the constitution for the new State of Kentucky, and resulted in the selection of Hubbard Taylor, Thomas Lewis, George S. Smith, Robert Frier and James Crawford. This convention met the following April and gave Kentucky its first constitution.

The trustees met on the last day of the year and elected Will Morton to serve in the place of Robert Patterson, who had resigned, and also issued an order for the secretary to "notify the carpenters to make every exertion towards finishing the market house." Nathaniel Wilson and Will Morton were ordered to "agree with some person to repair the bridge over Town Fork where it is crossed by Mulberry street." Dr. Daniel Preston's account, amounting to 20 pds, 12 shillings, for service to the poor, was ordered paid.

EVENTS OF 1792.

WITH the beginning of the year 1792, the Gazette mentions the severity of the weather, by reason of which "no mails have arrived from the eastern settlements for over ten days." The impassable condition of the roads into Lexington and the total lack of communication with the outside world during the winter months was also mentioned in the files of the Gazette, alongside some recent acts of Congress. In the issue dated January 7, 1792, William Scott announces he has "started a Fulling Mill, six miles below Lexington," and Isaac Telfair opens a store at upper (east) end of Lexington. John Moyland, in whose house Father Badin conducted the first Catholic services in Lexington, announces he has received a fresh shipment of goods at his store, "next door to the Buffalo Tavern, consisting of dry goods and groceries," and in the same issue Teagarden and McCullough announce they have dissolved partnership.

The election for trustees for the year 1792 resulted in the choice of Samuel McMillan, John Coburn, John Bradford, James Parker, Nathaniel Wilson and Will Morton.

On January 14, 1792, Thomas Sloo advises he would like to sell his "blacksmith shop and tools. Will those interested, please call upon Zebulon Barker?" John M. Reading advertises he has for sale "young Cherry trees, at corner of Mulberry and Main streets," which may be the basis for the old tradition that Postlethwait's tavern was erected upon the site of a cherry tree orchard.

On the 28th of the same month, Stephen Collins advises he will close his hotel business, and William Chenoweth says he has had "stolen from my wagon at Owen's tavern, between Lexington and Bryan's station, seven Indian blankets." William Leavy advertises he has "for sale excellent cotton grown on the Cumberland River," and offers to accept land warrants, public securities or young horses in exchange. On the 30th of the month, the trustees held a meeting and repeated their order "directing the carpenters to hurry up work on the Market house, and repairs to be made on the upper bridge." Some dispute seems to have arisen regarding the correct boundaries of Main Cross and Second streets, and they directed "the boundaries of these streets to be relocated." James Tompkins, carpenter and house joiner, advertises for apprentices, and Montgomery Bell, hatmaker, wants beaver skins, otter, raccoon, wildcat and muskrat hides.

On February 18, 1792, Major Peyton Short advertises he desires to "sell his tenement where I now live," also a distillery and a brewery, but does not give location of either. Mrs. Jane Todd transferred her right "to lot on Main street opposite the Court House," to James January, and trustees signed deed for same. On the 27th of the same month, the trustees directed the accounts of Elliott and Williams, amounting to 3 pds, 10 shillings, to be paid, and also the accounts of Stout and Higbee for building the market house, but the amount is not shown.

Charles Morgan prepared the tax book for the district of Fayette County bounded by the Bryan's station and the Leestown Roads, and reported a total of 1,683 white males, 1,682 slaves, slaves under 16 years of age, 904; horses, 3,747; cattle, 9,792; stage wagons, 4; Chaired wheels, 2; stallions, 25; acres 77,699.

Andrew McCalla prepared the tax book covering the portion of the county bounded by Tate's Creek road and the "road to General Scott's" (now Versailles Pike). The book shows—Whites, 2,210; Blacks, 2,435; horses, 3,774; cattle, 10,078; wheeled carriages, 2; ordinaries, 11; billiard tables, 1; stores, 20. This book covered the town of Lexington, judging from the names listed.

On March 10, 1792, the Gazette carried the advertisement of A. Scott and Company, who "have received an assortment of Dry Goods, iron mongery, saddlery, queensware, which will be exchanged for furs, and bear skins, country sugar and line, and ginseng." George Adams' tavern is mentioned in the advertisement of Daniel Weible, who advertised for his lost or stolen horse. The new town of "Newport" is advertised and prospective settlers are assured of good land at reasonable prices. Some unknown advertiser desires to exchange "Military land warrants for cash, young horses or young negros."

Early this year, the northeastern portion of Fayette county was used to form the new county of Clark, with a similar portion from the adjoining county of Bourbon.

The magistrates acting in Fayette county at this time, according to their seniority were Robert Todd, Robert Patterson, Eli Cleveland, William McConnell, James Trotter, Joseph Crocket, Abraham Bowman, Thomas Lewis, William Campbell, John McDowell, Edward Payne, William Ward, John Parker, Charles Morgan, Percival Butler, William Bush, James McMillon, John Maxwell, John Hawkins, Thomas Young, Walter Carr, and James McDowell.

John Coburn and Peyton Short resigned as trustees of the Town, and Christopher Keiser and Daniel Weissiger were elected in their stead. William Morton submitted his resignation from the same board April 23rd.

The militia report for Fayette County published that month shows a total of 1,954 privates and 179 officers. Writers of early Kentucky make frequent mention of the militia, which was the state's sole dependence for protection against the Indians. All male citizens between the ages of 18 and 50 years were subject to calls for military duty at the will of the County Lieutenant, to repel invasions, etc., and otherwise were subject to the call of the Governor of Virginia (Hennings Statutes, Vol. XI., page 476). They were paid at the rate of $5 per month when on active duty. During April of this year, Levi Todd, County

Lieutenant, made his return for the militia of this county and reported the following field officers:

First Regiment —Robert Todd, Colonel,
James McMillan, Lieut. Colonel,
John Mastin, Major.

Second Regiment—James Trotter, Lieut. Colonel.
John Morrison, Major.

Third Regiment —William Russell, Colonel,
James McDowell, Lieut. Colonel.
John McDowell, Major.

By the laws of Virginia of 1784, the militia was organized by counties, with the County Lieutenant holding the rank of Colonel. The militia was to hold musters every three months, with regimental muster during the spring, and a brigade muster some time during the fall of the year, usually after crops were gathered for the winter. The tactics were those used by the regular army, introduced into this country by Baron Steuben. The truth about these musters is hard to arrive at in this day and generation, but they were probably scenes of much disorder and confusion, if we can believe an eye witness. One writer says: "I suppose about 2/3's of the company appeared, some without muskets, and some with muskets without locks, and some with useless pieces—all without bayonets, uniforms, or cartridge boxes. After the roll call, the captain drew up his men in a hollow square for the accommodation of a candidate for election, then the company was again paraded and manoeuvred till about six o'clock, when they were dismissed. It was a dull business, for they had neither fife nor drum, nor did they whistle."

In the Gazette dated April 28, 1792, Elliott & Williams advertise they have at their stores in Lexington and Danville, "scarlet, blue, green, brown and drab superfine broadcloth, olive, butt, black, crimson and figured velvet, window glass, etc., and salt." Byers and Kirkpatrick announce their firm dissolved on account of the death of David Kirkpatrick, and on June 2, Benjamin Cox opens his saddle shop "next door to Edward West, with fine assortment of carriage harness, holsters, horseman's caps, etc." Melchoir Myers advertises to sell candles at seven pense per pound, and George Teagarden, "opens a store next door to the Sign of the Spinning Wheel."

That month, James Taylor, afterwards Quartermaster General of Kentucky troops during the War of 1812, arrived in Kentucky, and says in his diary:

"In a few days, I visited Lexington, then principally a log village. There were a few frame and some large log buildings, in one of which at corner of Poplar Row, a cross street (now Upper) with Main, Young and Brent kept a pretty good tavern. There was but one brick house in six at that time. One, called Mt. Hope, built by old Mr. January, but, in that year several brick buildings were erected, among other a market house was begun on south side of Main street in square below the court house. It was turned into the State House."[1]

During the spring months, the Gazette continued to publish many items of European politics and the doings of royalty, but failed to make mention of the approaching inauguration day for Kentucky's first governor. The convention, which had met at Danville April 19, 1792, and adopted a constitution for the State of Kentucky, provided that the General Assembly was to convene at Lexington on June 4, when the governor was to be inaugurated—for the first state to be admitted into the union of the states, from the enormous area west of the Alleghany mountains. Eleven senators and forty representatives from the nine counties composing the new state were to meet Isaac Shelby, of Lincoln county, who had been selected the first governor.

---

1 Unpublished MSS owned by Mrs. Jouett Taylor Cannon.

The Kentucky Gazette does not mention any preparations for this event by the citizens of Lexington, and the trustees' minute book is equally silent, beyond a resolution donating the use of the second floor of the market house, but we find in the issue of the Gazette, dated June 9, 1792, the story of the departure of Governor Shelby from his home, his arrival at Danville, and the reception accorded him there:

Danville, June 3, 1792.
"His excellency the Governor arrived in town this morning on his way to Lexington. During his stay the following address was presented to him by the inhabitants of the town.

To Isaac Shelby, Esquire,
Governor of the State of Kentucky.

Sir:

The inhabitants of the town of Danville beg leave in the warmest manner to congratulate your excellency on your appointment to the chief magistracy of this State. Unacquainted as to flattery or studied panegyrics they only wish in the plain language of truth to express the great satisfaction they feel on the appointment, and your acceptance of the office.

Alhtough they may not be the first to address you on this occasion, yet they will give place to no other part of the State in attachment to your person, and that they will at all times give aid and support in their power (which may be required) to assist you in the execution of the great trust committed to your charge.

And they beg leave to add their sincere wishes for your personal happiness, and to implore the Great Governor of the Universe to have you and the people over whom you preside in His Holy keeping.

By direction of the inhabitants,
Christo. Greenup
Thomas Barbee,
Greenbury Dorsey.

To which His Excellency was pleased to return the following answer:

Gentlemen:

I feel myself sensibly impressed with the duties of the office to which I am called by the voice of my country—I hope with the assistance of the Divine Ruler of the Universe to discharge the trust reposed in me, in such manner as may give general satisfaction to the good people of our infant state.

This being the first address which hath been presented me since the existence of the State of Kentucky, I beg leave through you gentlemen to return to the inhabitants of Danville, my sincere thanks for this mark of their approbation and personal attachment, and the readiness they have expressed to aid and support me in the execution of my office.

Should any circumstances occur which may require my aid to promote the happiness of the good people of this town, they may rely on my exertions to forward such measures as far as may be consistent with my duties.

I feel, from long residence in the neighborhood, a particular attachment to them, not only for the present mark of their esteem, but for the civilities which I have uniformly received from them.

I have the honor to be with esteem and regard, gentlemen, your most obedient and humble servant

ISAAC SHELBY.

June 3, 1792.

Christopher Greenup
Thomas Dorsey
Greenbury Dorsey
Gentlemen.

Immediately following the above, and in the same column:

Lexington, June 9th.

On Monday the fourth inst., the day appointed for the meeting of the legislature, Isaac Shelby, Governor of this Commonwealth, arrived in town from his seat in Lincoln county. He was escorted from Danville by a detachment of the Lexington troop of horse, and met a few miles from town by the county lieutenant, the troop of horse commanded by Captain Todhunter, and the trustees of the Town. The light Infantry commanded by Captain Hughs were paraded at the corner of Main and Cross streets and received him as he passed with military honors; after attending him to his lodging the horse and infantry paraded on the public square, and after firing alternately fifteen rounds, gave a general discharge in honour of his excellency.

After which the following address was presented to his excellency by the chairman of the Board of Trustees of the town of Lexington.

Sir:

The inhabitants of the town of Lexington, beg leave through us, to present to your Excellency, their sincerest congratulations on your appointment to the office of chief magistrate of the State of Kentucky.

Truly sensible, that no other motives than a sincere desire to promote the happiness and welfare of your country, could have induced you to accept an appointment, that must draw you from scenes of domestic ease and private tranquility, which you enjoy in so eminent degree. Having the fullest confidence in your wisdom, virtue and integrity, we rest satisfied, that under your administration, the Constitution will be kept inviolate and the laws so calculated as to promote happiness and good order in the State.

In the name of the inhabitants of Lexinton we bid you welcome; and assure you that we, and those we represent, have the warmest attachment to your person and character.

May your administration insure blessings to your country; honor and happiness to yourself.

By order of the Trustees of Lexington,
John Bradford, Chairman.

To which His Excellency was pleased to return the following answer.

Lexington, June 4, 1792.

Sir:

I receive with warmest sentiments of gratitude and respect, your very polite and genteel address, which added to the friendly treatment exhibited by you this day in conducting me to this place, commands my most cordial respect and esteem and altho I am thoroughly sensible of my want of experience, and abilities, to discharge the very important duties committed to me; the warm congratulations only of my country induce me to come forward with some hopes, that, by strict attention to the duties of my office and a firm adherence to public justice (both of which I trust are in my power) I may in some degree merit a part of that confidence which they have placed in me.

Unacquainted with flattery I use only the plain languages of truth to express my warm attachment to the inhabitants of this place and assure thro you sir, that I shall be happy to render them any service in my power which may not be incompatible with the interest of our common country.

I have the honor to be, with great regard and esteem, Sir, your most obt. servant.

ISAAC SHELBY.

To Mr. John Bradford, Chairman
of the Board of Trustees of Lexington.

The Gazette makes no mention of the kind of weather supplied for the inauguration of Kentucky's first governor, nor refers to any dinner, inaugural ball, or other entertainment for the legislators, or fair visitors. There is a five-column article presenting a plan for supporting a civil list and raising revenue for the State of Kentucky, but no authorship is shown. John Belli, deputy quartermaster for the United States army, advertises for horses, and Hugh McIlvaine announces he has been appointed administrator of the estate of Francis McDermid, deceased, and desires settlement with those that owe the estate. Simon Frost advertises he has taken up a chestnut sorrel horse on Clear Creek, with a "W" on one shoulder. John Crittenden advertises lands for sale on Kentucky River, Severn creek, Gunpowder creek and on waters of Licking.

There are many other interesting advertisements in the faded pages of the Kentucky Gazette for this date, but no news items are found regarding the sessions of the Legislature. No mention is found of office seekers, or lobbyists, and, for some reason not apparent, the address of the Governor and the reply of Mr. McDowell, the chairman at the joint session of both houses, do not appear in the issue of the Gazette dated June 16, and were not published until the issue of June 23. On that date these items were published, alongside many advertisements of local merchants:

State of Kentucky,
House of Representatives,
Thursday, June 7th.

The speaker laid before the House a copy of the address delivered by the Governor yesterday to both houses of the Legislature in the Senate chamber, which is in the following words:

Gentlemen of the Senate and
House of Representatives.

As the prosperity of our community will depend greatly on the manner in which its government shall be put in motion, it will be particularly incumbent on you to adopt such measures as will be most likely to produce that desirable end. Amongst the means which ought to be used for that purpose, none will be found more efficacious than establishing public and private credit on the most solid basis. The first will be obtained by a scrupulous adherence to all public engagements—the last by a speedy and uniform administration of justice.

The happiness and welfare of this country depends so much on the speedy settlement of our land disputes; that I cannot forbear expressing my hope, that you will adopt every necessary measure to give full operation to the mode pointed out by the constitution for that purpose.

It will be essentially necessary that you should pass laws, regulating the future elections of members to the State Legislature. The having those elections made without any kind of undue influence is an object worthy of legislative attention.

It is also incumbent on you and the interest of the State requires that you should as soon as possible appoint Two Senators to represent this State in the National Senate; and pass the necessary laws to prescribe the time and manner of election of this State's proportion of members of the House of Representatives.

A law obliging sheriffs and other public officers to give security for the due performance of the duties of their respective offices will be essentially necessary.

Your humanity as well as your duty, will induce you to pass laws to compel the proper treatment of slaves agreeable to the direction of the Constitution.

Gentlemen of the House of
Representatives:

It will be your peculiar duty to point out the manner by which the public supplies shall be raised. Small as our money resources are, I flatter myself you will find them fully equal to the necessary expenditures of the Government. I conceive that both the honor and interest of the State require, whatever may be the amount of those expenditures, that the funds for their payment shall be adequate and certain.

The Constitution has made it your duty, at the present session to cause to be chosen commissioners for the purpose of fixing the place for the permanent seat of Government.

Gentlemen of the Senate and
House of Representatives:

You may be assured of my hearty co-operation in all your measures, which shall have a tendency to promote the public good. The unorganized state of our Government and the season of the year, render every proper dispatch of the business that will come before you so much your duty and interest, that I shall forbear anything on that head.

ISAAC SHELBY.

Ordered—that the said address lie on the table.

Ordered—that the address from the Governor be referred to the Committee of the whole house on the state of the Commonwealth.

Saturday, June the 9th

Mr. McDowell now again reported the answer to the Governor's address in the following words;

Sir:

The representatives of the people of the State of Kentucky have considered the address made by you to both houses of the Legislature on the sixth inst.

We congratulate you upon the arrival of the period, when we see our wishes for years past consummated by the formation of a constitution and government organized.

It affords us pleasure that the voice of our country (almost unanimous) has called to the office of Chief magistrate, one who from early period, has experienced the inconveniences and danger we have in common been subject to, by our far removal from the assistance of government and our adjacent situation to hostile savages.

The communications made will be early and particularly attended to. We feel sensible to the force they ought to have on those whose only object will be the prosperity of the state, and we are happy in the reflection that every measure that will lead to its advancement will not only receive your cheerful concurrence but derive from your co-operation, sufficient efficacy to ensure happiness to our fellow citizens and beg leave to assure you, Sir, that we will leave nothing in our power undone which will tend to perpetuate the liberty and happiness of this commonwealth.

We feel anxious that you may be happy in the enjoyment of uninterrupted health; that your administration may be truly advantageous to the first republic in the western waters and leave sensations of gratitude imprinted and not to be obliterated by time.

Ordered—that the speaker affix his signature to the said answer and that Mr. M'Dowell wait on the Governor with the same.

The legislative session ended on June 30 and on July 7 the Gazette published the appointments of the governor for the various counties:

For Fayette—Robert Parker, surveyor; Robert Todd, Brigadier General; Levi Todd, Lieut.-Colonel; and to the Fayette Quarter Sessions Court were named Robert Todd, Thomas Lewis and John McDowell. To the County Court were named Edward Payne, James Trotter, Joseph Crockett, Abraham Bowman, Wm. Campbell, Percival Butler, Walter Carr, James McMillan and Hubbard Taylor.

William Lewis, Frederick Moss and James Hawkins were appointed tobacco inspectors at Wilkinson's warehouse located at mouth of Hickman creek in Fayette County.

The Gazette does not attempt to make much newspaper space out of the performances of the Governor, nor of state politics. It does mention the "cowardly murder" of Colonel John Hardin and Major Truman, by the very Indians they had visited on a peace mission. In the issue dated August 18, 1792, James Morrison advises he has a general store on the corner (northwest) of Upper and Short streets, "where goods will be exchanged for public securities, country produce and young horses." The Gazette refers to the treaty made during September with the Wabash and Illinois Indians, a treaty that was rejected the next spring by the United States Senate. In November the Gazette mentions the defeat of Major John Adair and about 100 of the Kentucky militia in a running fight with the Indians near Fort St. Clair (now Eaton, Ohio) and prints this article alongside an announcement of the establishment of the towns of Mt. Sterling, Versailles and Shelbyville.

On November 24, 1792, William Ross opens his shoe shop at the house of Robert Holmes, and Archibald Brown begins operating a hat factory at the corner of Water and Main Cross streets. John Moyland advertises for hands "to float his boats down the river to New Orleans," while Patterson and Byers announce receipt of a "large cargoe of goods from the East." Israel Wright, "taylor", makes his first appearance in the columns of the Gazette, as does George Hytel, "breeches maker" and glover opposite the Sign of the Spinning Wheel. On December 8, 1792, Jacob Thomas announces he will "teach music and Psalmody," and Anthony Molloy, "taylor" and ladies' habit maker, is to be found at the house of McDermid at Short and Market streets. Elliott and Williams announce they have moved their merchandise to the store "opposite the State House" and James H. Stewart, Printer and

Bookseller, says he has opened in a store lately occupied by A. McGregor. Catherine Wood advertises she "has salt for sale" next door to Dr. Richard Downing on west Main street. William Moore begins making wheels, while Basil Duke and Dr. Frederick Ridgely open "a general store with assortment of drugs, quicksilver, flower of Benjamin, oil of Vitrol, Spirits of Hartshorn, Salt of Steel, dragon's blood, etc." Christopher Keiser opens a store at High and Main Cross streets, and Irwin and Bryson take the "store lately occupied by Peter January and son, with merchandise lately from Philadelphia."

In the issue of December 8, 1792, the Gazette has this significant item:

"On Tuesday the 5th inst., the commissioners appointed by the House of Representatives of this State to fix the permanent seat of government, came to a final decision in favor of Frankfort."

With no other comment, the Gazette dismisses this subject, which at that time was felt to be a death blow to the prosperity of the Town of Lexington. No word of complaint was expressed against the member of the committee from this county, who voted in favor of Frankfort. Various acts of the Assembly were mentioned, among which was the one fixing the seal of the Commonwealth of Kentucky, which was made by David Humphrey, the Lexington watchmaker, and for which he was paid 12 pds.[1]

Some appointments were made for Fayette County: Lewis Bullock, adjutant; Benjamin Howard, paymaster, and Samuel Meredith, quartermaster, all for the 10th regiment of Fayette County Militia; and Justices Robert Patterson, Will Morton, Edmund Bullock and James Ware.

The Executive Journal under date of December 18, 1792, has an entry showing the revenue taxes collected by various sheriffs of Kentucky counties, which

[1] Kentucky State Historical Society Register, Vol. 22, p. 93.

gives us a comparison of the counties in central part of the state:

Fayette	£1,477. 4. 4.
Bourbon	850. 0. 0.
Woodford	584. 5. 1.
Lincoln	490. 9. 1.
Mercer	716. 6. 3.
Scott	231. 1. 2.
Jefferson	329. 1. 4.
Madison	516. 5. 2.

The final vote upon removal of the capital to Frankfort was taken December 22, 1792, and seems to have been entirely ignored by the Gazette in the following issues. In the issue of January 31, 1798, the Gazette placed the reproduction of the state seal between the two words of its name, which was continued until December 26 of the same year.

The Gazette closes the year remarking about the inclement weather and the "lack of mails from the eastern settlements."

James Lemon, who had been master of the Lexington Masonic lodge for the first half of this year, removed to Scott county and was succeeded by Daniel Weissiger, who served the last half of the year, but early in the next year removed to Frankfort.

EVENTS OF 1793.

THE new year of 1793 opened with the Gazette complaining about the severe weather, the non-receipt of mails "from the east," and a total lack of news. The annual election for trustees resulted in the choice of John Bradford, Basil Duke, James Hughes, Daniel Weissiger, Samuel McMillan, Christopher Keiser and Alexander Parker. The members of this board selected Benjamin Bradford as clerk, with James Trotter and John Maxwell as town assessors.

To the list of Lexington industries was added the earthenware manufacturing plant of John Carty, which gave employment to a number of hired slaves. Seitz and Lauman announce they have opened a merchandise store "in the house lately occupied by Walter Taylor 'In keeper'," and, on the 19th of January, the Gazette publishes a long advertisement asking for bids for the erection of a state house in the town of Frankfort. John Cope advertises himself as "a stone-mason, plaisterer and bricklayer," and John Nancarrow, "at the Lexington Brewery desires an apprentice to learn that business." Walter Butler, 'taylor', announces he is "now in the house opposite Keiser's Tavern, where he hopes to receive his former customers." On February 14 mention is made in the Gazette of "January's new brick store at Main and Upper street, nearly opposite to the court house.

The new board of trustees for the Town of Lexington recorded a lease to Robert Megowan, "for six months the Senate Chamber and the small committee room next to same," but the entry contains no information disclosing for what purpose it was to be used.

Daniel Weissiger removed to Frankfort and Samuel McMillan resigned, so an election was ordered, which resulted in choice of Hugh McIlvaine and Robert Megowan as trustees to fill the vacancies.

On April 1, 1793, Morgan's station, about seven miles east of Mt. Sterling, was captured and nineteen women and children were carried away by the Indians. This was followed by numerous other depredations, but all at some distance from Lexington. During April and May of this year, Lieut. William McMullens and twenty-six men from Lexington and Fayette county were sent as a guard at the iron works, on Slate creek, near Morgan's station. The Gazette refers to the depredations of the Indians and "hopes to be spared reporting any further such reports."

William Hughes and Company advertise "they have opened a store in the house lately used by Cornelius Beatty, with a fresh line of dry goods, Maderia Wine, etc," and at a meeting held 17th of April, the trustees directed the committee (not named) to make the final settlement with Stout and Higbee "for building the market house." On the 22nd of the same month, the trustees directed a committee composed of Basil Duke, Hugh McIlvaine and Robert Megowan, "to open Walnut street and Back (now Deweese) street through from Main street, the present crops to be removed by the owners of the lots through which the streets are to pass." Dennis McCarthy advertises he is the agent for John Moyland and is closing out his business, and in the same issue, Peter January and Son announce "The National Assembly" with William Theobalds as master, "a well-built beautiful boat of fourteen oars, and built in Lexington, came to the lower end of Lexington on her way to Frankfort on Wednesday, for freight and passage only."

In June Thomas Bodley was appointed Judge Advocate for the 9th Regiment of the Militia and Reuben Stivers was allowed 21 pds. for drums furnished the same regiment. Archibald Neal and Samuel Wilson were appointed captains, and George Vallandingham lieutenant of the 8th regiment.

The condition of the streets caused the trustees much anxiety, and they received some very unfavorable comments regarding them at this time. After several meetings and much discussion, the trustees

agreed upon a division of labor, beginning April 2.
Robert Megowan and Hugh McIlvaine agreed to supervise repairs to Main Cross and Mulberry streets; John
Bradford and Christopher Keiser, the streets below the
court house, and Alexander Parker and James Hughes,
Main street above (east) of the court house, also High
street. They fixed the tax rate for this year at 1 pd.
10 shillings per hundred pounds, with the poll tax at
3 shillings.

On May 24, 1793, Thomas Love announces he is
manufacturing nails but does not disclose the location
of his plant or its capacity. Daniel Spencer opens a
cabinet and chairmaking business at "Mr. Hustons on
Mulberry street, south of Main street." In a few weeks
he begins making reed-bottom chairs, and "repairs all
kinds of chairs." On June 29, 1793, William Leavy
advertises that, in addition to dry goods and groceries,
he has the following books and wares for sale:

Blackstone's Reports,	Vattel's Law of Nations,
Drinkwater's Gibralter,	Peter Pindar,
Pilgrim's Progress,	Culpepper Herbal,
Chesterfield's Letters,	Paine's works,
Rudiman's Rudiments,	Ainsworth's dictionary,
Boot's Reign of Grace,	Booth's Apology,
Olney's Hymns,	Wilson on the Sacrament,
History of Pamelia,	Dilworth's spelling book,
Sealing wax and wafers,	Ink Powder,
Slates and pencils,	Inkstands and quill pens.

On July 6, 1793, John Crozier and Company announce
they "have just arrived from Philadelphia with an additional assortment of shawls, camblets, wildbord,
callimancoes, durants, moreens, sattinets, which they
will exchange for cash, tobacco, hemp, beef, flour,
cheese, tallow and beeswax." On the same date,
Edward Howe announces the opening of a linseed-
oil mill, and W. and H. Parker begin tanning and
currying, but the locations of these plants are not told.

The Gazette for August 10, 1793, announces William
Ross "at the Sign of Boot, Shoe and Slipper on Cross
street, next door to the printing office, with men's

calf skin shoes at 13 shillings, woman's calf skin shoes at nine to ten shillings, childrens in proportion. Soles 3 to 4 pense, one-half soles, to boots or shoes, three shillings to three and six pense; red morroco for binding boots and white calf skins also for sale." William Hughes and Company remove their dry goods store from the corner of Main and Cross streets "to the house lately occupied by David Humphrey, next door to Andrew Holmes." George Wilson, boot and shoe maker on Short street, advertises he "is just two doors from Mr. John Morrison's."

Reuben Stivers invites "the public to visit his shop," but neglects to mention the stock he desires to display, or the location. David Sayers, cabinet maker and carpenter, extends a similar invitation. Nicholas Wood and Company begin baking "and have cakes and beer for sale, and also can provide entertainment for man and beast. These cakes can be procured at the Tavern of Isaac Ware, lately occupied by Nicholas Wood. They will also attend the Bourbon and Woodford court days, with bread, cakes and beer for sale." Boggs and Anderson state they "have purchased the entire stock of Joseph Byers, deceased, which they will sell for butter, eggs and cheese." Jacob Lauderman announces he " has started a tobacco factory on Main street, opposite the court house, one door above Wilkin's store."

James Reed, boot and shoe maker, is located at Main and Cross streets, opposite the printing office, and James H. Stewart announces he has lately "occupied the store opposite Love and Brent's tavern, on Main street, with a choice assortment of dry goods, groceries, cuttlery, queensware and saddlery, which he has just brought from Philadelphia."

The call for volunteers to join the expedition under General Anthony Wayne was made in Lexington in September, but the results cannot be determined. Evidently the response was not sufficient to fill the quota, since in the following month Governor Shelby ordered a draft, which supplied the numbers necessary. On account of the lateness of the season, the Kentuckians returned homeward in a short time.

On October 12, 1793, the Gazette announces Trotter and Ward have dissolved partnership, and James Lowry advertises he has begun making spinning wheel irons, also door locks and other locks of various kinds, at his shop "on Upper street, opposite Colonel Robert Patterson's."

The citizens of the Town of Lexington were much worried at this time regarding the "jockeys racing their horses through the streets," and on the 21st of this month, the trustees frankly announced "there is dangerous racing through the streets, and as they have no authority to prevent same," desire to call an election in order to have this authority conferred upon them. The election resulted in an overwhelming majority in favor of such action, and the trustees promptly met and issued strict orders, confining the racing to "the lower end of the Commons (west Water street) where stud horses can be shown."

In November of this year, a Democratic Society was organized in Georgetown, Paris and Lexington. In the last named meeting, considerable opposition to the domestic and foreign policy of George Washington developed and resolutions were passed "that the right of the people on the waters of the Mississippi, to its navigation, is undoubted, and ought to be peremptorily demanded of Spain by the United States Government." The Lexington society erected a Liberty Pole on Main and Cheapside and the members of the society wore the tricolor buttonieres.

Thomas Carneal advertised for "a good malster at the Lexington Brewery," promising good wages and steady employment. Nathaniel Wilson presented his account to the Town trustees, amounting to 20 pounds, "for repairing the Main streets, and the sewers (gutters) on both sides."

David Lines, "taylor and ladies habit maker," says he has lately set up his trade at Mr. Ware's tavern, "where prompt service will be given," and on December 7, 1793, Hugh McIlvane advertised "dry goods, and books, amongst the latter being Marrow of Modern Divinity, The Afflicted Man's Companion, The Religious Courtship, Bolton's Fourfold State, Christian Economy and School Books."

General Anthony Wayne's proclamation warning the citizens to "strict neutrality as between France and Spain, and cautioning the Kentuckians not to participate in any expedition against New Orleans," appeared this month in the Gazette, and without comment by the editor. In an adjoining column we find that Hugh Logan, who had served as Master of Lexington Masonic Lodge, was succeeded by William Murray.

On December 21, 1793, Joseph Hudson, "at Sign of the Buffalo, has dry goods, shawls, vest patterns, plush, table cloths, Sheridan's dictionarys, Young's Latin and Gough's Arithmetic for sale."

The Gazette made no comment regarding the session of the Legislature of Kentucky, which met at Frankfort for the first time on November 1, beyond publishing a list of the Acts, which included measures establishing the towns of Winchester, Cynthiana, Falmouth, Shepherdsville, Springfield and Wilmington (now Burlington), but mention was made of Indian depredations about four miles from where the workmen were engaged in building the State House, and the fact that a guard of soldiers was necessary for their protection.

Charles Morgan, who prepared the Tax book for this year for the territory covering the Town of Lexington and that portion of the county between the Georgetown Pike and the road to General Scott's (now Versailles Pike), reported a total of 2,579 slaves, 3,775 horses, 10,150 cattle, 94,671 acres, 12 ordinaries, 28 retail stores and 7 stallions. John White, a weaver, and Charles Wilkins each paid taxes on one Phaeton carriage.

The Reverend Harry Toulmin, who emigrated to Kentucky in 1791, and who was President of Tran-

sylvania University 1794—1796, wrote "A Description
of Kentucky" in 1792, containing 124 pages, with a
good map of the state, which was published in London,
England. He says on page 92:

> "Lexington is recognized as the capital of
> Kentucky. Here courts are held and business
> regularly conducted. In 1786 it contained 100
> houses and several stores with a good assort-
> ment of dry goods."

EVENTS OF 1794.

THE arrival of 1794 found the little Town of Lexington well established as a commercial center and the largest depot for supplies in the Ohio valley. Every commodity used by settlers could be found for sale in Lexington stores. This year witnessed many new firms starting their commercial careers, while some of the firms that had been supplying the wants of the community sold out and the members joined the flood of emigrants to the Spanish territory west of the Mississippi, or "down the river" to Natchez or New Orleans.

The trustees elected for this year were Cornelius Beatty, Alexander Parker, Robert Megowan, Hugh McIlvaine, Basil Duke, John Postlethwait and James Hughes, and their first meeting seems to have been devoted to "renting the State House."

Governor Shelby appointed Dudley Mitchem captain in the Fayette county militia, vice Ezekiel Haydon, resigned; James H. Stewart a lieutenant in place of Thomas Love, "who had accepted a position under the general government;" Hugh Logan, Lieutenant in room of Byrd Price, resigned, and Thomas Parker to the same rank, in place of John Boswell, who removed to Boone County, Ky. Justices of the Peace and County Court for Fayette county were David Walker, Henry Payne, John Postlethwaite, John South, Clifton Rodes and Francis McMurdy. Joseph Crockett was named to the Quarter Sessions Court.

In the issue of the Gazette dated March 4, 1794, is the advertisement of John and Samuel Postlethwait "who had removed to the middle part of the large brick house, nearly opposite to Young and Brent's tavern." On the same date, James Hardwick offers to "make Windsor chairs, next door to Mr. White's, the coppersmith." Thomas Christy, "goldsmith and jeweler commences business on Main street, opposite Dr. R. W. Downings," and Jacob Lehre re-opens his school on High street, opposite Mr. Fulton's.

On May 10 the trustees appointed a committee composed of Alexander Parker, Basil Duke and James Hughes "to lay out and make a platt on which the state house stands, and also, agree with John Bradford for renting him the state house and lot," the bid of Benjamin S. Cox "having been rejected." Some confusion arose regarding the lines of this lot, which is probably explained by the Minutes of the meeting of this board, held on the 19th of the same month when we find: "Resolved—Henry Marshall, to remove buildings located west of the line from his stone house to the southwest corner of the lot."

The Gazette is strangely silent regarding the activities of La Chaise, one of the four French agents dispatched to Kentucky by the French Minister, Genet, to engage men in an expedition against New Orleans and the Spanish possessions, but does inform the Lexington society that "unforseen events had stopped the march of 2,000 brave Kentuckians to go to take from the Spaniards the empire of the Mississippi, to insure their country free navigation on it." The opening of the Mississippi river was an important subject before our people and was constantly agitated by the speakers on rally days and by writers in the columns of the Gazette, but these last were usually signed "Poplicolius" or "Agricolous."

On May 24, 1794, the trustees met at Megowan's tavern and directed "Hampton and Garnett to clean up their premises." Abijah and John W. Hunt open a store on Main street, where Stephen Collins had his tavern (now 314 west Main), and Phillip Caldwell and Company advertise they have received "a large supply of merchandise, also bolting cloths." Peter Valentine proposes "to teach French, if he can get ten pupils, and he can be seen at Mr. Toulmin's on High street."

On July 12, 1794, the trustees held another meeting (tavern not mentioned) and "Resolved—That 12 feet of the streets to be reserved for foot passengers, the fence on Mulberry street to be removed, and, also, the horse stalls." John Woodrow was appointed Town surveyor, and "Robert Barr directed to remove the post and rails from in front of his door, and Thomas Lewis ordered to clean up his premises."

This same month General Charles Scott left Kentucky with nearly 1,000 volunteers to join General Anthony Wayne in his campaign against the Indians, but the Gazette gave scant notice to this expedition and did not publish the names of any Lexington soldiers. Colonel John Johnson, in a paper read before the Pioneer Association of Ohio, October 11, 1857, says: "I witnessed the arrival of the Kentucky Volunteers, 1,200 strong. They made a martial appearance. Their dress was a hunting shirt and leggins, with rifle, tomahawk, knife, pouch and powder horn. It was understood there was not a drafted man in the whole command."

Several meetings were held in the Town of Lexington during the early part of this summer, at which violent resolutions were voted "in reference to the injuries and insults offered to the citizens of the United States, by the Navy of Great Britain, and to free and undisturbed navigation of the Mississippi, to which they are entitled by nature and stipulation, and yet, since 1783, the Spanish King had prevented the exercise of that right."

On the night of August 11, 1794, the town trustees held a meeting and paid the account of Simeon Hickey, amounting to 11 pounds, 12 shillings, for repairs to the jail, and "directed Boggs and Anderson to remove their piles of logs from the public square." Elisha Winter was paid "five pounds for filling up the holes in Main street, opposite the Presbyterian meeting house." The Gazette dated September 13, 1794, mentions that Thomas Hart and son have started a nail factory and John Spangler begins making cabinets and furniture, while the Reverend Jesse Head,[1] "now in Lexington," desires an apprentice to learn the cabinet-

1 The Rev. Jesse Head who married Thomas Lincoln and Nancy Hanks.

making business. On November 8, Samuel Johnson opens his "house of entertainment," on Main street, in the house of Mr. Lewis, and M. Forrest announces a new store in "Collins old house, nearly opposite Jameson's tavern, with dry goods to be exchanged for cash or bank notes."

On November 29, 1794, Mann Satterwhite opened a general merchandise store "in the house lately occupied by William Hughes," and Henry and Thomas Hathorn, tailors, "open their store at Robert Holmes, on Cross street, two doors above the printing office." Hen. Fitzgerald and Rebecca Evans open a hotel at corner of Short and Back (now Deweese) streets, next door to "Captain M'Coy's billiard tables," and George Smart, "from Britian, opens a clock and watch repair shop back of the jail." C. Clark advertises his store at Main and Mulberry "lately occupied by Mr. Mansell," while Colonel James Morrison, who had been the Master of the Masonic lodge, announces he "will retire from the mercantile business."

The trustees' minute book shows they paid the accounts of Walter Taylor for "filling the holes on Short street," for which he was allowed 3 pounds. At the same meeting George Mansell was "allowed two pounds for repairing the bridge of Main street across Spring street, just below Dr. Downing's."

The Gazette closes the year with some comments regarding the severe weather and "lateness of the mails from the Eastward." It also refers to the Battle of Fallen Timbers, where a victory over the Indians was won by General Wayne, and hopes a permanent peace will arise from it, but does not mention the names of the members of this command from Lexington.

The trustees held a meeting on the last day of the year and issued a deed to out-lot No. 21, five acres of ground on the northeast corner of Walnut and Main streets, to William Murray, who was assignee of John McKinney, who was assignee of James Morrow, the original drawer of this lot.

EVENTS OF 1795.

WITH the beginning of the year 1795 a long spell of rainy weather visited Lexington, and the Gazette comments upon the unpleasant business conditions in the state, alongside the proceedings of the United States Congress. The birth of a new industry was reflected in the advertisements—the first of a legion of its kind, which lasted until the automobile made its appearance—when John Kennedy "opens his livery stable," but neglects to mention its stall capacity or its location.

Some new faces appeared among the newly-elected trustees when Henry Marshall, John Smith, John Cocke, Robert Patterson, James Morrison, George Teagarden and James Hughes were sworn in for the new year at a meeting held in Megowan's tavern, with the last-named as chairman. No business was transacted with the exception of the election of Jacob Lehre as clerk.

Appointments by the Governor for Fayette county were: Ezekiel Harrison, tax commissioner; Joseph Crockett, Justice of the Quarter Session Court; George Vallandingham and Archibald McKee, captains; Thomas Baxter and John Darnaby, lieutenants; Isaac Scholl and William Denison, ensigns.

Adam Winn, who resided at Cross Plains (now Athens), calls attention in the columns of the Gazette to his store which was established in 1794. Samuel Downing, who had a store next door to Henry Marshall's tavern, died, and his stock was advertised for sale. This is the first time his name was mentioned in the Gazette, since he did not advertise.

A very good description of Lexington life as it pertained to students for the year 1795 is to be found in the Robert McAfee manuscript:

"In February 1795 I returned to Lexington and was placed in an English school kept by Mr. —— Duty on Water street, opposite the

public square. I boarded with Mr. Samuel
Ayers on High street, but he moved on to
Main street opposite the Seceeder church,
which was built the next year for the Reverend
Adam Rankin. My father left me at James
McCoun's store (my cousin). My teacher was
excellent and Mrs. Ayers very kind to me and
in three months I entered Transylvania under
Reverend Harry Toulmin."[1]

The tax book for the Town of Lexington for this
year shows, among other interesting items, 26 stores,
9 ordinaries and two brick yards working 281 negro
hands, with 34 (clay) wheels.

On March 16, 1795, the trustees voted "that part
of Water street below Cross street to be appropriated
for the purpose of shewing stud horses." Henry
Marshall presented his account "for repairing the
public spring," and was allowed two pounds, nine
pense. John Smith resigned from the board, and
Benjamin S. Cox was elected in his stead. Joseph
Putman advertised he was manufacturing wool machine
cards, and also doing cabinet work. He married Susan
Hull, daughter of the High street butcher. He used
many apprentices and was remembered for the care
he took in training them in his trade and also in
religious instruction. Several of these afterwards became prominent in the business life of Lexington,
among them Joseph Milward, for many years leader
of charitable and civic enterprises.

This year brick houses began to take the place of
log houses, if we can believe the tales of travelers who
passed through Kentucky. The Gazette contains many
advertisements of brick layers, and also brick yards,
but none quotes any prices.

On February 10, 1795, James Anderson, from
Carlisle, Pennsylvania, "opens his shoe and boot making business in the house formerly occupied by Mr.
Patterson, and more lately by John Allison, the
wheelright." In the same issue Dr. Frederick Ridgely

1 Kentucky State Historical Society Register, Vol. 25, page 78.

announces his intention of "visiting the East for three months and his business will be looked after by Drs. Duke and Watkins." William Tod sells watch glasses in the store opposite Love & Brent's tavern, and Dailey and Stewart announce they have purchased "the Billiard Table lately occupied by Captain McCoy, where they propose to keep a coffee house." Edward West moves his silversmith's shop to Main street, opposite Bradford's printing office, and Thomas Leishman, bookbinder moves his shop outside the town and "requests all orders for him to be left at the Printing Office."

The trustees, at their February meeting, voted "to build the new Market house on the Public Square (now Cheapside). They also appointed a committee to visit all streets and report at next meeting "upon necessary repairs." Reid and McIlvane, "lately from Philadelphia, announce they are making saddles on Main street, opposite Bradford's printing office," and David Sutton advertises "his store is now open" but fails to mention contents nor location.

On May 18, 1795, the Trustees ordered Thomas Lewis "to remove his porch off Main street, at the corner of Mill," but it was still there the following January, when this order was repeated. William West "opened a new store between Major Morrison's and Walter Taylor's tavern" and early in June the Trustees devoted one meeting to the consideration of draining the water off lots on Main street and voted a notice to John Castleman and John McNair to drain their property.

Lexington's second newspaper began its existence that summer when James H. Stewart started his "Kentucky Herald." This newspaper lived until 1802, when John Bradford purchased it and consolidated it with the Kentucky Gazette. On June 27, 1795, the Gazette advertised "John Bradford, at the large brick building near public spring on Main street, where books and stationery can be bought." On July 24, 1795, Abijah and John W. Hunt announce they "have opened a choice assortment of new merchandise on Main street, in the house formerly occupied by Stephen Collins as a tavern, also a choice line of iron mongery and books purchased in Philadelphia."

Under date of July 3, 1795, the trustees appointed a committee composed of John Cocke, Robert Patterson, James Morrison and George Teagarden to supervise the building of the new market house, and also issued threats to prosecute "any one doing washing at the public spring." The conditions at these springs caused the trustees to appoint supervisors from among the board. Henry Marshall and George Teagarden were to supervise the spring at the school house, while Benjamin S. Cox and Henry Marshall were to watch the spring at the State House. Michael Raber was notified to "abate the nuisance of his slaughter house." This month McCoun and Castleman advertise they have "removed two doors west of the 'Sign of the Buffalo' where they will welcome their old customers." Jacob Keiser announces he is a distiller with excellent vinegar for sale by barrel or gallon.

On October 31, 1795, Thomas Hart and Son announce they "have received and are now opening an extensive assortment of general merchandise, which they will sell low by wholesale or retail; also a large assortment of bolting cloth and copper, which they will sell at a more reduced price than they have before been sold in this country." Elisha and J. Winter dissolve their partnership and George A. Weaver opens a bake shop in the house of Ben. S. Cox, at corner of Main and Cross streets, "formerly occupied by Isaac Ware, where the public may be supplied with bread, cakes, beer, as well as biscuits for travelers at shortest notice." John Crozier mentions the fact that he intends starting for Philadelphia on November 1st and asks that all that owe him to settle with Samuel Downing." Young and Bright "open a shoe and boot shop on Main street, two doors from Cross, in the building where Ben S. Cox had his saddle shop."

Benjamin Stout advertises he is "located next door to Henry Marshall's tavern with an assortment of glassware, boots and shoes, calf skins and boot legs, and also, hops—which he wishes to dispose of for cash, whiskey, bear skins and country-made sugar." Richard Terrill announces he will move from Lexington to Bear Grass, and will continue in business at that point. George Smart, "at corner of Main and Mulberry streets, has a neat assortment of 13 inch plain and double moon and seconds for the center, eight-day and thirty-hour clocks." Thomas Hart and Son advise "they have commenced the manufacture of cordage and desire well cleaned hemp, for which they will pay a generous price in cash and merchandise in the store of Thomas Hart and Son, or the store of Samuel Price and Company."

William West advises his "new store is now at the corner between Major Morrison's and Taylor's tavern, and he has brought into this State a handsome assortment of merchandise, which he determines to sell on reduced terms as he is anxious to sell out in order to return to the 'settlements' next fall."

The Gazette comments in its columns during November of 1795 upon recent acts of the Legislature, one of which "requires the Auditor, the Treasurer and the Secretary of State to reside at the seat of Government," and an increase in the salary of the Governor to $1,333 per annum. Another act was passed obliging every white male, over sixteen years of age, to kill a certain number of crows and squirrels each year. Many issues of the Gazette about this time carried advertisements "for good cooks," just as they do in this day and generation. The Gazette also mentions the removal of Major Thomas Love, Master of the Masonic Lodge for this year, to the town of Frankfort.

During November the trustees held their meeting at Love's tavern, and deeded in-lot No. 61, to Charnock Self, as assignee of Alexander Maxwell. This lot is now the west side of Upper street extending from Vine to High street.

The Gazette carried a number of open letters attacking the action of a mass meeting in Lexington on the last day of the September term of court, which was held as a remonstrance against Jay's Treaty with England. Also, there was published this startling bit of information:

> "That noted horse thief M—— M——- is said to have been in this town early in the morning of Thursday last."

The executors of Colonel William Ward announce sale of the effects of the deceased, and Thomas Whitney, cabinet maker, announces sale of the house of John Van Pelt, "next door to Jacob Lauderman, the tobacconist, and opposite Lawyer Hughes." The Gazette also announces:

> "A large company well armed will start from Crab Orchard on the first, early in the morning."

However, subsequent issues fail to disclose how many took advantage of this protection to return "over the mountains."

A four-column article signed by Humphrey Marshall on "The Treaty of 1783" is followed by an article sustaining the Treaty and attacking Colonel Marshall. On October 17, 1795, the Gazette says: "No mails having arrived down the River last week, we are without any late foreign intelligence and the scaricity of paper prevents our giving a supplement this week by which sundry political peices are omitted."

Another industry is disclosed to us when the Gazette had this item in the issue dated November 7, 1795: "On Tuesday last J—— S—— was executed in this town for horse stealing, agreeable to sentence of late court of Oyer and Terminer. About twelve months ago, he was under sentence of death and received the Governor's pardon for a similar crime."

On November 21, 1795, Andrew McCalla advertises his store at Short and Market, "near the stray pen, which carries an assortment of drugs and 167 patent medicines, including British oil, Turlington's Balsam Bateman's drops, Imperial Essence, Ryan's sugar plants, Anderson's pills, Essence of Lemon, Smelling bottles, Tamarinds, Almonds, Red Lead, Whiting, Pepper, allspice, and desires to buy corn for cash." On the same date, John Todd "informs the public he has employed John McMillen, fuller and dyer, from a Northern state, to carry on the business on Kentucky River near Todd's ferry and he will dye greens, claretts, pompadores, etc." William Scott, "six miles south of Lexington, will dye bottle green and blue." Nicholas Bright sells shoes at Short and Upper streets, "opposite Major Morrison's." On November 28, 1795, Baird and Owens open a new store "next door to McNair's tavern, opposite the court house, where they will sell for cash a general assortment of merchandise. They return thanks to their friends for the encouragement they have experienced at their store at the lower end of Main and Cross streets, where they first opened." On the same date James Collins advertises "land for sale in Clark, Bourbon and Fayette counties, which he will sell low for young negroes and good horses, as the land is all military claims."

The Kentucky Gazette during this period was filled with many letters full of recriminations, and the political situation must have been acute. "A democratic society at Georgetown and another at Paris, all to be considered as offsprings of that in Lexington; inheriting its principles, and embracing its projects. They condemned and abused the president's proclamation of neutrality; his decisions in relation to Genet, the excise, the Army and whatever had the name of Federal."[1]

The manuscript of Robert McAfee, in describing his life in Lexington in 1795, says: "In the latter part of this year our government secured from the Spanish the liberty of deposit and more liberal regulations at New Orleans, and in Lexington we had a bonfire with boxes and tar barrels in celebration of the event."[2]

1 Marshall's History of Kentucky, page 95, Vol. 2.
2 Kentucky State Historical Society Register, Vol. 25, page 78.

The political situation seems to have worn itself out, and the open letters and cards became shorter and finally ceased. On the 20th of December the Gazette announced that the Governor had appointed Hugh McIlvaine, Samuel Blair, James McDowell, William Lewis, Jr., Thomas Caldwell, James Hogan, William Roberts, Isaac Webb, William Lewis, Sen., James Morrison, Ambrose Dudley and John McNair as Justices for Fayette county, and Fielding Lewis Turner as ensign in the Militia. Also, the Gazette announced the Town of Newport had been established, "on the Ohio River, above the mouth of Licking."

The last issues of the Gazette for this year contain the advertisements of James Collins, who, in addition to exploiting his Real Estate Agency, says: "Have just furnished my shop with a new assortment of medicines where I practice as usual surgery and physic." In the same issue James Morrison advertises for 30,000 pounds of pork, also hemp, tow linen, butter, country sugar, corn and flax seed. John Cockey Owings advertises for slaves to work in the "Iron works on Slate," and Benjamin Snelling, saddler, advertises for a runaway apprentice, for whom he offers one pense reward, but does not give the name of the fugitive. Robert Calloway states he has just received a "new assortment of merchandise, which is now being opened at Hugh Shannon's mill on South Elkhorn." John Kennedy announces he has taken possession of his livery stable, "which for the last three years has been in the possession of Billy Bailey," and hopes to receive again the patronage of his friends. Samuel Ayers informs "his friends and the public in general, that he has moved his shop higher up on Main street next door to Mr. Moore's, and nearly opposite the Freemason's lodge." In this same issue of the Gazette "Citizen C. Barbiere offers thanks to those who have encouraged him and states he will shortly open one day school and one night school for teaching French, also will give private lessons at twenty shillings per quarter." Robert Holmes states he has received paints, "white lead and red lead, Prussian blue, Yellow Ochre, Pattent Yellow, Rose, Pink, putty, Spanish whiting, Spanish Brown and lamp black, at his shop on Cross street, a few doors from Dr. Downings."

The only item appearing on the minute books of the board of trustees for their last meeting of this year was an allowance of 3 pounds 15 shillings to Thomas Stephenson, "for 25 perches of stone work on the Market House."

EVENTS OF 1796.

IN the first issue of the Gazette for the year of 1796, the usual complaint appears regarding "the non-receipt of the mails from the east, and the consequent inability to supply the readers with any late news." The Gazette announced the results of the recent election by which Hugh McIlvaine, James Morrison, Robert Patterson, Thomas January, George Teagarden, James Hughes and Alexander Parker were chosen by the citizens as trustees for the year of 1796. This board appointed Benjamin Stout and John Maxwell as assessors, John Arthur as surveyor and Thomas Love clerk of the Market house. James Hughes and Thomas January were appointed a committee to secure correct weights for use in the stalls of the market house. At same meeting A. Woodrow filed a new plat of the town, which was ordered placed upon the record.

The following item appeared in the first issue of the Gazette, and well illustrated the difficulties of communication between the various settlements until the establishment of the Post Offices:

"Ben King who married my daughter and moved to this county about twelve months ago, will please call or send word to me at Jacob Sodowski's on Sinking creek, on road from Lexington to De Lancy's ferry, where I shall continue until the last of February.
FRANCIS COLE."

In the issue of the Gazette dated January 9, 1796, appears the following: "Lawson McCullough begs to inform the public that he could not get a house on Main street and was obliged to rent a room from Captain Smith on High street and Cross, where he is making Ladies fashionable riding coats, with vest and habit; Gents tight and loose coats, vests and small clothes, tight overalls and pantaloons with feet. Price 30 shillings per suit, coat 16 shillings 6 pense; plain

suit 27 shillings. Whiskey, wheat and oats taken at
market prices." This is the first appearance of a citizen
who afterwards became prominent in the civic affairs
of the Town of Lexington. On the same date, Major
Walker Baylor announces the "opening of a house of
Entertainment for gentlemen at the house lately
Taylor's tavern. A few genteel boarders will be accepted, with special attention given to horses." His
death, in Bourbon county, was announced in the Kentucky Gazette dated October 14, 1822, with a short
sketch of his Revolutionary War services as head of
a troop of cavalry.

The town trustees directed "a post and rail fence
to be built around the Market House, 12 feet from the
sides of same; also, the pike at each end to be built,
and the ground around the house to be made level."
The trustees also selected James Morrison, chairman,
Jacob Lehre, clerk, and Thomas January, as a committee to manage the Market house and select materials for the fences.

George Adams announces he has opened a tavern
on Main street, a few doors below Cross street, and
Joseph Hudson advises "those who owe him to call
and settle at once as he desires to leave for the
eastern settlements on March 20th."

Early in February the trustees arranged to have
the stalls in the market house numbered, and the
minute book shows they were leased as follows: John
Hostetter, No. 1; George Coons, No. 2; Samuel Biles,
No. 3; John Johnson, No. 4; Stark Gillam, No. 5;
Solomon Boshart, No. 6; Robert McNitt, No. 7;
Barney Rairden, No. 8; John Hull, Nos. 9, 10 and 11;
Robert McNitt, No. 12, and John Carty, No. 13. None
of the entries discloses the commodities sold by any
of the above named.

On February 29, 1796, the scheme of the Lexington
Masonic Lodge No. 25, F. & A. M. (now Lexington,
No. 1), to raise $2,250 in order to pave the streets
(sidewalks), build bridges over Town Fork of Elkhorn and sink some public wells in Lexington, was

adopted by the board of trustees. On same date Major Cornelius Beatty announces he "intends going east to Baltimore and Philadelphia early in the month of March and desires all that owe his firm to call and settle." The minutes also show that Anthony Geoghagan, William McDaniel and Anthony Martin paid their taxes on "Ordinarys."

On March 19, 1796, Archibald Brown advertises "his hat factory at Cross and Water streets, where he makes ladies and gentlemen's wool or fur hats." This plant evidently stood near where an old letter says "there was a deep bathing and swimming hole, just west of Cross where it joined Water street."

On March 26, 1796, the free navigation of the Mississippi was secured by reason of a treaty between the United States and Spain, and "New Orleans is a free port." The Gazette mentions this fact with much gratification and speaks of the benefits to the farmers of central kentucky. On the same date appeared this item :

> "All persons who own wagons and teams are requested to attend at Kirtner's tavern in Lexington on Saturday next, 2nd April, in order to take into consideration and establish uniform rates."

Succeeding issues of the Gazette are silent as to the results of this attempt at organization of the teamsters. Seitz and Lauman dissolve their partnership and "request all that owe them to settle at once, as they propose to take the shortest method of securing their own." M. Forrest announces he is quitting business at his store next door to William Leavy's, and Kincaid and Allen dissolve partnership, with James Kincaid continuing the business.

Robert McAfee says:

> "In 1796 I worked at the store of my cousin, James McCoun, and his partner, Mr. Castleman. It was a small frame building with the gable end to Main street, opposite the Court

House, and the stock of goods was not large. Mr. Castleman did not stay at the store much. Mr. Ayers charged me $60. per year board. The Reverend Harry Toulmin was deficient in tact and his school run down until there was only 18 or 20 students. I afterwards studied law under Mr. Breckinridge who had 8 or 10 students under him."[1]

This description of a building opposite the Court House for this year is evidently a fair sample of the buildings that composed the business district of the Town of Lexington.

The enterprise and energy displayed by our early merchants was very remarkable considering the difficulties under which they labored and the distance they were from their sources of supplies. A hazardous undertaking—even when making the journey on horseback with guards and unaccompanied by any transport or supplies other than that carried by each individual, it became extra hazardous when attempting to carry bulky packages and coins through the Indian infested woods or "down the River" past the haunts of outlaws, who were even more heartless than their savage competitors. The treaty made at Greenville, Ohio, with the Indians during 1795 stopped all further raids of large bodies of Indians from across the Ohio, and Kentucky thereafter had to contend with only small groups of prowlers, who committed many petty depredations for several years after the treaty. The constant and never ending vigilance that had been kept up for many dreary years was somewhat relaxed and business enterprises began to take on a much wider scope. The enterprise of one citizen is found in a letter written this year to Governor Blount of Maryland by Colonel Thomas Hart:

"We arrived June 1st and brought between 3 and 4,000 pounds worth of goods, about 2,000 of which we put in retail stores and balance sold by wholesale. The nailing business is

[1] Kentucky State Historical Society Register, Vol. 25, page 78.

properous and our rope manufacturing will be started as soon as winter breaks. I shall set up a blacksmith shop and will keep four forges going."

Another new firm appears this year, as John and David Coons, "Coppersmiths from Berkely county, Virginia, beg to inform the public they have opened a shop near Mr. Leavy's." George Mansell advises the public "he desires to purchase a quantity of ashes and will call and collect them twice each week from all houses in town."

On March 28, 1796, the Gazette published an open letter signed by Eli Cleveland, in which he says "his mill was burned last night by some enemy, as no fire had been in or near the building." He announces he will sell land and warehouse on the Kentucky River twelve miles from Lexington. On April 8, the trustees adopted a series of regulations for those using the Market house, and after electing John Arthur clerk of the Market issued instructions regarding the sale of unwholesome food, but neglected to record these rules in the minutes of their meeting. On this same date the Gazette published the announcement of the resignation of the Reverend Harry Toulmin as President of Transylvania University. He accepted appointment as Secretary of State under Governor Garrard, and while so employed published a digest of the Laws of Kentucky. He afterwards was appointed United States Judge for the Territory of Alabama.

Trotter and Scott announce they have sold their store and "desire all who owe them to settle with William Scott, who has the books." Jacob Keifer and Joseph Jeffs "open a tan yard on High street, opposite Colonel Robert Patterson's." William Tod advertises he is "from Scotland and has now erected in Lexington,[1] machinery for spinning cotten, and will charge—two dozen, 2s, 6 d; three dozen, 3s; cotten to be cleaned from seed; also, dyes blue of flax and cotten yard.

---

[1] On Vine Street east of Mill.

Recommends farmers and others in Kentucky and
Tennessee to raise cotton, as there will be a good
market for same."

Henry Marshall and John Bradford file their agree-
ments with the trustees for renting the public land on
Main street[1] on basis of six shillings per foot, payable
annually beginning October 1.

On April 23, 1796, Jacob Boone lost one box of
supplies sent from Limestone and requests the finder
to leave same at the tavern of Richard Coleman. On
May 6, the Gazette says "George Poff and William
Weathers have leased stall No. 4, in the market house
for one year, at a cost of $12." This issue of the
Gazette cites several regulations passed by the trustees
at their previous meetings governing the use of the
market house, mentioning that "no beer, ale, cider or
other spirits could be sold in stalls of the market
house."

In the same issue the Gazette published this bit
of information but did not reveal its source:

"Following is the number of immigrants
into Kentucky through the Wilderness during the year 1795:

January 72, February 88, March 365, April
1,218, May 717, June 489, July 141, August
94, September 739, October 3,103, November
1,442, December 562. Total 9,010."

An interesting description of this immigration is found
in the Journal of Isaac Weld, a traveler who was in
the Shenandoah Valley in 1795-97, saying:

"I met a great many people traveling on
the high road from the northern states to Kentucky and the new state of Tennessee. Many
going to Philadelphia or Baltimore for supplies and others in the contrary direction 'to
explore,' as they call it—that is, to search for
lands conveniently situated for new settlements
in the western country. These people travel

[1] The old State House, now site of J. D. Purcell Store.

on horseback with pistols or swords, and a
large blanket folded under the saddle. There
are now houses scattered along nearly the
whole way, from Fincastle into Lexington, in
Kentucky. It would be dangerous for any person to venture singly; but if five or six travel
together they are perfectly safe. Formerly
travelers were always obliged to go forty or
fifty in a party."

On May 6, 1796, the Gazette published an item
from Madison county regarding "the squirrel hunt
held a few days ago in which 7,941 squirrels were
killed in one day."

Webber and Lintel dissolve their partnership of
baking and cooking cakes and bread, with Laurence
Lintel continuing the business. The firm of Scott and
Thurston also decide to part company but the Gazette
fails to mention their business. Irwin and Bryson
sell out to Thomas Irwin. James Morrison resigns
as treasurer of the board of trustees. His death
in Washington City was announced in the Gazette for
May 5, 1823. On June 11, 1796, John W. Semple
opens "next door to Brent's tavern[1] with an assortment of drugs, which he desires to sell for cash or on
orders from physicians." On the 15th the trustees held
their monthly meeting and decided to "order the water
standing on Short street, near Walker Baylor's old
stand, to be drained and the hole filled." This was
accomplished by cutting down the hill on Short street,
just west of Limestone, and using the materials to
make the street level. On June 17, the committee appointed by the trustees made their report and recommended that the ground on Mulberry and also on
Upper street (on east side of court house) be cut
down to permit free flowing of drainage. Love and
Brent and also Walker Baylor bid on this work, but
minutes do not disclose to whom the contract was
awarded. The agreement read only that "the contractor is to take the high part of the street and move

---

[1] Now North-East corner Main and Upper streets.

it to the lower parts." Captain McMurtrie's chimney
was ordered "to be declared dangerous." Sewers
(gutters) on Mill, Main and Cross streets were ordered
to be repaired.

Josiah Bullock advertises that he will do washing
and "take a few genteel boarders, at reasonable rates,
next door to Hugh's saddlery." On July 9 the Gazette
carries the advertisement of William White, who
offers "to sell the house and lot where I live on Short
street, a frame building 20 by 32 feet, with shed the
length of the house, 12 feet wide." William Ross also
advertises his house on Mulberry "For sale—lot is
40 by 66 feet and house is 24 feet front and 26 feet
back, built of squared logs and one story high." Jacob
and Henry Hoover advise they "have a quantity of
French burr mill stones for sale, for which please
see Henry Strouse now at Baird and Owens store in
Lexington." In the same issue Elijah Craig announces
he is "manufacturing paper at his mill in Scott county
and same is for sale at the store of Abijah and John
W. Hunt in Lexington, on Main street." The old day
book of the latter firm for the period of July, August,
September and October, 1796, has been found recently
and contains many interesting items. It discloses not
only the names of their customers, but the articles
they purchased and the prices in vogue at that period
of the little Town of Lexington. The names alone,
make a very good directory for this community at that
time: Captain John Garner, Daniel Weible, Wm.
Stewart, David Stout, Achilles Hawkins, Stephen
Collins, James Alexander, Cornelius Coyle, Lloyd
Holmes, Oakey Hoagland, Captain John Fowler (by
wife), Dr. D. O. Wonens, Nathaniel Lowry, Thomas
Sthreshly, Elijah Craig, William Daingerfield, John
Hayfield, Richard Rice, Christopher Rice, George G.
Taylor, George and Adam Winn, Benjamin Stout,
Rebecca Green, Cuthbert Banks, Thomas Ammon, Joel
Craig, Martin Hoagland, Sr., Hiram Mitchell, Peter
LeGrand, Gwin Tompkins, Kenneth McCoy, Mann
Satterwhite, George Heytel, Christopher Weaver, David

Meade and wife, Ransom Colerain, James Pharre, N.
Shaw, Jesse Head, Edward West, William White, Seth
Thornton, Wm. Gewet, Chartnea Pane, Achilles Hop-
kins, Beverly Chew, David Hitchkiss, Dr. R. W.
Downing, Phillip Caldwell, Charles Bird, Richard
Tomlin, James McEntire, Trotter and Scott, Thomas
Stockdell, James Gray, Christian Willman, James
Brown, Edmund Purdy, Harris Kinlock, Daniel Weis-
siger, Elisha Winters, Golson Stopp, John Brown (by
daughter), George Pendergrass, Hathorn, the "taylor,"
Mary Burmen, Francis Jones, Leavy Conover, widow,
Rachel Conover, Wm. Juett, Nicholas Lewis, John
Kennedy (by wife), Charles McKinney, John Harrison,
Andrew Adams, Downing and Moody, Solomon Sla-
back, Elizabeth Gilmore, Jacob Lauderman, Capt.
Henry Brock, Captain Gilbert Low, James Stapp, John
Bradford, Hubbard Taylor, Ezekiel Simpson, Charles
Sanders, Jacob Wodson (Wolston), Archibald Rideford
(Rutherford), John Tanner, Cor. Pentecost, Wm.
Barklon, Ambrose Dudley, John Keiser, Col. Geo.
Nicholas, John Johnson (at Washington), James G.
Hunter, Andrew Hare, Cochran and Co., James Bacon,
George Adams, Nathaniel Shaw, Wm. Bell, John C.
Owings, Aseriah Higgins, Dr. Thomas Huff, George
Watts, Jonathan Rolston, James Bell, Richard Allen,
Edmund Hockaday, Roger Mallory, Barnabus Worland,
Hugh Markelin, Major John McDowell, Chancelor and
Davis, James and Richard Smith, Todd and Mott;
Meeker, Cochran and Co., Thomas Bradley, John
South, Wm. Whitney, Martin Greder, Reuben Runion,
John Mayfeald, Eley Stiles, Thomas Howard, Wm.
P. Smith, Charles Sumption, Jesse Guttery (Guthrie),
Jacob Keiser, Isiah Yard, Dr. J. W. Scott, Samuel
Rice, Nicholas Bright, Charles Byard, Absolum Ballou,
Henry Marshall, Garrett Conover, Asa Cox, Alexander
Mahan, John Breckinridge, Thomas Carneal, John
Stilfield, John Cocke, John Harries, Catreny Wood
(widow), John Kennedy, George Sowerbright, Walker
Baylor, John Crooke, Levi Todd, Jacob Fisher, Anthony
Bass, George Howard, John Clay, Robert Henderson,

John Caldwell, Col. Gabriel Madison, Joseph Simpson, Montgomery Bell, John Liby, George Lickes, Benedict Vanpradelles, Eley Lyons, John Beachem, John Ishmal, Abner LeGrand, Mrs. Ann Wood.

Some of these names appear many times during the three months. Not all of them were residents of Lexington, as several well known inhabitants of adjoining counties appear, many of whom had "by son" or "by daughter" written after the entry. Sometimes the name of a servant was found written after the charge. The item that appeared most frequently was "one qt. of whiskey," which was charged at .50 cents, but in only one instance was it delivered to a servant.

The prices paid for the various articles mentioned in this book make an interesting exhibit of the differences in the cost of living in 1796 and today:

6 yards of muslin	12 shillings,
1 roll tobacco	9 "
3 skeins thread	6 "
1-2 pd. tea	7 "
1 doz. needles	9 "
1 briddle	10 "
1 handkerchief	2 " and 3 pence
1 yd. stripped dimity	7 "
1 pr. silk stockings	18 "
2 yds. black ribbon	2 "
1 bu. salt	one pound
1 yd. cambric	12 shillings,
1 pr. scissors	2 "
1 pr. spurs,	12 "
12 jews harps	4 "
1 onz. alum	1 shilling, 6 pense,
1 bottle snuff	3 "
4 pds. sugar	3 "
2 yds. calicoe	9 "
1 snuff box	3 "
1 barrel salt,	2 pounds, 6 shillings, 9 pense,
1 scrubbing brush,	2 shillings, 3 pense,
1 pr. white silk mitts	6 "
1 saw file,	3 "
1 42-inch Dutch Oven	1 pound, 2 shillings, 9 pense,

1-2 doz soup plates	7 shillings, six pense,	
1 red plume	12 "	
2 reams writing paper	2 "	, 2 pense
6 tin cups,	6 shillings,	
1 tea pot,	4 "	6 pense,
1 packet pins,	15 shillings,	
10 yds, toe linen	18 "	4 pense,
1 wool hat	7 shillings, 6 pense,	
3 tumblers,	3 pense,	
1 set knives and forks	15 shillings,	
12 plates	14 "	
1 pitcher	4 "	
1 pr. gloves,	3 "	9 pense,
1-2 yd. cloth	5 "	
6 panes of glass (window)	5 shillings	
1 sad iron	8 "	
1 quart decanter	6 "	
24 small nails	3 "	
1 Webster spelling book	1 "	6 pense,
1 "Man of the world"	7 "	
1 pr knee buckles,	1 "	3 pense,
1 doz. flints,	1 "	
1 pair garters,	9 "	
4 pounds cheese,	3 "	4 pense.
1 yd. cross barred muslin	8 "	6 pense

Several of these accounts were carried from Virginia pounds into dollars and cents, as we find Captain John Fowler credited with $20 which amount was carried out as 6 pounds. One horse was purchased, for use by the firm, at $100 and the amount was entered at 30 pounds. Many of these accounts are interesting as indexes to the wardrobes of the purchasers and the cost of such apparel. Henry Marshall purchased on September 13th "by Ring" three yards blue cloth at 4 pounds, 16 shillings; 3 yards brown Holland at 11 shillings, 3 pense; six coat buttons, 7 shillings, 6 pense; two pieces of tape, 4 shillings, 6 pense; four buttons, three pense; two sticks twist 2 shillings, 3 pense; eight skeins thread, 1 shilling, 4 pense; 5-8 yard scarlet cloth, 16 shillings, 3 pense—a total of 7 pounds, 2 shillings, 10 pense. Evidently this was for a uniform coat. Hubbard Taylor bought one cast-iron frying pan for 14 shillings, 6 pense; Elijah Craig received credit for writing paper 1 pound, 6 shillings, 4 pense. Alexander Mahan purchased seven pairs butt hinges at 14 shillings, twelve pairs 'less' hinges at 9 shillings, seven dozen screws 5 shillings, ten pense, and one brass knob 3 shillings, 6 pense.

Mrs. Ann Wood received credit at 7 shillings 6 pense for making "one bed tick," and she purchased one pair children's stockings for 1 shilling, 3 pense, and two horse collars at 21 shillings. Some one whose name could not be deciphered purchased two gallons of brandy at 18 shillings, one pint of peach brandy for 1 shilling, 2 pense, one black silk handkerchief for 9 shillings, one plume for 12 shillings, and 3 1-2 yards of corduroy for one pound 10 shillings. Gabriel Madison purchased one patent tea pot for one pound, 10 shillings, and one side of sole leather for one pound. Gwin Tompkins purchased nine yards of silk at 12 shillings, and Kenneth McCoy three quarts of whiskey at 4 shillings, 6 pense. Nathaniel Lowry, received credit for 6 wool hats and 6 black hats, and Nathaniel Shaw credit for six bushels of oats, but the amounts were not carried out into money. The Reverend Jesse Head purchased 1,000 saddle tacks.

The Gazette announced in August that the Governor had made the following appointments in Fayette County; James Trotter, Justice to the Quarterly Court; William Dudley, Justice to the County Court, and Justices of the Peace, Leonard Bradley, Richard Overton, Hezekiah Harrison, Richard Higgins, Peter Mason, Robert Frier, Wm. Hambleton, Alexander Montgomery and William Allen, the latter declining such appointment. In addition to the above, officers to the Fayette Troop of Horse were named: Samuel Price, captain; John William Hunt, lieutenant, and William Daingerfield, ensign.

It was during the latter part of this year that more than local prominence came to one citizen because of his inventive genius. Nathan Burrows, who had settled in Lexington in 1792, began to develop his inventions, the first of which seems to have brought him nothing but trouble. The machine for cleaning hemp was successful but caused a financial loss. He later invented a very superior method for the manufacture of mustard for the table, and "Burrow's Lexington Mustard" became well known throughout the world. Lexington's famous condiment inventor received the appointment of mustard maker to Queen Victoria of England, and the bright yellow cans still bear her coat-of-arms. It is to be regretted this industry was removed to Louisville, where its excellence was submerged by competition. Along with Burrows should be mentioned John Jones, who invented a spindle speeder and a stone-sawing machine; E. S. Noble, who invented a beading machine for use of tin workers; Thomas E. Barlow, who invented a nail and tack making machine, a rifled cannon and the planetarium, and Dr. Joseph Buchanan, whose medical classes did not interfere with his inventing a musical instrument of glasses of different chemical compositions, and a capillary steam engine of enormous power at an extremely cheap cost of operation.

All of these added to the fame of Lexington and were some of the reasons why Lexington of that period was the metropolis of the Western Country.

One visitor to Lexington this year was not deeply impressed with the future possibilities of the town. General Victor Collot says:

"We reached Lexington. This town is situated in the midst of a vast plain, as open as that of Philadelphia, and on which there is not a tree to be seen for miles around. A whitish soil without water and a burning July sun in 1796 are all we found and felt in the neighborhood of Lexington. The town contains 3 to 400 houses the greater part built of wood and arranged regularly in parallel lines running southeast and northwest. A square is left at the central point in the midst of which a court house is erected. As this town has no navigation it is presumed that its increase will not be great and that Frankfort will be the real place of commerce."[1]

On July 16, 1796, William Leavy advertised that he "desires all that owe him to come forward and settle as he intends going to Philadelphia for a fresh supply of goods." William West advertises he is now "opening a fresh assortment in the store house adjoining Marshall's Tavern, which has been lately occupied by William Threshley, and formerly by Benjamin Stout." In the same issue Jesse Guthrie and Benjamin Batterton announce they will "purchase pewter, copper and brass, and they have a brass founder who will cast still cocks, and rivets, mill inks, spoon molds and mountains."

Another industry is mentioned for the first time on August 13, 1796, when Emmor Trego offers to do "sign painting of all descriptions at Captain Wm. Allen's in Lexington." McCoun and Castleman dissolve partnership, with James McCoun continuing the business. William Macbean advertised he was "at the old court house on Cross street with a fresh assortment of dry goods suited to the Fall seasons, 'Best Durham Mustard' in bottles and cakes, looking glasses and engravings in gilt frames and thermometers." Benj. S. Cox advises he had "just opened where I formerly kept a saddle shop at Main and Cross streets, an assortment of dry goods, hardware, Milliner's work, bonnets, hats, caps, cap feathers and other ornaments for ladies, watches and gold rings, and an assortment of medicines." Jacob Keiser and Joseph Jesse decided to separate and the first-named took charge of the business. "The Kentucky Miscellany" is advertised for sale by Thomas Johnson, Jr., and the Gazette mentions the interest with which this publication is received "by the well informed."

On September 1, 1796, the town trustees held a meeting and repeated their former order to clean up

[1] A Journey in North America, Vol. 1, p. 102—Victor Collot.

the streets, and also notified Melchoir Myers to clean up his slaughter shop. Nicholas Bright announces he has "moved his boot and shoe making shop to Cross street at the lower end of Colonel Hart's rope walk." Israel Hunt, boot and shoe maker on Cross street, advertises for six or eight good journeymen and this advertiser has the distinction of being the first one in the Gazette to use a cut in his advertisement. The cut was roughly made, showing a boot 1 1-4 inches tall. John McMillan advertises a fulling mill at Todd's ferry on the Kentucky River "where blue or green dying will be done, if the goods will be left at C. & H. Curtner's." George Poff advertises for a journeyman tobacconist, and Lewis West announces watches and clocks for sale.

On October 8, 1796, the Gazette advises that Joseph Crocket and James Knox as a committee, announce "the Wilderness Road is now complete from Cumberland Gap to the settlements in Kentucky, and will hold wagons loaded one ton in weight, where pulled by four horses. Supplies can be purchased along the road." On same date R. Elliott and Son advertise they have employment for one good apprentice.

On November 1, 1796, the trustees "Resolved— that Mann Satterwhite be charged $2. for the plank contained in the arch boards made by J. Spangler, and which he appropriated to his own use." Seitz and Lauman advise "they have need for able-bodied men to conduct their boats to New Orleans," and on the same date Francis Carson advertises one pense reward for an apprentice boy that had run away, but fails to name the fugitive.

On December 3, 1796, Larazus Rogers announces he is "in the fulling business," but does not give his location. William Ross advertises, "My house for sale where I now live on Limestone, the lot 40 by 55 feet."

Basil Duke and John Coburn announce they "have been appointed a committee to build an Academy at Washington, in Mason county, and will receive bids for erection at that point." James Morrison advertises that he wishes "to decline the mercantile business and for some time will sell his entire stock of goods cheap. He desires also to purchase Continental Bounty warrants, better known as Knox's warrants, for which he will pay cash or goods." Moody and Downing repeat their former advertisements and announce they "will accept in exchange for goods wheat, butter, hog's lard and oats." The junior member of this firm was Dr. Richard W. Downing, who resided on north side of Main street just west of Broadway. The Gazette of December 20, 1796, announced that "Members of the Order of Cincinnati will meet at the home of Robert Megowan, to form a society."

The Lexington Library began to function this year for the benefit of the little Town of Lexington. Organized as a result of a meeting held on January 1, 1795, in the Old State House, John Bradford, Robert Barr, John Breckinridge, James Brown, Dr. R. W. Downing, Thomas Hart, Thomas January, James Parker, Samuel Price, Dr. Frederick Ridgely, Rev. Harry Toulmin and Colonel James Trotter "Resolved, to organize a library called Transylvania Library." In a few days they secured a subscription of five hundred dollars, a purchasing committee was appointed and the money was forwarded to the East. Nearly a year passed before the books arrived, when, for lack of room, they were placed in Transylvania Seminary buildings. Additions were made to this stock of books during the next year. In 1798 further additions were made and it was then voted to house the library down-town. On November 29, 1800, the library was moved into the second story of a building on the northeast corner of Market and Short, the lower floor of which was occupied as a drug store by Andrew McCalla and he agreed to serve as librarian. The directors at this time were Thos. T. Barr, Fielding L. Turner, Samuel Postlethwait, William Macbean, Caleb Wallace, Robert Barr, James Trotter, John McDowell, James

Morrison, Robert Patterson, John A. Seitz, John Bradford and Thomas Hart, Sen. At a general meeting of
the shareholders, held at the tavern of John McNair
on the first Saturday in 1801, it was found that the
library owned seven hundred and fifty volumes, and a
re-organization was effected with the election of a
new board of directors. In 1803 the Library was
removed to the second floor of the Old State House.

The close of the year of 1796 found the Kentucky
Gazette uttering a vigorous complaint at "the frequent
delays in receipt of papers from the east," and the
hope expressed "that the Government will take steps
to correct this evil." The winter season seems to have
almost entirely shut the little Town of Lexington off
from the East, but neither the cold nor the mountains
could stop the westward flow of emigrant trains. A
very vivid description of the hardships of the journey
over the mountains at this period, is found in the
story of Moses Austin.[1] Starting on December 8, 1796,
with a lone companion, Josiah Bell, Austin went by
Abingdon, Cumberland Gap, Danville, Frankfort, Louisville and Vincennes to St. Louis, which he reached
January 15, 1797. Despite the intense cold, he crossed
most of the streams on the ice and says that "the road
through Kentucky was thronged with emigrants, many
in the most wretched condition." The night of the
17th of December was spent by Austin and his fellow-
traveler in a one-room log cabin at Rockcastle with
sixteen companions, and the next day he recorded his
reflections concerning "the many distress'd families
that he passed. Women and children in the month of
December traveling through the wilderness through
ice and snow, passing large rivers and creeks, without
shoe or stocking, and barely as many rags as will cover
their nakedness, without money or provisions except
what the wilderness affords, to say they are poor is
but faintly express'g there situation. Can anything be
more absurd than the conduct of men—here is hundreds

1 American Historical Review, Vol. 5, page 518. See also—
   Barker's Life of Stephen F. Austin, page 8.

traveling hundreds of miles, they know not for what nor whither, except its to Kentucky, passing land almost as good and easy obtained, the proprietors of which would gladly give on any terms, but it will not do, its not Kentucky, its not the promised land, its not the goodly inheritance, the land of Milk and Honey."

From the same "Memorandum of M. Austin's Journey," we also learn St. Louis had at this time "about two hundred houses, most of which were of stone, but there was no tavern in the town."

The long lines of immigrant trains must have been an interesting sight in the little Town of Lexington. While some of these stopped in Lexington, others continued on to the Spanish Territory west of the Mississippi, where the generous policy of the Spanish Government in donating land to settlers attracted all those who were dissatisfied with living conditions on the Atlantic seaboard. Many of these trains of immigrants paused in Lexington only long enough to purchase fresh supplies, repair wagons, shoe and refresh the stock, and then pass on towards the setting sun, frequently accompanied by a settler from Lexington who had been disappointed in acquiring acreage and to whom the charm of the Blue Grass had diminished. "The Blue Grass became a token of what was to be found farther on, if sought early. Willing to again resume the backwoods life in hope of getting cheap land which would grow as dear as central Kentucky," they passed on to the west and south, and many of their names appear in the records of Mississippi and Missouri in later years.

The business of our merchants was conducted largely by credit and barter, as currency was scarce and the merchants were frequently unable to meet their obligations. The trouble incident to their failure to collect accounts caused some to "retire from the mercantile adventure" and resort to the Courts, "in an effort to collect their own." In 1796 we find court records showing many attempts to collect debts, and it is to these records we owe the discovery of a number

of names of firms doing business in Lexington. These
records also disclose the names of a number who "did
not believe in advertising in the Gazette."

Miller and Company, Boggs and Anderson, Russell
and Taylor, Percival Butler and Nathan and William
Ewing are some of the names found in the records of
the Circuit Clerk's office, either as plaintiffs or defendants, for this year.

The Gazette announced the death of General
Anthony Wayne, near Erie, Pennsylvania, "who had
command in the recent Indian War and his success
led to the treaty of Greenville."

EVENTS OF 1797.

WITH the start of the year of 1797 we find the Gazette complaining at non-receipt of the mails "from the east" and expressing a hope from the Editor that some change that would guarantee more frequent delivery and more regular service would be effected. Early in January the Gazette announced the following appointments for Justices of the Peace by the Governor: Walker Baylor, Andrew McCalla, Robert Russell, John Richardson, Peter January and James Hord. John Hickman and John Moss were made inspectors of flour and hemp, at Kentucky river warehouses.

The annual election for trustees for the Town of Lexington resulted in the choice of the following: Robert Patterson, chairman; Hugh McIlvaine, George Teagarden, Alexander Parker, James Morrison, James Hughes, John A. Seitz, treasurer, and John Arthur, clerk. In the issue of January 11, 1797, the editor of the Gazette published a brief sketch giving the history of the establishment of his paper.

A description of Lexington during this year is to be found in the Western Gazeteer, page 91, written by Samuel R. Brown:

"I had occasion to visit Lexington in the summer of 1797; it then contained about 50 houses, partly frame and hewn logs, with the chimney outside; the surrounding country was new; a village lot could have been purchased for $30, and a good farm in its vicinity for $5.00 per acre. The best farmers lived in log cabins and wore hunting shirts and leggins."

The minute book of the Board of Trustees shows an inventory of the property belonging to the town, taken during the month of January, listed as follows: Two oxen, one two wheeled cart, one wheel-barrow, one sledge, one mattock, one crow bar, one shovel, and one two-foot rule.

The tax books show that the ordinaries were run by Henry Marshall, Robert Megowan, Hyram Mitchell, James Thompson and Adam Webber. McCoy and Cosby paid tax on one billiard table. The same books show there were twenty-eight retail stores in Lexington that year. Other statistics show there were 4,654 slaves and 8,064 horses in the county. The number of white inhabitants over 16 years of age was given at 2,620 and the value of the town lots as 21,751 pounds. For the first time the tax books contained a list of the merchants with stores, doing business in the Town of Lexington; Patrick McCullough, Joseph Oliver and Company, Poyzer and Company, Samuel Price and Company, Alexander Parker, Robert and Andrew Porter, Seitz and Lauman, George Teagarden, Trotter and Scott, James Weir, William West, George Anderson, John M. Boggs, Beard and Owen, Cornelius Beatty, Christopher Curtner, Richard Coleman, Robert Barr ("Lameman"), Joseph Hudson, Andrew Holmes, John and Abijah Hunt, Andrew Hare (Hickman Creek), Peter January, Jr., James B. January, Thomas January, William Leavy, Hugh McIlvaine, James McCoun and Moody and Downing.

On January 20, 1797, thirty or forty citizens of Lexington sent proposals to the House of Representatives at Frankfort, in which they agreed to erect a state house, Governor's mansion and public jail, and refund any money paid by the citizens of Frankfort on condition that the capital be removed to Lexington. This proposal was tabled on January 21, as was another similar offer made during the year of 1809.

In this year the Lexington Immigration Society was organized with Thomas Hart, president, and John Bradford, secretary. This society made very strong exertion to attract "industrious farmers to locate on lands in the vicinity of Lexington." They published various assortments of information relative to labor conditions, the soil, climate and other necessary and useful data. Their figures show that the average acre in Central Kentucky would produce 25 bushels of wheat on ground that previously had been used for corn, or 35 bushels otherwise. Corn ran as high as 60 bushels to the acre, rye 25 bushels, barley 40 bushels, oats 40 bushels, potatoes 250 bushels, hemp 800 pds, tobacco 2,000 pounds and hay three tons.

In February, James Hughes, who became the author of the first Kentucky Law reports, resigned as Trustee and was succeeded by Mann Satterwhite. Alex. Macgregor was elected Master of Lexington Lodge, and was one of the organizers of the St. Andrew's society. That spring the Gazette carried many advertisements for "good cooks," and also the advertisement of William Allen, "who has opened a house of entertainment for man and beast on Main street, next door to Dr. Downing."

The Gazette announced it would change from a weekly to a semi-weekly, and in the same issue announced that Andrew McCalla, "at his store near the stray pen, has been furnished with the stock of drugs formerly owned by Mr. Sample and Mr. Cox;" also, that "the partnership between Drs. Ridgely and Watkins is to be dissolved and all who owe the firm will settle with J. Watkins."

The trustees voted at the February meeting "to allow the constables 2 shillings and 3 pense for each hog found straying on the streets of the town, and 9 pense for each pig." No record has been found disclosing the number found straying during any period.

On February 18, 1797, Robert and Andrew Porter announce "they have just imported from Philadelphia and are now opening in the brick house lately occupied by the Messrs. John and Samuel Postlethwaits, next door to Mr. Stewart's printing office, merchandise at the lowest prices heretofore sold in this district." Samuel Price and Company announce "they have just received at Limestone, a large assortment of brandy and feathers, merchandise and hardware, which will be opened in this town in a few days." Lewis Castleman advises he wants a foreman and Will Mann, "the barber, has a stray grindstone that had been used and which broke into his yard, which the owner will please remove." Peter January, Jun., opens "a new assortment of goods in the brick store opposite the court house, suitable for the present and the approaching season" and John Robb advertises for men to work in his brick yard. On March 8 McGuire and Connelly, tailors, open their new store in the house opposite Bradford's printing office, on Main street, and Richard Coleman advertises that he "has secured that very commodious house lately occupied by Captain Walker Baylor on Short street, where he will have entertainment for man and beast." James Parker's death is announced in this same issue. His remains were interred in the burying ground at Mr. Rankin's meeting house, at Short and Walnut, and the business was closed by Alexander Parker, his brother.

Dr. Duhame announces he will "in the future, practice medicine in Millersburg," and Rodes Thompson illustrates an ad concerning his stallion "Gallant" with the first wood cut advertising a horse, ever used by the Gazette. John Hargy advertises the opening of his school under the patronage of the Reverend Adam Rankin, John McCord, and Archibald McIlvaine, quoting the tuition at 12 shillings per quarter. This advertisement ran for a number of issues in the Gazette, several of which make mention of the prosperity of the school. Nathaniel Shaw advertises he has been authorized to purchase horses for use of the United States Army, and can be seen each day at Megowan's tavern. The well digger, John Robert Shaw, has an advertisement in which he mentions "wells recently dug at Mock's Mill, on Town Fork of Elkhorn, and Bourne's Mill on Main Hickman creek." Born in Bristol, England, and impressed into the English Army, he claimed to have been wounded a number of times, shipwrecked three times, and thrice captured by the enemy. Finally he joined the American Army, and after service in the expedition under General Harmar against the Ohio Indians, he was discharged and settled in Lexington, where he married. He was in turn a well digger, innkeeper, and operator of a stone quarry, in which he was blown up several times. He claimed also to have the ability to locate underground streams of water. His advertisements in the Gazette frequently were in rhyme. Shaw wrote the story of his life, which was embellished with some crude woodcuts showing him in the uniform of an English soldier, then as a sailor and finally as a frontiersman. This little volume now commands a considerable increase over its published price. Mr. Shaw was survived by eight children, all of whom had "Robert" for their middle name.

In this same issue of the Gazette, Patrick McCullough threatens to sue all who owe him unless they settle before March 1st, "upon which date he desires to start to the East for a fresh supply of goods." Charles Sumption, blacksmith, says he has "set up his business on Mulberry and Water streets, next door to William Reed, the chairmaker." T. M. Woodson and John S. Wills advertise land for sale in the grant of Judge Symmes, in the Ohio Territory. John Watkins, Jun., advises he "has been authorized to sell the 200 acre military grant of Dr. Tennant, of Virginia, which is located on the Ohio River a few miles above Louisville."

The first wood cut of a house to appear in the columns of the Gazette was used in the issue dated March 15, 1797, when John A. Seitz advertised he would sell on the 25th inst., "at Innes Brent's tavern, the store house formerly the property of Irvin and Bryson, and now occupied by Samuel Price and Company." This house cut shows a two-story house of brick, with two chimneys on outside of walls, five windows in the second story and four in the first, with a door in the center of the first floor. On this date, the Trustees issued, again, their order prohibiting hogs from running at large. John Robert Shaw advertises he will "sell a house on Main street a little below Dr. Downing's, lot 26 feet wide back to Short street, of hewn logs, 18 by 16 feet, with stone chimney and a good spring just before the door. Lot is enclosed with a post and rail fence." On the same date, Jonathan Nixon advertises he will wind up the business of Richard Abbott, deceased.

The Gazette on this date announced "the wedding of Dr. Frederick Ridgely to Miss Short, sister to Major Peyton Short of Woodford county." Much valuable genealogical information would be available to the present generation had the Gazette's editor given local items as much space as was devoted to political changes in war ridden Europe.

On March 20, Hughes and Fitzhugh, of Hagerstown, Maryland, begin to advertise nails made in their factory and shipped into Lexington. Peter January, Thomas January and Peter January, Jun., dissolve their partnership, with Thomas January assuming charge and to continue the business "at the old stand." Mrs. Welch advertises her school "for little misses, where they will be taught reading and needle work." The brew house of Mr. Earderman was destroyed by fire and the Gazette says, "the many idle spectators had better been at home as they encouraged others to act in the same manner." Lucy Gray announced "a school for girls, where reading, writing and needlework, drawing springs, flowers, etc, at the house of James Gray, four miles from Lexington—tuition and board, four pounds per quarter." Andrew McCalla advises that "in addition to drugs, he has for sale French brandy, Gin and Cordials." Robert McAfee says in his journal: "I attended a singing school in Lexington this year, which was kept by Chapin, and again the following year, when School was taught by Joshua L. Wilson, as a means of aiding his education." Andrew Holmes advertises the firm of Charles Humphrey and Company "is being dissolved and will all those who owe the firm please call and settle at once." William Leavy advises he has on hand a "quantity of Maderia, Port Lisson and Sherry wines, also good old spirits, etc." George Weigart advertises for "lambs wool, and can use an additional apprentice in the hat making business."

On May 1, 1797, "the tan yard" is mentioned in the Gazette, and on the same date the trustees announce "a bridge is to be built across Main street, opposite John A. Seitz's residence, with four pillars, and abutments, fifty feet across Main street and four feet wide covered with timber, two walls to be stone, two feet across the streets, at a cost of 30 pounds." On the same date, the trustees authorize a suit to be brought against J. Spangler to compel him to "finish the market house, and that Mulberry street at Leiby's brick yard be repaired." Hugh McIlvane and John A. Seitz resigned, and Cornelius Beatty and William West were elected in their stead.

Travel down the rivers to New Orleans continued to increase as did the shipments of Kentucky products. Travelers passing up and down the Mississippi river have told the story of their experiences in diaries and letters, some of which contain interesting information. Among these was one written June 14, 1797, by Captain Isaac Guion, an officer engaged in patrolling the river near Natchez, saying "Elijah Craig from Kentucky, who was bound for New Orleans, passed down." Another, June 21, 1797, said: "Phillip Stucker of Woodford County, Ky., left New Orleans on the 5th of April and took route across Lake Ponchartrain but was stopped and sent back. He left New Orleans the second time at the beginning of May and came up the River to Natchez. Three galleys at that place. He left Natchez on 10th of May and passed thru Choctaw and Chicksaw nations. He thinks the Creeks will soon strike. He is now on his way down the river with flour boats."[1]

In a letter addressed to James Wilkinson, Captain Guion says: "I directed the Commissary to purchase fourteen head of cattle for the payment of which I drew a bill on the Secretary of War and sold it to Mr. Elisha Winter, who was ascending the River."[2]

[1] Letters of Isaac Guion—7th Annual Report Missississi Archives, p. 29.
[2] *Ibid.*

On September 4, the Trustees voted to cut off the night watchmen, and elected William Allen as clerk of the board. On the 7th of the same month, the accounts of the watchmen were delivered at a meeting of the board, who ordered Nathaniel Barker to be paid 16 pounds, 13 shillings and 4 pense, and Thomas Ockletree to be paid 12 pounds, 17 shillings and 9 pense.

Notice was received of appointment by the Governor of Joseph McMurtry as major of the 10th Regiment of Militia, vice James McDowell, resigned.

On September 29 Israel Hunt opened his boot and shoe store on Cross street, four doors from Main, and mention is made of Jacob McConathy's steam mill being erected in Lexington. A. E. Saugrain advertises shot of different sizes, "made by him in Lexington and sold by Andrew Holmes, at his store at corner of Main and Mill streets." On the same date, Dr. Samuel Brown "begs to inform the public he will practice medicine and surgery in Lexington and occupy the house which Mr. Love lately occupied opposite Stewart's printing office. He will instruct one or two pupils who come well recommended." Charles Humphreys announces he has commenced business "in the brick house opposite the court house, lately occupied by Hugh McIlvane, where he will dispose of dry goods, hardware, groceries, and a small quantity of patent medicines." This mercantile "adventure" did not prevent him from practicing law, and also operating a chain of blacksmith shops in the county. Nathan Burrows opens a store at the house "formerly occupied by Ben S. Cox, at corner of Main and Cross streets, opposite the 'Old' Court house, with groceries, window glass, saddles, martingales, and a case of port wine." Tatham and Banks announce they are prepared to do "auctioning," while Samuel Beeler advertises "new stills for sale, with all necessary vessels fitting the same, at my place on Cane Run, four miles from Lexington." William Reed, the chair maker on Main street, "next door to Lawyer Hughes and opposite J.

Postlethwait's, wants an apprentice to learn the house painting business."

On September 30, 1797, Mann Satterwhite announces "at my store opposite the Market House, a good assortment of merchandise, suitable to the present and approaching season, will be sold for cash only."

On October 4 a reform wave swept over Lexington, and at a meeting of citizens at Postlethwait's tavern resolutions "against the practice of Gaming" were adopted and signed by the following: Thomas Hart, William Leavy, James H. Stewart, James Trotter, Peter January, Samuel Price, James Morrison, Samuel Downing, George Anderson, George Mansell, John A. Seitz, Frederick Ridgely, John McChord, James Brown, James Hughes, Samuel Ayers, James Moody, Joseph Hudson, Robert Barr, George Nicholas, Thomas Sthreshley, John W. Hunt and John Bradford. Nothing has been found in subsequent issues of the Gazette indicating any permanent reduction in any of the "indoor sports."

In October the Governor announced appointments for the 8th Regiment of Militia of Surgeon Dr. Frederick Ridgely, Surgeon's Mate, Walter Warfield, and Quartermaster Edmund Bullock.

On October 21, Nelson Thomason announces he will wind up the business of West and Guthrie, and on November 2 some unknown citizen advertises "for a pair of pocket pistols, lost four miles from town on the Limestone Pike, which the finder will please leave at Joseph Capley's the tailer in Lexington and receive reward." The trustees directed Robert Patterson and William Allen to provide for the safety of the town-owned oxen "during the winter, and to settle with Kenyon, the present driver, and also to collect and care for what tools belong to the trustees." Arrangements were made "to have the pavement around the court house built up to the railing, and the sewers (gutters) opened all the way around." John Ball advertises he has "for sale one coach and harness complete, to be sold on twelve months credit." John

Geary advises he has for sale "all distillers supplies, at A. McCalla's apothecary shop, near the stray pen," and Samuel Price announces he desires "to buy hemp seed and deliveries can be made at any time." William Morton advertises "the receipt of a large supply of Tanner's Oil."

On December 16, 1797, the Gazette published the following result of the election held in Fayette county for representative to the General Assembly, to fill the vacancy caused by resignation of James Morrison:

John Breckinridge	594
Alexander Macgregor	359
Walter Carr	141
Hugh McIlvane	110
John Bell	106
Robert Patterson	13

David Humphreys advertises his clock and watch-making business "in the house of Captain Kenneth McCoy, on Mill street second house above Short." The trustees, at a meeting held December 29, voted to pay "Simon Hickey one pound, 13 shillings for repairing the Market House and clearing out the spring," condemned the chimney to the house belonging to the heirs of Joseph Byers, deceased, and signed a deed conveying "in-lot No. 66 to Dr. Walter Warfield." This lot is now on southwest corner of Vine and Mill streets.

The Gazette, in its final issue for this year, comments upon the passage by the General Assembly of the "Occupying claimant" law, which excused the occupant of land from the payment of rents and profits prior to receipt of notice of adverse title, and requiring the successful claimant to pay for all valuable and lasting improvements made prior to service of such notice. The same Assembly also abolished the death penalty, excepting in cases of murder in the first degree, from a long list of crimes.

In the fall of this year Mr. Henry Clay removed to Lexington and began the practice of law.

EVENTS OF 1798.

THE beginning of the year of 1798 found Fayette County again called upon to give up a portion of its area for the purpose of the establishment of a new county, when Jessamine county was formed out of the southern and southeastern portions of this county. The Jessamine creeks settlements had grown considerably by the acquisition of the Moravian settlers, who had been brought to this county from Hagerstown, Maryland, by Doctor Peter Trisler, and who occupied a commanding influence when the new county began to function as such on January 1, 1798. The energy and thrift of these German Protestants and their descendants have done much to bring that county into the front rank of Kentucky's agricultural communities. These substantial qualities were carried by them or their descendants into the states to the south and west, and did much to improve the best elements of those newer settlements.[1]

The first vineyard planted west of the Alleghanies is reputed to have been planted within the present limits of Jessamine county by John De Four and his Swiss Colony, in the year of 1796, which effort was not as succesful as he had expected. He removed to Indiana and was the founder of Vevay, on the Ohio River, where he propogated the celebrated Cape grape, which is still a commercial factor in Southern Indiana. Naming the new settlement for the place of his birth in Switzerland, he established it on a firm basis, with every settler owning the same acreage and hearing the same denominational tenets preached each Sunday. His story of his adventures and experiences makes a welcome addition to the history of the Ohio valley.

The election of Lexington's town trustees, held in January, resulted in the choice of William Allen, Robert Patterson, Cornelius Beatty, Alexander Parker, George Teagarden, Samuel Postlethwait and Archibald

[1] Young's History of Jessamine County, page 45.

McIlvane for this year. Their first meeting was devoted to ascertaining a list of property owned by the
town and a survey of the "conditions of the streets
and pavements."

The new year also brought forth an announcement from the editor of the Gazette that hereafter the
paper would be published once each week. In the
same issue Poyzer and Company advertise "cotton for
sale for cash or produce." On the 15th, the trustees
held their meeting at some unknown tavern, and voted
to pay the account presented by Samuel Vanpelt,
amounting to nine pounds, thirteen shillings, "for repairing the town pumps on Main street." He owned
considerable acreage on the east side of the town, and
in 1811 opened a street southward from Main, which
was called "Van Pelt" street, but is now known as
Rose street. James Pilling advertised "imported merchandise, hardware, nails, gartering and window glass,
for sale at the store next to McNair's tavern, lately
occupied by Baird and Owen." Jacob Lauderman
announced a "tobacco factory on Main street, next door
to Lawyer Hughes," which site is now covered by a
portion of the Phoenix Hotel. With the issue of the
Gazette dated January 31, the Gazette appeared for the
first time using the Seal of Kentucky between the words
of its title. This specimen of the first seal is interesting, as the original seal was destroyed by fire in 1832,
and only a few copies remain.

In the same issue of the Gazette the total vote
cast in the last general election was published as follows: Bourbon 1113, Fayette 813, Franklin 449, Madison 1,153, Clark 610, Montgomery 707, Campbell 876,
Jefferson 373 and Woodford 578. The Gazette also
published extracts from the act of the General Assembly giving an endowment of 6,000 acres of public land
to "Kentucky Academy" and a like quantity to acad-
emies in Franklin and Fayette counties.

The end of January also found the firm of John
M. Boggs and his auctioneering partner, George Anderson, dissolved by mutual consent, and Hiram Shaw

announcing "the making of all kinds of furr and wool
hats, at his factory on northeast corner of Main and
Cross streets." David Dodge and Company advertise
"they have a quantity of hemp to break for which they
will pay 7 shillings, 6 pense per one hundred and
twelve pounds."

On February 3, 1798, Captain Walker Baylor, John
Bobb, Thomas Hart and Thomas Briggs advertise
they "have a brick-making machine and are prepared
to deliver brick on shortest notice," and on the 13th
the Kentucky Vineyard Association requested the stock-
holders to "attend a meeting to be held at Postlethwait's tavern, where a specimen of native grown wine
will be displayed." Benedict Vanpradelles announces
he is attorney for John Cockey Owings "and will handle
accounts due him." This attorney received appointment from the Federal Government of Register of the
Land Office and Commissioner for settling land claims
in the Territory of Orleans, and died while on that
duty January 24, 1809. Macbean, Poyzer and Company
advertise they are now at the "Old Court House, at
Main and Cross streets, with a new assortment of
general merchandise" and John Jordan, Jr., says he
"has received a varied list of merchandise from Philadelphia, which he is now opening, and which will be
sold for cash." Joseph Oliver advertises a fresh lot
of cabbage seed for sale, "next door to the Printing
Office." Nathan Burrows states he has "a fresh assortment of merchandise, suitable for the present and
approaching season, at his store at Main and Cross
streets, opposite the old court house, which he will
exchange for cash or fresh furrs."

On March 14, 1798, Samuel Wilson published his
"Kentucky English Grammar" and the partnership of
Robert Barr and Company was dissolved. The Town
trustees published an order directing the assessor "to
report on the number of inhabitants in the town and

county," which report was not published until the
issue date May 9, as follows:

Males above 12 years	462
Females above 12 years	307
Whites under 12 years	346
Negroes	360
	1,475

These figures represented the residents of the Town
of Lexington and the addition of the county inhabitants
raised the total to 2,247. The taxable property is
listed at 189,666 pounds.

The Trustees fixed the tax rate for the town at
3 shillings on each 1,000 pounds' valuation on all
property "within the bounds of the in- and out-lots,"
and three pense on each tithable.

In the same issue of the Gazette we find a population comparison of Fayette county with the surrounding settlements, in the publication of the votes
cast for representatives of the General Assembly:

Fayette, 2,247; Clark, 799; Franklin, 590; Mercer,
896; Madison, 950; Bourbon, 1,673; Nelson, 913; Montgomery, 765; Fleming, 513; Scott, 1,040; and of the
poll in the election for Sheriff in this county, result-
ing as follows: Tompkins, 387; Carr, 378; Colby, 110;
Clark, 57; Logan, 48; McMurdry, 17. In the race for
Coroner, Benjamin Stout received a total of 462 votes,
while the old pioneer, John Maxwell, received only 91.

The Gazette announced appointments by the Governor for the 10th regiment of Militia as follows:
Captains Robert Russell, Christopher Chinn, Morgan
Bryan and Robert Tucker; Lieutenants John Hamilton,
Abner Browning, and John Shrock; Ensigns Wm.
Stephenson, Moses Masterson, Seth Stephens, Samuel
Patterson and Peter Sidner. William Dudley was
nominated Major for the 8th Regiment. In the same
issue of the Gazette P. D. Robert advertises he has
"for sale, lands in Tennessee and in the Illinois territory, near the village of Kaskaskias; also, 450 pounds

of very good gun powder." Samuel Wilkinson advertises he has begun business as a whitesmith "next door
to Colonel Hart's on Mill street, where he makes
wheel irons and does iron work for printers, cotton
workers and rope walks." R. Gilbert informs "the
young gentlemen of Lexington, he has opened a fencing school in the upper brick house on Main street,
where lessons will be given from 5 to 7 P. M."

Hugh McIlvane is announced as the Master of
the Masonic Lodge for this year.

On June 5, 1798, Dr. Peter Trisler gives notice
that "all who owe him for medicines which they got
last year, to come forward and settle as I need money
for my creditors." His home was on main Jessamine
creek, where he maintained a flower garden of unusual
beauty and variety. Peter Higbee announced he will
"undertake to build brick houses and can use four or
five hands." On June 13, John Arthur advertises he is
"the collector of the (Federal) revenues for this district and has opened his office at Major Morrison's on
Short street, and all those who are distillers are notified that the law requires stills to be entered for taxation annually in June, whether in use or not." This
tax amounted to $1.00 per year and caused great
indignation and many hard words at the avariciousness
of the government. George Heytel advertises for a
journeymen tanner and currier, and on July 2, the
trustees voted "the watchman be allowed to draw
the balances due them for nine months services as town
watchmen." Some unknown advertised as lost "a
very green small umbrella on the Georgetown pike,
near Joshua Humphrey's" and on July 18 Margaret
Carothers "begs leave to announce she is now manta-
making at house of Mrs. Welch on High street." In
same issue "The Fried Meat Tavern" is mentioned
on the corner of Upper and Church streets.

"A few Franklin stoves" are advertised by Charles
Humphreys at his store on Main street, "which have
been made at the Laurel Furnaces and which he
desires to sell on very moderate terms for cash only."

Judge Charles Humphreys also advertised for slaves to work at the blacksmith business. This same month, John Bradford published his book on "The Revenue laws of the United States," and on the 5th of August brought out the "Acts of the Assembly passed at the last session." Henry Clay advertises for "A red morocco pocket book lost between Lexington and Winchester," and Price and Company dissolve partnership. On August 27, John Arthur, United States Revenue Collector, announces that September 1, is the time appointed for entering carriages for taxation, and he will attend for the next month at Major Morrison's house.

On September 11, 1798, John Mullanphy advertises "he is located on Cross street, next door to Mr. Burrows, where he had a choice and handsome collection of new books, just opened, consisting of many thousands volumes of law, physic, divinity, history, novels, plays, German and French chap books, the whole to be sold at Philadelphia retail prices; also, parcels of music for the violin, flute, etc., new songs, loaded horse whips, playing cards, men's shoes, fine and coarse. As I am returning to Baltimore this fall, I will give bargains either wholesale or retail. These goods to remain in town but two or three weeks."

The Gazette on this date mentions that "between 4 and 5,000 people met in Lexington on August 5th to discuss National Issues" but gives no clue as to any action taken or resolutions passed. The Gazette does refer to the passage by Congress of the two acts since known in Political history as the Alien and Sedition laws, and publishes many cards for and against this act, all of which were signed by such names as "Pro patria," "Publicus," and "Agricolous."

On September 19, 1798, William Campbell advertises "his fulling business at Major Morrison's mill, 5 1-2 miles from Lexington on the Tate's Creek pike. Clothe to be left at George Anderson's store in Lexington, near the Market House." On the same date, a committee of the Lexington Academy announce they have employed Mr. Leroy Johnson to open an English school on October 1, under the direction said Academy, "with the indorsement of the Reverend Adam Rankin."

Thomas Reid advertises as a "copper and tinsmith, opposite the Gazette, where all work will receive prompt and careful attention." On October 17 the Gazette announces "there is now opened in Colonel Patterson's old house on High street, a sunday school for use of people of color." Thomas Lewis advertises in this same issue for "good clean wheat to be delivered at his mill, three miles below Lexington." On October 22, 1798, the trustees employed George Teagarden "to build a stone gutter across Main street at Cross street, on a good foundation, and also a bridge to be built across Mulberry, Upper and Milne (Mill) streets over the Canal."

On November 7, Gardner and Boardman open "on Main street, next door to Stewart's printing office, an elegant assortment of British and India muslins, clothes, bed ticking, comforts, handkerchiefs, Jew's harps, pocket knives, and cuttlery." James B. January announces he "will buy hemp and tobacco, and has for sale red clover seed of this year's growth."

The Town of Lexington was considerably enlivened on November 9 when the news arrived that the Kentucky Legislature had passed the resolution introduced by John Breckinridge, protesting against the Alien and Sedition Laws. A bonfire was arranged to be followed by a parade, and many of the inns kept open house in celebration of this event..

On November 17, 1798, the St. Andrew's society of Lexington was organized by the local Scotchmen, with John Maxwell as chairman of the meeting. George Muter was elected first president, and on the night of November 30 this society had a dinner at Megowan's Tavern with many toasts and "much good cheer." The members at the time of this organization were Alexander McGregor, John Cameron, William Macbean, John Maxwell, David Reid, Richard Lake, John Arthur,

William Tod, Thomas Reid, George Muter, Miles McCoun, James Russell, Alexander Springle and James Bain.

On December 3, 1798, the Board of Trustees notified James Lowry and Joseph McMurtry that the chimneys to their houses constituted a fire hazard and directed they be built of stone. At the same meeting Mrs. Woods was allowed $15, "for cleaning and repairing the State House."

The Governor appointed William Moore and Ezekiel Patterson as captains in the Militia Regiment known as No. 10, with Peter Goodnight and Joseph Reyburn as lieutenants, and Braxton Pollard, George Rodgers and Moses Randolph as ensigns. Cuthbert Banks was commissioned a Notary Public, Nathaniel Barker as Jailor, and Cornelius Beatty as a Justice of the Peace. For the 8th regiment, the Governor appointed Captains James Alexander, Charles Tylor, Hugh Muldrow and Hugh Thompson; Lieutenants William Chinn, William Porter, Abraham Weagly and Jesse Fitzgerald, and Ensigns James Carothers, James Stone and John Brown.

On December 12, 1798, the firm of John Oliver and Company was dissolved by mutual consent with "the stock of goods for sale cheap for cash." The Gazette complains of the severe weather and closes the year with considerable space devoted to the military exploits of Napoleon, European politics, and acts of Congress, but does not mention any local happenings such as the union of the Kentucky Academy and Transylvania University. It does refer, however, to the convention to be held July 22, 1799, "for purpose of erecting a new constitution for the State of Kentucky."

Thomas Bodley served as Master of the Masonic lodge for the last half of this year. He had been the first secretary of the Democratic Society, and also was Captain of the Lexington Light Infantry.

EVENTS OF 1799.

THE opening of the year of 1799 found the Gazette complaining of "the continued severe weather and the non-receipt of the mails from the east," and praying "that the authorities will make some improvement in the service." The trustees elected for this year were Robert Patterson, George Teagarden, Alexander Parker, Cornelius Beatty, Thomas January, Andrew McCalla and Samuel Postlethwait. Their minute book shows they met promptly after the first of the year, began to pay considerable attention to the condition of the streets and pavements, and directed many sections of the latter to be put down in brick, forbidding the use of cinders and small stones in the business district. Mention frequently is found of narrow board walks in front of residences and "the remarkable number of instances in which these said boards disappear, especially during cold weather." Some of the houses had large flat stones for sidewalks, of which the board appeared to approve. A bridge was built from the southwest corner of Main and Mill streets across to the public square.

On January 10, the Board of Trustees directed "Mrs. Woods to be paid $10. for cleaning the State House," but no mention has been found as to the use that had been made of these rooms. On January 21, Henry Hyman advertises in the Gazette that "he has gold and silver for sale, also clocks and watches, being lately from London, and will reside in the house of Robert and Andrew Porter." Josiah Bullock advises he has "for sale, boats for use on the rivers to New Orleans." Thomas Tibbats says he has "opened a tavern at the Sign of the Sheaf of Wheat, where travelers always can be furnished with biscuits, bacon, ham, venison, dried beef, beef tongues, cheeses and cakes." Ashton and Overall advertise "Iron mongery in the house lately occupied by Dr. Brown on Main street, next door to William West." John Goodman says he has "a fine quantity of cabinet work, desks, tables, chairs, etc., at John Coon's, or at my factory on Cross street, opposite Colonel Hart's nail factory." On February 14, George Young and also James Fleming and Company advertise they have boot and shoe factories on Water street, "opposite Brent's tavern, and next door to Mrs. Thomas." John Robert Shaw advertises "lime for sale at Colonel Patterson's quarry at 10 cents per bushel, and he will do well-digging at 2 shillings 6 pense per foot."

On March 14, 1799, Transylvania Library extends its thanks to Mr. Allen Bowie Magruder for a present of "Taylor's Summary of the Roman Laws." The Gazette for April 16, 1822, has a notice of Magruder's death at Opelousa, Louisiana.

The Governor appointed Walter Carr, James Martin and Abner Venable as tobacco inspectors at Cleveland's ferry; David Logan, John Chinn, James Wood and James McCoun, Jr., as Justices of the Peace, and Robert Todd, Justice of the Court of Quarter Sessions, in place of Joseph Crocket, resigned.

On March 28, 1799, John Hargy and his daughter "open a school in Robert Patterson's late home on High street," and on the same date Dr. Frederick Ridgely advertises for sale his house and lots and offers to receive in payment, "lands northwest of the Ohio river, young negroes or six horses, or stock in the Bank of the United States." On April 18, John Scott and his son, Thomas, "announce they are in business" but do not divulge its character or location. On same date, the trustees' minutes book records that Daniel Siers was allowed "13 shillings, six pense, for making a plow for use on the streets of Lexington," and William Ross offers to "sell the brick house on Short street, opposite the Presbyterian church, and nearly opposite the Market House."

Charles Humphrys announces he has "removed his store to the house lately occupied by Major Cornelius Beatty, where he has for sale an assortment of fine goods and other commodities." James Ross, "shoemaker, lately from New York, opens a store on Cross street, two doors below Nathan Burrows; also, another store on Main street, next door to Leavy's store."

The election held in Fayette County for Congressional representative and for members of the General Assembly of Kentucky resulted in the following state of the polls:

For Congressman—

John Fowler	793
Richard Johnson	275
P. Thomas	36

For the Legislature—

J. McDowell	751
J. Bell	545
B. Thurston	742
J. Breckinridge	698
H. Harrison	573
Walter Carr	501
J. Parker	352
Edmund Bullock	457
John Bradford	263
James Hughes	236
Robert Todd	166
W. Barbee	106
C. Graves	204

At the same time delegates to the Constitutional Convention were chosen and the following were selected as representatives from Fayette County: John McDowell, Buckner Thruston, John Breckinridge, Walter Carr and John Bell.

On May 16, 1799, the Gazette moved its home back to Main street and the editor announces: "The editor presents his readers with the Gazette executed on paper equal to any western newspaper and with new type. He offers to accept the following for subscriptions; Corn, wheat, country-made linen, linsey, sugar, whiskey, ash flooring and cured hams."

Nathaniel Hart advertises he has "opened a store at the place lately occupied by Gardner and Boardman, and adjoining Major Beatty's store, where he has an extensive assortment of dry goods, paints, Crowley steel and patent medicines." Dr. C. Freeman announces he "has had such success that he will be compelled to start for the Indian towns in the northwest to secure a fresh supply of herbs."

At their May meeting, the trustees fixed the tax rate at 13 shillings, six pense per thousand pounds on in-lots and ten shillings, six pense on out-lots; tithables 3 shillings each. They ordered "the dirt around the court house fence to be removed and the ground leveled off even with the street."

On May 28, George Anderson "calls on those that owe him to come and settle as he desires to start East for fresh supplies at once." On June 3, Colonel Robert Patterson, chairman of the trustees, published notice that "all owners of lots on Main street must have their pavements completed by August 1st and sewers freed from rubbish." William Macbean, George Poyzer and John Anderson file notice of an agreement to dissolve their partnership, which had been engaged in the business of conducting stores—the one in Lexington as Macbean, Poyzer and Company, and another in Nashville under the name of John Anderson and Company. "Macbean and Poyzer will continue business at the Old Court House." James B. January announces "he has sold out his business for the express purpose of collecting what is owing to him." On June 21, 1799, the trustees met in the "lower floor of the court house," and issued an order prohibiting the game of "Long Bullits" from being played in the streets of Lexington. This game consisted in laying a cannon ball on the ground and then, without lifting it, attempt to jerk it the greatest distance. It was the favorite game for testing strength of the competitors and usually drew a large crowd of loafers from the blacksmith's shop and corner stores. After a number of innocent bystanders had sustained severe injuries, the trustees finally banned the sport.

On July 2, 1799, Dr. Michael Schaag, Physician and Surgeon, advises "he is on Main street, where he can be found in cases of Mad dog bites, flux, jaundices, coughs, dropsy, white swelling, etc." James Morrison advertised flax seed oil for sale, and on July 16, Dr. Joseph Boswell says "he has removed his office to the corner of Short and Market streets, opposite the Market house." On August 7, George Weigart, "the hat maker, has removed to the house lately occupied by Jacob Keiser, on High Street, next door to Melchoir Myers." The Gazette publishes a notice of Jacob Myers, merchant, and refers to his store but does not mention its location. At the time of the death of Jacob Myers, June 1, 1827, the Gazette said "He emigrated to the West in the early settlement of this town, and encountered all the dangers of savage cruelty and was made a captive, and remained with the Indians for a considerable period."

On August 22, 1799, the Gazette refers to the new constitution that the convention had voted upon on August 17, and mentions that "the governor will be elected by the voters directly, instead of by the college of electors, and will be chosen every four years." Grainger and Whelan open "at the store lately occupied by Robert Barr, with teas, coffee, sugar, wines, brandy, ladies hats, clothes, prints and hoses, gartering and stays." The little Town of Lexington was also advised that "Dr. C. Freeman has returned from the Indian tribes with a fresh assortment of herbs to cure all diseases. He is now located on High Street, in a healthy part of the town." William Massie advises "he has been authorized to sell Booker's patent threshing machine in Kentucky—one has already been built for Thomas Hart and Cuthbert Banks."

The Honorable George Nicholas died on August 1, 1799 at his home which stood on the site of Sayre College. James Morrison was appointed administrator of his estate. The files of the Circuit Clerk's office show

the following as plaintiffs or defendants in various
actions brought during this year: John Clay and Com-
pany, Irvin, Hockaday and Wood, Adams and Craigs,
Fisher, Cogar and Company, Nabb and Company,
Meredith and Breckinridge, John Miller and Company,
Clay and Fowler, West and Guthrie, Rankin and
January, Baker and Company, Hicks and Campbell,
Green and Willoughby, Henry and Boggs, Craig
and Toliver, Fink and Rice; Daley and Stewart, Hart
and Price, Searcy and Royles, Phillips and Busick, Four-
nor and Smith, Jonathan Holmes, Davenport and
Thruston, Lacy and Holman, and Cochran and
Thursby.

On September 5, the Gazette mentions the "very
low stage of the water in Kentucky river" and the
interference with navigation, and Colonel Thomas Hart
announces "he is obliged to give up the manufacturing of cordage account of the shortage of hemp."
The tax of carriages, as passed by Congress on May
28, 1796, is announced at $15 for carriages, $12 on
chariots, and $9 for phaetons. Other carriages hav-
ing panel work above with glass blinds or curtains,
were taxed $9.

Andrew Holmes advertises for "hops to be delivered at his brewery on Mulberry street" and Stephen
Young announces "boots and shoes are made at his
factory on Main street, next door to Brent's tavern,
and directly opposite Morton's store." In the issue
dated September 26, the Gazette announces the death
of "Captain Samuel Price, of Yellow Fever, while on
a trip to New Orleans," and in the issue of October
24, the death is announced of Colonel John Campbell.
The latter owned a large portion of the City of Louisville, and he willed this estate to his brother and the
children of his sister, Sarah Beard. Litigation over
his property lasted for many years and enriched several
generations of lawyers. John Jordan, Jr., advertises
"Northern Furr for sale" and James Crutcher, Hugh
Crutcher and John Metcalf dissolve their partnership,
with the last name continuing the business.

On October 26, 1799, Cuthbert Banks announces the following returns from the taxable property in the state of Kenucky:

Number of acres	17,674,634
Dollars	21,438,253
Dwelling houses of $100 valuation and over	3,081
Slaves	28,517
Bodily exemptions	1,654
Between 12 and 50 years	15,858

Cornelius Beatty and Company dissolve their partnership and advertise "they will close out their stock cheap, consisting of old whiskey, salt, iron, castings, and stills." John Clay "opens merchandise for sale in house of Robert Barr, and opposite George and Samuel Trotter's." Robert Frazier announces his "removel from Paris to Lexington into the house on Main street, opposite the District Clerk's office, where he will do watch and silversmith's work." Alexander Frazier, his brother, took charge of the Paris shop. On the same date, Edward West announces "sale of iron rings to prevent Rheumatism." Elijah Craig "received an allowance from the Board of Trustees of 4 pense per load for 250 loads of clay, handled by his teams to fill holes in Main and Short streets."

On December 19, 1799, Christopher Smedley, "Taylor," advertises "he is next door below the old court house and prepared to fill orders on shortest notice." William Compton advertises "for a good baker willing to work in Nashville." James Bliss, attorney, advertises he is prepared to draw up all kinds of commercial papers. He also served as Master of the Masonic lodge the last half of this year.

As usual, the Gazette closed this year with complaint regarding the severe and disagreeable weather and "lack of news from the East or from foreign shores, because of the non-receipt of the mails."

The Gazette this month issued another "Kentucky Almanac" for the year of 1800, containing 36 pages.

This feature of the Printing office had been inaugurated by John Bradford in 1788, and was issued with
certain changes and additions in the years of 1789,
1794, 1795, 1796, 1797, 1798, 1799 and for several years
thereafter, before it was taken up by his competitors.
No compiler is named in any of these issues, and it
is supposed John Bradford himself was responsible for
the material they contained.   The title pages usually
announced, "The Rising and Setting of the sun, and
Moon, the Lunations, Conjunctions, and Eclipses, the
Rising, Setting, and Southing of the noted fixed stars,
together with length of days, judgment of weather,
festivals and other remarkable days.   Also, Court days
with useful observations on, and directions for, propa-
gating Fruit trees by grafting on its different branches.
Directions for making and refining sugar, etc., etc.,
etc.   Calculated for Lat. 37 degrees north and a Meri-
dian of 15 degrees west from Philadelphia and will
serve without any sensible variation for Virginia, North
Carolina and the settlement on the Cumberland River
(Nashville), St. Vincents and the Kaskaskies, the
territory south of the Ohio, and the western parts of
Virginia."   Frequently, the pages contained original
poetry but the authorship is never disclosed.   On Page
32 of the Almanac for the year of 1799 is the following:
    "The Printer to His Customers.
    "My worthy Friends;
    "We strive to merit your applause,
    And own 'tis but a second cause
    From which we act—for to be just,
    The Ready Rino is the first.
    Great Pains we've used, our friends to treat,
    That they may read and we may eat;
    For, Printers strangely are inclined
    To wholesome food of every kind!
    Therefore, our work we wish to sell ye,
    To clothe the back and fill the belly;
    For, if to purchase you incline,
    We hope to breakfast, sup and dine."

EVENTS OF 1800.

THE year of 1800 opened with considerable political activity under the leadership of Mr. Breckinridge, as the death of Colonel George Nicholas during the previous year, left Mr. Clay and Mr. Breckinridge at the head of the opposition to John Adams in this state. "There was not half a dozen Federalists that dared to avow their opinions,"[1] and evidently the political complexion of Kentucky must have appeared very one-sided. The Gazette has many political cards during this period and devoted much space to "National Affairs." It also refers to the "severe storm of snow" that visited the Town of Lexington during the early part of January, and the severe cold weather following. The trustees elected for this year were Robert Patterson, chairman; George Teagarden, Alexander Parker, Alexander Macgregor, John Hull, Robert Campbell, John M. Boggs and John Arthur, the latter clerk. They appointed a committee (not named) to investigate the condition of the public springs and to ascertain if "washing was being done in any of them."

On January 21st John Slater advertises he has "just arrived in Lexington from Sheffield, England, with an assortment of knives, forks, hardware, kerseymere, swansdown for waistcoats, all of which are now being sold in the storeroom lately occupied by Charles Humphreys." The town trustees held their monthly meeting at Megowan's tavern and voted "to join the procession on Saturday next from respect of the Revolutionary hero, George Washington, Commander in Chief of the Revolutionary Army of the United States, who lead his country to Independence and then resumed his station as a private citizen in 1783."[1]

The same issue of the Gazette requests all citizens to meet at the Masons' Hall at 10:30 A. M. "to join in the procession from there to the Presbyterian Meeting

---

[1] McAfee MSS.
[1] Trustees Minute Book page 124.

house, where an oration will be delivered to the illustrious Washington."

Nathan Burrows advertises "he has just received from Philadelphia a handsome assortment of merchandise which is now for sale in the house lately occupied by Mr. Andrew Hare, amongst which are kerseymeres, cashmires, velvets, corduroys, plush, linen, calicoes, coarse muslin, books, jaconet handkerchiefs, family and school bibles, writing paper, augurs, screws, cuttlery, saws, tea, coffee, loaf, white, Havana and Muscavodo sugar, rosin, brimstone, copperas, and a few excellent double and single triggered rifle guns."

The partnership of William Smith and Joseph Arthur is dissolved with the latter continuing the business, and a committee advertises "a bridge is to be built across the Kentucky River at Frankfort, according to the Acts of the last General Assembly, which will be 400 feet long, 16 feet wide, and clear six and one-half feet the highest water known. To be oiled, tarred or pitched with a good convenient roof."

Among the many travelers who visited Lexington this year was D. B. Warden, who returned again in the year 1810. Of his visit this year, he says: "In 1800 Lexington had 1,795 inhabitants of whom 23 were Indians and 439 were slaves."[1] His book of travels contains much of interest in pioneer Kentucky and the South.

Up to this time, the shipments of flour from this vicinity to New Orleans had much exceeded the shipments of tobacco,[2] but after this year the development of "Kitefoot" light leaf and the increased acreage due to clearing of the forests caused tobacco and whiskey to assume first rank as export crops from the Blue Grass. During this year the shipments of tobacco amounted to 2,113 hogsheads. William Ross advertises his "brick house for sale, on Short street opposite the Presbyterian Church, and nearly opposite to the Market House." This corner was afterwards occupied

---

[1] Descriptive—Statisque—Historique, et Politique des Etate Unis.
[2] Johnson's—History of Kentucky.

by Drs. James Fishback and Joseph Boswell, the latter of whom gave his life in an attempt to stay the cholera scourge in 1833. The Security Trust Company now occupies this site. In the same issue of the Gazette, William Leavy advertises he has "just received from Philadelphia a general assortment of merchandise, which had been purchased at such low terms, that they will be sold lower than other stores in this community. Amongst the items are law books, histories, Books of Divinity, Schools books, writing paper of the best quality, also, wafers, quills, slates and slate pencils, and an elegant coach with plated harness." On the same date, John Clay advertises "he has just received from Baltimore an extra large shipment of assorted merchandise, which is exposed for sale in the house formerly occupied by Robert Barr, opposite Samuel and George Trotter, which he will exchange for country produce, hemp, tobacco, good clean wheat, to be delivered at any mill in the county, or in Woodford county." He also "offers to buy beeswax and tallow for which he will give one-half cash." Lawson McCullough, 'Taylor', also, advertises that "he takes this method of informing his friends and customers that he has rented a room on Main street, upstairs in the house where Robert Barr formerly lived, two doors from Trotter and Scott's store."

On February 6, 1800, John Jordan, Jr., announces he is "willing and ready to purchase a few thousands of clean dry ginseng, and will pay cash for same." In the same issue, Thomas Hart offers "to exchange salt and cash for a few thousand pounds of good pork." Richard Allen, John Keller, Abraham Bowman and John Young advertise they are "trustees to receive bids at John Higbee's on South Elkhorn, for the building of a brick meeting house, the plans of which are to be shown on date of the opening of the bids." On same date, notice was published directing the "Citizens of Lexington to meet at Bill Bailey's at 6 o'clock Saturday next, to form themselves into fire companies. It would be insulting to the good sense

of the citizens of this town to attempt to enforce
the idea for the necessity of such meeting, to be informed there is not a properly organized company
in this place is sufficiently alarming to show that
necessity."

At the meeting of the Board of Trustees, held on
March 11, 1800, the board inaugurated a cleaning up
campaign, by having the gutters cleared, and directed
"that every person in occupation of the several lots in
the town, shall, on every Saturday after the 25th inst.,
wash and clean the pavement before such lot."

During this month, Robert Frazier and his nephew
of same name, announce "they have arrived from
Ireland, and will do watchmaking and Jewelry at Main
and Upper streets." The will of General George
Washington was published in the Gazette for March
6, and following it was the notice of the death of
"Robert Parker, the county surveyor, an early adventurer."

On April 7, 1800, the trustees held their meeting
and appointed a committee (not named) to locate a
house for the fire engine, and on the 18th directed
"bridges to be built on Main Cross street, to be 40
feet wide in the clear, and the ones on Mill and on
Upper streets to be 20 feet wide. All foundations to
be of stone with brick arches." The committee appointed to locate the new fire engine house reported
"they recommended such building to be built on Main
street, next door to Bradford's printing office, and
that it shall be 14 feet deep and 11 feet wide."

In the issue for April 14, the Gazette published
this item:

> "At ten o'clock yesterday the duck fac-
> tory, a brick building 160 feet long, in which
> ten persons were employed, was blown down.
> Two persons perished and the overseer had his
> thigh broken. The loss is estimated to be at
> $5,000."

On May 8, 1800, the Gazette announced the result of the election for State offices, as shown by the returns from some of the surrounding counties:

	Garrard	Greenup	Todd	Logan
Bourbon	360	117	34	9
Henry	119	94	6	40
Gallatin	20	45	4	3
Woodford	107	119	129	13
Jessamine	91	273	51	42
Scott	366	312	83	51
Fayette	423	642	194	46

On May 22, the trustees announced they have been compelled to raise the tax rate to 18 shillings per thousand. On May 29, the Gazette gives the official count in the recent election for the Governorship:

Garrard	8,390
Greenup	6,745
Logan	3,996
Todd	2,166

This was the first election held after passage of the new Constitution, which remained in effect until the year 1850.

In the issue of the Gazette dated June 3, Nathan Burrows advertises "he has just received from Philadelphia and Baltimore, at the stone house at Main and Mill streets, formerly occupied by Seitz and Lauman, and lately by John Jordan, Jr., a cargoe of merchandise, groceries, lard, glass, queen and china ware, salt, castings, nails, etc., and other articles too numerous and tedious to mention." William West advertises for 20,000 pounds of ginseng, and John Jordan, Jr., advises "he has received his brother George into partnership, and, also, a large shipment of merchandise, suitable to the present and approaching season." On June 18, 1800, George Weigart advertises "for one or two lads to learn the hat-making business, at his shop on High street." John Lowry advertises in the same issue "for Mole skins, to be delivered at my hat factory." On July 3, 1800, John Bradford announces he "has just published a primer on an entirely new plan, calculated to teach children the different sounds of all the letters, with more ease to the teachers." On July 7, the Gazette announced a "meeting of the United Company of the Kentucky Iron works, to receive proposals of Cuthbert Banks, James Morrison, and B. Vanpradelles, for a furnace, splitting mill, grist mill and appurtenances." The Gazette also announced the publication of "An Easy Method with Deists," also, "The Truth of Christianity Demonstrated." The partnership of Abijah and John W. Hunt was dissolved this month, with the latter continuing the business, and the former removing to Mississippi. On the same date, the trustees met and voted

> "Whereas, there is an assemblage of negroes in Lexington on the Sabbath day, and they have become troublesome to the citizens, a committee composed of John Hull and Robert Campbell, appointed to secure a watchman."

On July 28th this committee reported they had agreed with William Davis to serve Saturday and Sunday nights, each week, at the rate of $2 per week for a period of two months.

On August 14, Jacob Ashman announces he "will do dying in the house near the public spring, back of Bradford's printing office, where blue, red, yellow and other dyes will be done on short notice." Samuel Postlethwait was Master of the Masonic Lodge this year and later removed to Natchez, Miss., where he assisted in establishing another lodge.

The firms mentioned in the various court actions as defendants or plaintiffs for this year were Logan and Lydick, Blanton and Borell, Price and Owens, Huston and Chambers, Crittenden and Harris, Morrow and McClelland, Craig and Moseby, McConnell and Greenup, Clay and Clark, Kincaid and Stafford, Simon and Brown, Alexander and John Patrick, Charleton Beeler and Company, Dunn and Craig, Moore and Beeler, and Simeon Frost.

On August 21, Francois Langlois advertises "he is leaving the State and has on hand vinegar, candles, glue gum, annise seed, cordials, neat's foot oil, which he desires to exchange for cash immediately, or for whiskey or sugar." On September 5, the Board of Trustees directed the "Union fire company to erect their building 14 feet by 11 feet, on Main street, adjoining the "gavel' end of the house of John Bradford." On the same date, John Bobb and his brother William advertise for flax seed to be delivered at the oil mill. In after years, the former achieved local fame by his manuscript gift to the Lexingon Library, and which was only recently deciphered.

A white lead factory was established in Lexington this year. The crude ore was hauled to the plant located on what is now Saunier street at rear of the Lexington Opera House, and was there powdered and hauled to the yards located in west end of Lexington and placed in small crocks and covered with a weak solution of vinegar, which acid slowly decomposed the ore and the solution was then treated with linseed oil. This white lead had considerable sale for many years, until cheaper methods of production drove the local commodity off the market.

In the fall of this year, Joseph Bruen started his iron foundry on the west side of Spring street, just south of Main, hauling the hematic ore to Lexington from Eastern Kentucky.

The method of examining applicants for license to practice law at this period is explained in the manuscript left by Robert McAfee, of Mercer county, which was published in the Register of the Kentucky State Historical Society, Volume No. 25. He says: "On September 14, 1800, I met Judge McDowell in Lexington and we retired to a tavern east of the court house, and he asked me what kind of a suit I would bring under a supposed case, and signed my license."

On September 22, the Gazette announced the partnership of John Taylor and David Kilgore, but does not state the nature of the business, nor its location. In the same issue a long list of books published at the office of the Gazette are named:

Winchester's Dialogues	.50 cents
Slavery Inconsistent with Justice and Good Policy	.18 cents
A Short and Easy method with Deists	.38 cents
A Letter from George Nicholas	.25 cents
Correspondence between George Nicholas and his friend R. G. Harper	.25 cents
Voyages and Adventures of the French Emmigrants	.25 cents
Adventures of John Smith	.50 cents
Persecuted Wanderers	.25 cents
Wilson's grammar	.42 cents
Constitution of Kentucky	.12 cents
Laws of Kentucky	$4.
Primer	.06 cents

Ch. V. Lorimer advertises in the Gazette dated October 6, "he has started a dancing school in Mr. Martin Hawkin's house, opposite the district clerk's office, also, an evening school for young gentlemen." Macbean and Poyzer advertise "the receipt of a large assortment of merchandise from the East, containing books, English and French grammers, United States Gazette, Junius Letters, Washington's Will on white silk, school books, a few prints of George Washington, and a line of medicines which they will exchange for cash, tobacco, ginseng, or country made linen." John A. Seitz advertises "he has received from Philadelphia and Baltimore, at his store in the stone house at Main and Mill, formerly occupied by Seitz and Lauman, and lately by John Jordan, Jr., a varied assortment of Merchandise, glass, china and hard wares, castings, coffee, maderia and port wines, coarse muslin, India nankeen, white nankeen, dimities, calicoes, scarlet cordinals, tambored and jaconet muslins, raw silk hose, etc., Hamilton's worm destroying lozenges, Infallible ague and fever drops, Sovereign Ointment for itch. Dr. Gann's anti-billious pills, Hamilton's grand restorative for dissipated pleasures and immoderate use of tea, Damask lip salve, general eye water and tooth ache drops."

The Gazette announced that Thomas Jefferson had received the vote of Kentucky and was chosen President of the United States over John Adams.

Cornelius Beatty and Company dissolve their partnership, and a new firm makes its appearance when P. Yeiser and Son advertise they "have commenced the currying business at southwest corner of Main and Cross streets, in the house formerly occupied by Archibald McIlvane with a varied assortment of leather goods." On October 21, the trustees of the town had the editor of the Gazette publish the revised laws of the town, which make a very interesting comparison with those now in effect. On same date, the Gazette published a list of the prices received for Kentucky products when delivered in the New Orleans port:

Tobacco, per 100 pds French weight	$4.
Bale Rope " " " "	16.
Small castings " " " "	10.
Bar Iron " " " "	8.
Bacon " " " "	12.50
Salted Pork (barrels)	14.
Flour (barrels)	10.
Whiskey (gal.)	1.25
Gun powder (pds)	.75
Lead (one pd. bars)	.10
Salt petre (pds)	.50
Brimstone (pds)	.50
Lime (bu)	.50
Corn (Unshelled) bu.	.50
Shingle nails (pds)	.40
Flooring brads	.50
Country made linen (yds)	.40

Insurance on cargoes from New Orleans to Atlantic states rated at 10 to 12 per cent.

The freight rates charged to New Orleans from
Kentucky river points amounted to average of $5.50
per hundredweight for tobacco, and on hemp $4 per
hundredweight.

On November 17, 1800, Jacob Tregor announces
"he will begin the manufacture of all kinds of stockings, of thread, cotton and silk, at the corner of Main
and Upper streets." George Norton begins the operation of his nail factory, employing six hands. John
Bradford announces he will move his newspaper and
printing office to Main street and the price for the
paper will be $2 per annum payable in advance. The
Gazette also, says "Kentucky now has a population
of 220,955, an increase of 200 per cent in ten years,
42,343 being slaves and 793 free colored, in the forty-
two counties then composing the State."

The next few issues of the Gazette contains many
references to the severe weather accompanied by
storms of rain and snow, and the usual remarks regarding the non-receipt of the mails from the East
and the lack of news. Very little reference is made
to the new constitution. No notice is found regarding the "Great Revival" of religion which began in
July of this year in the Green river country and which
spread over all of Kentucky and into some of the
surrounding states. Cane Ridge is mentioned in a small
paragraph but nothing more. "The effects of these meetings through the country were like a fire in dry stubble
driven by a strong wind. Great excitement at every
meeting and there was many eccentricities, yet the
good effects were seen and acknowledged in every
neighborhood." One small item announces Congress
had repealed the Circuit Court system of the United
States, and also, the act which established a circuit
court for the United States in Kentucky, which threw
Judge William McClung out of office.

The Gazette for December 22, 1800, carried the
following advertisement which should have attracted
more than local attention:

"I am a neat taylor, my charges are low,
Which I am desirus the public should know,
A neat suit of clothes for three dollars I make,
When the clothes are delivered, the money I take.

"To every one punctual, who doth me employ,
Of those who have tried me, not one will deny,
On Main street in Lexington, Now I abide,
Next door to Brent's tavern, and on the same side.

                    LLOYD HOLMES."

Just what success was secured by this effusion, "the record does not divulge," but he afterwards relapsed into prose, and as his advertisements continued in that form for several years, we may suppose it was successful.

The fall of this year witnessed the independence of Masonic Lodges of Kentucky from the Jurisdiction of the Virginia Grand Lodge. On September 8, fifteen delegates from the five lodges of Kentucky met in Lexington for the purpose of forming an independent grand lodge. John Hawkins, of Scottt County, was elected chairman and the resolutions prepared by William Murray, were transmitted to Virginia, expressing the intention of the Kentucky lodges. On December 11, the Virginia Grand Lodge heartily endorsed the movement for independence, and the grand lodge of Kentucky was the result of this endorsement. William Murray was chosen Master of the Lexington Lodge for this year with Alexander McGregor as deputy master.

EVENTS OF 1801.

THE year 1801 started with a severe spell of cold weather accompanied by a heavy snow, and also an election for town trustees, which resulted in the following "state of the polls"

Cornelius Beatty	30 votes
Alexander Parker	29 "
Robert Patterson	27 "
Andrew Holmes	25 "
Robert Campbell	24 "
John M. Boggs	24 "
John Bradford	18 "

There was no editorial comment upon the result of this election, which was announced in the Gazette over the signature of John Arthur, clerk of the board. The editor, in this same issue, did comment upon the lack of news, saying "Three mails are now due from the East. What can be the occasion of this irregularity we cannot divine."

On January 12, 1801, Thomas Reed advertises "for a journeyman tinner, also, three boys to learn the tin and copper business." Bledsoe and Taylor advertise "they will buy peach brandy, twilled baggs or bagging and will exchange merchandise for the same." Henry Marshall, blacksmith, announces "one penny reward for James Carson, a runaway apprentice."

In the issue of Gazette dated January 19, there is published a copy of the Treaty with France, which did not attract any editorial attention, and in same issue we find the advertisement of Christopher Keiser announcing "One penny reward, for Isaac Brown, a runaway blacksmith apprentice." Inasmuch as there were several other similar advertisements, there must have been some particularly attractive inducement, such as a well equipped wagon train, passing through Lexington at this period and which enticed these boys to seek their fortunes in the western country. On February 16, Thomas Hart advertises for "three or four boats, to be 45 feet long and fourteen feet wide, to be delivered at his warehouse at Boonesborough," and David Reid, 'saddler,' announces removal from corner of Main and Cross streets "to the house formerly occupied by J. Pew, opposite the Presbyterian meeting house." Peter January advertises for a few thousand pounds of clean hemp. On Monday, February 23, the Gazette says: "The mails arrived on Wednesday which ought to have arrived on January 21st, and brought no paper of later date than January 5th, **1801**. There are now four southern mails due and yesterday the eastern mails failed to arrive again."

John Jordan, Jr., and John A. Seitz advertise "for 150 good water tight hogsheads" and Andrew McCalla says he has "received a new shipment of fine linen, flax seed and red clover seed." Jonas Davenport wants "a good English teacher, who can come well recommended, and only sober men need apply." John Hull, the High street butcher, died and Catherine Hull, his widow, announces she will wind up the estate and desires all who owe to please call and settle.

On March 16, 1801, the Gazette announced "No mails arrived yesterday. On Wednesday last we had a mail from the South, the principal part of which consisted of papers and letters dated in December," a statement that will illustrate the inadequate method of communication of that period. George Heytel, attorney for Melchoir Myers, desires "all that owe him to come forward and settle," and John Wyatt advertises for a "good coach maker, who is sober and industrious."

On March 23, 1801, Robert Barr advertises "two good stills for sale, for cash," and in same issue J. J. Du Four, of the Kentucky Vineyard company, advertises "rice for sale at the vineyard, five miles below the mouth of Hickman Creek." Peter January advertises "for good clean hemp, and two good rope makers, who are sober." The Gazette of April 6, says: "The editor has a few copies left of Mr. Jefferson's

inauguration speech, printed on white satin." George
Norton advertises the product of his nail factory with
the following prices:

```
10 and 12 penny nails—1 shilling, 3 pense per pound
 8          "          1    "     4    "    "    "
 6 and 4    "          1    "     6    "    "    "
 3          "          1    "    10    "    "    "
```

In the issue dated April 27, 1801, the Gazette
publishes the result of the recent census in Lexington
as follows:

White	males	under 10 years	212
"	"	10 to 16 years	85
"	"	16 to 26 years	264
"	"	26 to 45 years	189
"	"	45 and over	55
"	females	under 10 years	189
"	"	10 to 16 years	75
"	"	16 to 26 years	121
"	"	26 to 45 years	123
"	"	45 and over	31
Free colored			23
Slaves			439
		Total	1,806

In the same issue the Gazette announced that "Kentucky tobacco is now bringing $4 per French hundred-
weight at New Orleans, bacon $12 per same and
whiskey .75 cents per gallon."

On May 11, John Cocke advertises he is "doing
blue dying at the house lately occupied by Mr. Megowan
on Main street, and will welcome old customers."
The Gazette published the following list of Kentucky
exports and quantities shipped from the port of Louisville, from January 22 to May 6, 1801:

Flour, 41,140 barrels; whiskey, 42,562 gallons;
peach brandy, 2,553 gallons; beer, 8,932 gallons;
hogsheads of tobacco, 779; pork, 92,300 pounds; bacon,
91,356 pounds; hog lard, 10,881 pounds; cordage.
34,092 pounds; butter, 2,587 pounds; cheese, 1,344

pounds; candles, 2,654 pounds; salt petre, 19,266 pounds; nails, 3,237 pounds; beef, 14,860 pounds; gun powder, 3,042 pounds; biscuits, 8,179 pounds; country-made linen, 2,588 yards; flannel shirts, 65; hats, 216; corn, 1,030 bushels; cherry planks, 15,000 feet, and barrel staves, 1,000.

On May 24, 1801, John Postlethwait advertises "for sale, the house and lot in Lexington, used as a tavern," which item represents the first of the many changes in management of the Phoenix Hotel. In the same issue an item says that "on 8th inst. citizens of Mercer and Lincoln county had a shooting match of twenty on each side, and in the course of the day 5,442 squirrels were killed, and bets were freely offered that the same company could kill double that number on the following day."

In the issue dated June 1, 1801, the Gazette published a long list of property owners of Harrison, Pendleton, Campbell and Boone counties, who had not paid the direct land tax up to October 1, 1798, which list makes very interesting reading to the genealogists. In the same issue, Richard Ashton advertises that "John W. Stout is now his partner, and they are lately from Philadelphia and will begin the manufacture of coaches and do repair work, opposite David Stout's on Limestone street, also, opposite Bastrop and Nancarrow's factory." Charles Cernenit Lorunier opens his dancing school, and George Weigart "on Water street, advertises for wool, for which he will pay three shillings for well broke wool, and twenty-eight shillings, if picked. Will pay 1/2 cash and balance in hats." On June 15, William Leavy "has turned over all his accounts to Robert Gatewood for collection," and Peter January executed a deed of trust to George Teagarden and Thomas January. Francois Langlois announces "he intends leaving the State in one month and desires all that owe him to call and settle. He still has a quantity of glue for sale for cash."

The Gazette for July 6, announces "on Friday last, there arrived several families from Switzerland, principally wine dressers. They brought several boxes of vines and choice fruit trees, and left this morning for the Kentucky Vineyard. Among them were three brothers and three sisters of John James Du Four, manager of the Kentucky Vineyard, and they expect to be followed by 100 of their countrymen." John W. Hunt announced in the same issue that "he has moved the Post Office to the office of the Kentucky Gazette," and Lewis Saunders and Company advertises "they have just received from Philadelphia, at their new and cheap store, lately occupied by Bledsoe and Baylor, and formerly by Patrick McCullough, a new and varied assortment of dry goods, groceries, hardware and school books." On July 13, 1801, Walker Baylor announces "the firm of Bledsoe and Baylor is to be dissolved, and he will continue the business of green coffee, chocolate, old Port, Sherry, Maderia, French Brandies, peppers, pimentoes, alum, coperas and mader." Neal McCann advertises for "two apprentices to learn the hat making business, and also, one penny reward each for William Emberson and Samuel Hardister, who ran away last January, if delivered to him in Lexington."

On August 10, the Gazette announces the result of an election held in Fayette county during the previous week, when the following named were elected Representatives: Benjamin Graves, James Hughes, Benjamin Howard and John Bell. James Trotter was the successful candidate for State Senator.

In the same issue, the Gazette has this interesting announcement:

"Edward West, on Thursday last (August 6th) exhibited to the citizens of this town a specimen of a boat worked by steam, applied to oars. The application is simple and from the opinion of good judges will be of great benefit in nevigation of the Mississippi and Ohio Rivers. Mr. West intends to apply for a patent for this discovery."

The Gazette has nothing to say regarding the "Great Camp Meeting" at Cane Ridge in Bourbon county, which sarted on August 6th[1], was attended by over 20,000 people, and at which over 3,000 persons made a confession of their faith, but has almost an entire column on the election to Congress of John Fowler, who received 7,125 votes to 2,050 for Garrard and 1,351 for Thomas. In the same issue, John Batista Kalb advertises "for a stocking weaver, who is sober and comes well recommended." The Gazette dated August 31, announces the "Death of John McNair, a tavern keeper and among the early settlers here." In an adjoining column is printed a notice of the death of Benedict Arnold "in England," without further comment. John Lowry advertises "he is making hats on Main Cross street, near Short." Robert Frazier says he has "moved to the house lately occupied by Stewart's printing office, opposite to Brent's tavern, where he will continue in the watchmaking and silversmith's trade." On September 7, 1801, the Board of Trustees ordered paid the account for a cart and horse that had been used in filling the spring on Main and Spring streets. George and Jacob Sowerbright were "allowed thirteen pounds, for serving sixteen days as watchman and patrolmen in March last." Peter Cartner and George Sowerbright were "appointed watchmen from this time until first of January next at $26 per month. They to parade at least three nights in the week, from 9 o'clock to six in the morning." On September 28, 1801, "Private entertainment at the Sign of the Buffalo" is announced and location given as opposite to the court house. On October 5, 1801, the Gazette published a list of the officers of the Government of the United States for the district of

---

[1] Life of Barton Stone—also, Collins' History of Kentucky, p. 25.

Kentucky as follows: Harry Innes, Judge; Joseph H. Daviess, Attorney, and Joseph Crocket, Marshall.

In the same issue the prices of Kentucky products at the market of Natchez, Miss., is given:

Cotton—$20 per hundredweight
Tobacco—$4 per hundredweight
Bacon—$14 per hundredweight
Salt Pork—$13 per barrel
Flour—$8 per barrel
Whiskey— .75 per gallon

The issue refers to a political rally "held at Washburn's tavern, on the road from Lexington to Bourbon court house," and on October 12, the Gazette changed its publishing date to Friday, and announced a list of uncalled-for letters in the Post Office. The firms and professional men listed were John Anderson, merchant; John Clay and Company, Benjamin Howard and Company, George Lewis, merchant; Alexander Marshall, attorney, and James McChord, attorney.

On October 30, an advertisement said that Jacob Boshart, "blue dyer, next door to John Keiser's on High street, will call for work to be done and deliver same when finished." John and William Bobb solicit "flax seed at their mill near town," Caleb Williams announces he is a "boot and shoe maker on Main street, nearly opposite to the court house, in the large brick building formerly the property of Peter January." On November 6, 1801, William Dorsey stated that "he has begun the cooperage business and can supply barrels of all sizes." The Gazette describes "a fire to the store of John Arthur, which was filled with cotton." On November 13, 1801, George Madison, Auditor for the State of Kentucky, published his report dated November 1, 1801, showing taxes collected by him amounted to a total of $50,724.58.

Nancy Mason, a returned Indian captive, was in Lexington this month, looking for some of her relations, but the Gazette in future issues does not mention her progress in the quest. Seitz and Lauman dissolve partnership "with George M. Johnson taking charge of the business, who still has a few cases of Maderia wine on hand." In the same issue, mention is made of the Masonic lodge of which Captain Levi Todd, the county clerk, and John Jordan, Jr., were the Masters for this year. The latter was chairman of the committee to select the seal for the Grand Lodge of Kentucky.

On November 29, 1801, "Mrs. Harriet Beatty, consort of Colonel Cornelius Beatty, died," and "The St. Andrew's society held its annual meeting at the tavern of Mrs. McNair, opposite the court house."

The records of the Circuit Clerk's office show the following named were either plaintiffs or defendants in the various mercantile actions brought during the year: Noell, Simpson and Company; Stephen Win and Company, Ross and Carneal, John Arthur and Company, Bastrop and Nancarrow, Walker, Spears and Bristow; Naff and Polk, Elliston and Weathers, Hurt and Tierman, Thomas and Phillips, Kelly, Kincaid and Todd; Montgomery and Newbold, and Quarles, Threshley and Company.

The trustees requested the editor to publish the following announcement in the issue of the Gazette, dated December 30, 1801:

> "The Trustees have strong reasons to think a negro man by name of John Sutton, now in town, has small pox. Resolved: that the negro and those who have attended him be sent out of town at once."

The Gazette makes only slight comment upon the act of the Legislature which abolished the district courts and the general court, and established the Circuit courts. The editor closed the year with a strong plea for "Universal peace and fondly hopes he will be denied the painful task of detailing any account of effusion of human blood." He also took "this opportunity of warning his readers of counterfeit Spanish dollars, minted with date of 1799."

EVENTS OF 1802.

"WITH the thermometer around zero for several days, and the weather extremely unpleasant," the Gazette began the year of 1802 by announcing that "the town trustees were compelled to change the stable of the Oxen that were used on the streets."

On January 8, 1802, the "Presbyterian Church roof was set on fire by an unnamed negro who was shooting at pigeons, but little damage was done, and that only to the roof." John Speed advertised "clean dry salt from Mann's lick, for sale for cash." The Gazette also published the following result of the election for town trusees:

Alexander Parker,	60
John M. Boggs,	59
Robert Campbell	55
Robert Patterson	52
Robert Holmes	45
William Huston	44
William Macbean	39

In the same issue, the Postmaster advertised the following uncalled-for letters: George Taber, clockmaker; Robert Hanna, "taylor"; Andrew Hanna, "tanner"; Henry Mockquort, tanner; William MacDonald, carpenter, and George Parkerson, hatter.

On January 29, 1802, William Voorhies and Company, opened "a saddle and harness shop at William Ross' house on Short street, opposite the Presbyterian meeting house, and nearly opposite the market house." On February 5, 1802, the Gazette says in the editorial column, "No southern mail has arrived for over two weeks, and no Eastern mail for one week. What can be the cause of the irregularity?" Peter January and William Bealert dissolve their "ropemaking business' with the first-named continuing the rope-walk at the old stand. On this same date, John Bradford published an editorial calling attention to "the Insurance company now being formed in Lexington, to insure shipping on board boats, plying the western waters. Shares can be had by applying to John Jordan, William Macbean, Cuthbert Banks and Henry Purviance." The officers of this company were President William Morton, Directors, John Jordan, Stephen Wante, Thomas Hart and Thomas Wallace, Cashier John Bradford, and Clerk William Macbean. The office was on north side of Main street, between Mill and Broadway, until they had constructed a building on the Main street end of the alleyway between Limestone and Upper.

On February 12, 1802, the Gazette announced the "house of George Hamilton on north Elkhorn was destroyed by fire during the absence of Mr. Hamilton in Pennsylvania," and in the same issue, "Mr. Robert Bradley succeeds Major Wagnon in the commodious brick house and stables, with revision of assistants and servants, which emboldens him to anticipate patronage from genteel guests only." On March 1, Boggs and Holmes make a contract with the town trustees "to furnish 100 perch of cracked stone from a quarry, to be used on the streets." Mrs. Gray advertises "her school for young misses, four miles from Lexington, at $20 per quarter." On March 12, 1802, Dr. Joseph Boswell advertises "I shall now commence the innoculation with vacine, being perfectfully satisfied that it will eradicate the principle which the small pox acts on." Catherine Wood advertises "for sale, her house built of logs, on southeast side of Market street, 66 feet front and lot 98 feet deep, with house 16 feet square and with brick chimney." On April 2, 1802, the Gazette publishes a card signed by John Bradford, announcing the Gazette has been turned over to his son, Daniel Bradford, "who will in future conduct the same." Alexander Parker advertises "he is trying to wind up the estates of James and William Parker, and will all who have claims against these estates please present same, and will all those who owe these estates please come forward and settle at once." On April 9, 1802, the Gazette published the report of a committee composed of trustees of Transylvania College, regarding some "unlawful societies." The Gazette publishes a list of prices which Kentucky export products are bringing in the Natchez market: Flour at $4 per barrel and tobacco at same price per hundredweight. "Sixteen boats have been lost between the mouth of the Ohio river and New Orleans." In the same issue, Benjamin Grimes advertises "for sale, a New Orleans boat, 45 feet long and 14 feet wide, with four oars, now at Tedgerson's ferry near Cross Plains."

The death of Mrs. Elijah Craig, at Georgetown, is noted in the Gazette of April 30, 1802, and on May 7, "Peter Paul and Son, lately from London, England, begin cutting stone on the Woodford Road, near Lexington, where tombstones, grave stones, marble chimney pieces, safes to preserve papers, etc., will be promptly supplied." In this same issue, John Walker Baylor announces "he has employed Robert Bledsoe to rent or sell his property," and on May 14, the Gazette publishes an editorial calling attention "to the machine invented by Edward West for cutting nails at the rate of 1,000 pounds in 12 hours, and on yesterday, in presence of a number of guests, cut five pounds in 50 seconds, which is at the rate of 4,320 pounds in 12 hours." Mr. West gives the reporter an interview and says: "Notice, as I have invented a machine for the cutting of nails, which will on moderate calculation cut one thousand pounds of iron into nails of any size in 12 hours, and have shewn a model thereof to a number of my friends and acquaintances, also, have taken proper steps to obtain a patent for the same, I do hereby forwarn all persons from making use of said invention under the penalty of what the law directs in such cases." This interview was subsequently published as an advertisement and dated March 24, 1802. On the same date, William West announces "he has received a very large shipment of dry goods, hard, queens, and chinaware, etc., and will extend credit to no one." Alexander Hawthorn advertises he is making nails at Morgantown,

Virginia, 76 to the pound at 12 pense, 80 to the
pound at 10 pense, 106 to the pound at 8 pense, and
300 to the pound at 4 pense. Announcement in this
issue also is made that "The Kentucky Insurance
Company informs the public they are now organized
and ready to insure cargoes up or down the Mississippi,
or at sea, upon application at the office." On May
28, 1802, the Gazette announces the appointment of
John Jordan, Jr., as postmaster in place of John W.
Hunt, and in the same issue Edward West announces
"he has sold the rights to his invention for cutting
of nails for $10,000." The death of Mr. Nathaniel
Shaw is announced, "at his farm south of Lexington.
He was the army Contractor for this district and
had purchased many horses for the service." John
Jordan, Jr., announces "he has moved his store opposite the public square, to the house formerly oc-
cupied by Innes B. Brent as a tavern." Cuthbert
Banks, who had been elected first secretary of the
Jockey Club organized in 1797, was elected Master
of the Masonic lodge this year.

On June 4, 1802, the Gazette published without
comment, a copy of the treaty of Amiens between the
British and French governments, which was dated
March 25, 1802. The Gazette also announced the
"death in this city of John Hargy, a merchant" and
the death "at Mt. Vernon on Saturday last (May 26th)
of Mrs. Washington, widow of the late illustrious
George Washington."

The celebrated traveler, Francis Michaux, who
visited Lexington during the summer of this year, says:
"In the year 1802, Lexingon had two printing offices,
two newspapers, a paper manufactory, two extensive
rope walks, several potteries, two powder mills, and
several tan yards."

From the port of Louisville was shipped this year
to New Orleans 72,000 barrels of dried pork and 2,485
barrels of salted pork, all from Central Kentucky. On
June 18, the Gazette published the announcement that

Joseph Hamilton Daviess had removed his law office to Lexington.

Several alarming rumors had reached Lexington of conditions in the South, which caused the town trustees to hold a meeting at which the following was adopted:

"Whereas—the slaves in the south are strongly bent on insurrection; wherefore, Re-solved—that no slaves from any of the States or any other state, be permitted to be sold in this place contrary to the 26th section of an act of the Assembly, passed on 8th day of Feb-ruary, 1802, without being subject to the pen-alty imposed by law, and this action of the Board to be published for two weeks in the Kentucky Gazette."

On July 16, 1802, John Adams and George Adams, Jr., advertise "they have opened a shop opposite Bradford's printing office where they will make and sell all kinds of wool and furr hats." Samuel Down-ing offers "Mann's lick salt in exchange for country linen or hemp." D. M. Ciccar advertises "coppers for sale at Hickman Mills, near Lexington," and in the issue of the Gazette dated July 30, George Mansell an-nounces "he had invented a machine for breaking, milling or cleaning hemp or flax, for threshing grain, and sawing wood or stone. Guaranteed to break and clean 1,000 pounds of hemp per day."

On August 6, the Gazette announced the result of the recent election held in Fayette county for State Representatives, when the following were chosen: Benjamin Howard, William Russell, James Hughes and John Bradford. In Scott county the Representatives chosen were Robert Johnson and Fielding Bradford.

In the Gazette for August 25, is published report of the Surveyor of the Port of Louisville, giving the amounts of central Kentucky commodities shipped from that port between January 1, and June 30, 1802, as follows:

Barrels of apples, 841; gallons of beer, cider or porter, 7,971; barrels of beef, 80; pounds of butter, 3,300; bushels of corn, 1,237; barrels of flour, 85,570; gallons of flax seed oil, 100; hams and bacons, pounds 272,222; hemp pounds, 42,048; pounds of lead, 55,052; barrels of pork, 2,482; bushels of potatoes, 342; pounds of soap, 2,399; manufactured tobacco, 2,640; loose tobacco, 503,618 hundredweight; plank boards, 13,666 feet. Total value $590,965.

James Dover "respectfully announces he has commenced the grinding business at Mr. Tibbatt's tavern, where all kinds of cuttlery will be neatly ground." In the Gazette for September 3, the recent census of the Baptist denomination is published: Elkhorn Association, 5,310; Green River, 800; Salem, 2,023; Bracken, 753; Tate's creek, 1,803; Southern Kentucky, 2,382; total, 13,076. The authority for this census is not disclosed by the editor.

On September 10, Fielding L. Turner, attorney at law, announces "he has removed from the country ino Lexington, where he has fixed his residence, in order to be more convenient to his clients." On the same date the Gazette published the census of the United States, which gave the population in 1790 as 3,680,653, and 1800 as 5,305,482. Kentucky was shown at 220,959.

Fishel and Gallatin, "Copper and tin smiths, commence business on Main street, opposite Captain Marshall's tavern, where they make stills, kettles and will purchase old copper and pewter."

In October of this year, notice was received in Lexington that "Morales, the Spanish intendant at New Orleans, had closed the port to all Americans." This was almost a paralyzing blow to the Kentucky producers. Its effects immediately caused business stagnation throughout the Blue Grass, and many of the merchants who had on hand large quantities of tobacco, hemp, butter, pork or beef, were ruined.

Lexington, from the year 1800 to 1820, was economically unlike all the other towns of this region, and far different from the Lexington of the twentieth century. From the first named year, it had been the distributing point for all of Kentucky and parts of Tennessee, Ohio, Indiana and Illinois territory. It was the manufacturing capital of the west, and this meant everything west of the Alleghanies. It acquired some prominence at this period because the west was then in the packhorse stage of its transportation, and as Lexington was located upon the natural highways from East to West, it received the benefits from the vast wave of immigration to the new and fertile west.[1] Lexington was the "grand depot" for supplies to these immigrants, who purchased everything they expected to use when they would be far from any source of supplies. Horses had a ready sale, as did all kinds of dry goods, groceries, powder, lead, medicines, coffee and teas.

While it is true that the Lexington merchants were so few in number they could fix their own prices for commodities urgently needed, yet the competition was sufficient to cause extensive credit to be granted and this caused the downfall of many of them. Their goods usually were purchased in Baltimore or Philadelphia on 12 months credit and payment was generally demanded on time, if we may judge by the actions brought for recovery of accounts in the Circuit court. "It became a common occurrence to see packhorses with loads of cut silver enroute back to the Eastern settlements to balance accounts of Lexington merchants. One report has it that a Lexington merchant shipped 100 pounds of cut silver to Philadelphia in spring of 1806."

The ukase of Morales left many of our merchants with considerable quantities of merchandise on hand, and with no produce of Kentucky that would bear the expense of shipment over the mountains. Soon after the notice of this order was received in Lexington, the Gazette's columns bear testimony to the efforts of our

1 McDougal MSS.

merchants to reduce stocks of goods by "cut price for sale for cash only." This sentence appeared in nearly all merchants' advertisements for several months during the latter part of this year, and bespoke loudly their extremity. Several mass meetings were held and much oratory expended, but beyond passing some strongly worded resolutions nothing could be done except appeal to Congress.

On October 19, 1802, the town trustees' minute book shows "they had agreed to Reuben Runyon and Miles McGowan, who had offered to serve as watchmen at the rate of $14 per month, and will patroll the town at least three nights each week." Walker Baylor and Son advertise "for any quantity of hemp to be delivered at their store opposite the market house, where they have for sale blankets and red and white clover seed." On the same date, J. J. Du Four, of the Kentucky Vineyard Company, announces "he has discovered a method of drying all kinds of grains by kilns, so as to secure same from weavel, and he warns all from infringing on his discovery, as it will dry, also, fruits and other desirable things. Demonstrations will take place on the Kentucky River, four miles above mouth of Hickman creek." On this date also Mrs. Jean McNair, widow of John McNair, was granted a deed to in-lot No. 17, now 411 West Main street, and James C. Rumsey, "the brush maker, advertises for combed hog bristles for which he will pay 18 cents per pound. He is located at Mr. William Edwards' opposite the Bradford's printing office on Main street." Maccoun and Tilford announce "they have just received from Philadelphia, a very large shipment of dry goods, groceries, Ketland's gun and pistol locks, Crawley and blistered steel, hardware, and queens ware." On November 2, 1802, the Gazette announced "the death of Captain James Moody, for many years an inhabitant of this town." John Downing takes over the management of "The Sign of the Buffalo" from Mrs. McNair. The Gazette says, "this is a commodious house opposite the court house, large tables with

separate stalls for travelers and ample stable room."
Another importer and merchant, Mr. Joseph Tilford,
died on Saturday, November 6, 1802, and on the same
date Mr. Samuel Munet announces "he teaches the
French languages, next door to Mr. Wyatt's, the coach
maker, at upper end of Lexington." On December
7, 1802, Colonel Robert Patterson released the ground
"between James Looney's lot and Keiser's old tan
yard, to be called Locust sreet, extending from High
street to Water street, to be used as a lane or street
forever." The Kentucky Soap and Candle Manufacturing Company, Ebeneezer Tipping manager, "located
near the tanyard, advertises large quantities of soap and
candles for home consumption, or for exportation.
They also make and sell British hard white soap,
British hard yellow soap, Scented Windsor soap,
Scented wash balls, scented moulded candles, and
scented dipped candles." In this same issue the Gazette
announces the death of General Benjamin Logan of
apoplexy at his home in Shelby county.

The Circuit Court records show the following
firms named in actions brought this year: Davis and
Cope, Marshall and McMullen, Hunter and Steele,
and James and Hunt.

The year closed with an election for trustees for
the Town of Lexington, and "the polls returned the
following: Robert Patterson, Alexander Parker, John
M. Boggs, John Jordan, Jr., Robert Holmes, John
Bradford, and Joseph Hudson," for the year of 1803.
On December 7, 1802, Jasper Tingle and Thomas
Ochiltree were appointed to be watchmen "at $12
per month working every other night." On December
12, the Trustees decided this force was not sufficient
and reinforced them by the addition of Reuben Runyon
and Edward Harrison for two months at the same
rate of pay.

The closing issues of the Gazette for this year contain many cards of complaints regarding the embargo
on the New Orleans port for Kentucky's produce.
All of these referred to this order as "an act of broken

faith" and indicated there had been considerable indignation all over the State of Kentucky when the order was first published in the newspapers. These cards contain many suggestions designed to correct the situation. Most of them intimated that the best method was "for armed troops to invade the Crescent City." This had been advocated openly since the settlers learned of the terms of the secret treaty made in October, 1800, by which Spain ceded Louisiana to France.

However, at the very time this condition was causing so much loss to the Kentucky producers, President Jefferson already had taken steps to recover this market by the purchase of the Louisiana territory from Napoleon. The purchase was effected in April, 1803, but formal possession was not secured until December of the same year, when Governor Claiborne, of the Mississippi territory, and James Wilkinson, of the United States Army, took possession in the name of the United States. During this period of suspended shipments to the southward, the Lexington merchants were loud in their complaints, and of course ceased buying, which left the farmer-producer with his crops on hand and no market in sight.

The elevation of Mr. Jefferson to the Presidency of the United States had made him very popular in Kentucky, and he became more popular when the news of the purchase of the gateway to the gulf reached the backwoods settlements and the conditions were understood. His popularity was further increased when the Internal taxes were removed, which event seems to have been especially appreciated in the Blue Grass section.

This year should be remembered also for the inauguration of banking in Kentucky. On December 16, 1802, the Kentucky Legislature granted a charter to the Kentucky Insurance Company, which had been organized in Lexington during February, 1802, a charter that conferred banking power upon this company by the inclusion of a very cleverly worded clause

in their application which tradition says never would
have been approved had the members of the Legislature thoroughly understood the meaning of the clause.
The purpose of this corporation was to cover with
insurance, property shipped on board boats or other
vessels navigating the western waters and the sea.
The following year the Legislature granted an increase in the capital stock to $50,000, by the sale
of additional shares at $100 each. In this year Thomas
Hart, John Jordan and William Leavy were appointed
a committee to draw up plans for a house and vault
for the Company and to make inquiry as to whether
a building could be rented on Main street, between
Cross and Mulberry. This was effected by securing
a lease on a building on the north side of Main street,
just west of Mill. Afterwards the company erected
a building on Main street at the east corner of the
alleyway between Upper and Limestone. The insurance company prospered to such an extent that on
January 13, 1804, one hundred and forty-three shares
sold at public auction at $105 per share. In this same
year a dividend was declared of 65 cents per share,
which in the following year increased to $8 per share.

During the year of 1805 the officers were William
Morton, president; Alexander Parker, Thomas Hart,
Jr., John Jordan, Jr., and James Morrison, directors;
Thomas Lewis, Thomas Wallace and John Bradford,
auditors. Considerable opposition to the company
developed as soon as they began doing "Banking"
business, which finally resulted in a bill being introduced in the Legislature to repeal the charter, but
the latter failed to pass by a safe majority. The opposition was not satisfied with this defeat and, re-
organizing their forces, they undertook to set up competition. At a meeting of citizens held January 16,
1806, at Satterwhite's tavern, "to consider the propriety of petitioning for a branch of the Bank of the
United States," sufficient pledges of cooperation were
secured to warrant their being forwarded to Philadelphia, the location of the "Mother Bank." This move

resulted in success and before long the Town of Lexington had two banks, but even this did not satisfy the disgruntled opponents of the Insurance Company, whom four years later we find objecting to the Bank of the United States, because it employed "foreign" capital, and the dividends went to the mother bank at Philadelphia. The twelve local directors were elected to the Board of the mother bank, thus creating an aristocratic "junto" that destroyed "a lucrative branch of profit to other institutions" by "knocking up" the business of advances on Bills of Exchange. This opposition finally faded away and both banks enjoyed a period of prosperity before they joined the ranks of the "has beens." The Kentucky Insurance Company lasted until 1818, and left Kentucky plastered with paper money of no value and this community in the "slough of a financial morass." The institution was succeeded in 1822 by the Bank of the Commonwealth of Kentucky, and in 1835 by the Northern Bank of Kentucky, which latter remained until within the memory of many of those now living.

A detailed description of the Town of Lexington for the year of 1802 can be found in "Travels to the West of the Alleghany Mountains," by F. A. Michaux, who says:

"Lexington has two printing offices which publish newspapers twice each week. Part of the paper is manufactured in the county and dearer by one-third than in France. That which they use for writing is imported from England by the way of Philadelphia. There are two extensive ropewalks and several tan yards where there is a severe want of hands. A Lexington man has just invented a nail cutting machine which bids fair to make considerable change in the method of turning out nails. All the articles that are manufactured at Lexington are very passable.

"I boarded at the best house in Lexington for two piasters per week.

"There are several common potteries, one or two powder mills and other industries. A majority of the

inhabitants of Lexington trade in Kentucky, and from
Lexington the different kinds of merchandise is dispatched to the interior of the State, and the surplus
to Tennessee. It is very easy for merchants to make
their fortunes; first, they have twelve months credits
from the house in Philadelphia and Baltimore; second,
they are so few in number they can fix in their favor
the course of produce which they accept in exchange
for their goods. As there is an extreme scarcity of
specie, most transactions are by way or barter. The
merchants use every exertion to get into their hands
the little specie in circulation. All specie collected
in course of trade is sent by land to Philadelphia. I
have seen convoys of this kind consisting of 15 to 20
horses. The distance from Lexington to Philadelphia
is 650 miles and usually those that go do so in the
fall, taking three weeks to a month to perform the
journey.

"There is not a single species of colonial produce
in Kentucky, excepting Ginseng, that will bear the
expense of carriage by land from that state to Philadelphia, as twenty-five pounds weight would cost more
expediting that way than one thousand pounds floated
down the River.

"They reckon six shillings to the dollar, or piaster;
the 1-4, 1-8 and 1-16th part of a piaster forms the
small white money, and it is extremely scarce, being
supplied by the very indifferent means of cutting
coins. As every one can do this, it is done for sake of
gain, and the seller in trade will frequently abate the
price of his merchandise for the whole dollar, rather
than take some of this cut coin."

This "picture" of Lexington can be found in the
London, 1805, edition of Micheaux's travels, which
portion was edited when the Mauman edition was reprinted in 1812.

EVENTS OF 1803.

THE year 1803 started out with a financial depression in the Town of Lexington and all over Central Kentucky by reason of the continued closing of the Port of New Orleans, and the Gazette comments upon the hardships of the local merchants and "those who export to the southward." The "severe and unusual weather" and the "non-receipt of the mails from the Eastward" also come in for comment in the columns of the Gazette. It was during this month the merchants made some united efforts to relieve their condition but no permanent result seems to have been attained. On January 18, the Gazette amended its name by the addition of "and General Advertiser," which was continued until April 11, 1809.

The election for town trustees resulted in the choice of the following:

Robert Patterson,	63
Alexander Parker,	54
John M. Boggs	53
John Bradford,	51
Robert Holmes,	45
John Jordan, Jr.	43
Joseph Hudson	33

The Shareholders of the Lexington library held their annual meeting this month and elected Fielding L. Turner, John McDowell, Robert Patterson, Thomas L. Barr and William McIlheney, Jr., as directors, who promptly elected John Tilford as secretary, Benjamin Stout as treasurer and Andrew McCalla as librarian.

In the Gazette for January 11, 1803, the announcement of Joseph Charless, "late of Philadelphia," discloses that he has established "a new printing office and book store on Main street, between Bradford's printing office and Captain Marshall's tavern, where I propose to sell books and print a newspaper called The Independent Gazeteer." Francis Peniston was a partner in this enterprise. This firm in 1806, printed

Lexington's first city directory. Early in 1808 Joseph
Charless emigrated to St. Louis, where on July 12, 1808,
he introduced the first newspaper to be printed west
of the Mississippi river, "The Missouri Gazette," today
known as the St. Louis Republic.

On February 1, 1803, the Kentucky Gazette published an item that presaged a calamity to genealogists,
when it announced the fire on the night of January
30, that destroyed the records in the county clerk's
office, then located out the Richmond pike two miles
from town, on the farm of the clerk, Levi Todd. One
tradition explained it: "The Clerk's office was burned.
It was the place where Wickliffe afterwards lived.
'Twas believed the office was set on fire to destroy
land claims. Those who could get oral testimony
were enabled in that way to again establish their
claims."[1]

Subsequent issues of the Gazette contain requests
from the County Clerk for "all those that have ori-
ginals of such papers as were filed in his office to
please bring them in and copies will be made."

On February 8, 1803, the Trustees agreed "with
Thomas Ockletree, John Newell, Edward Harrison and
Robert Craig, to serve as watchmen, three months at
$12 per month each, they to parade at least three
nights each week." On March 1, 1803, the Gazette
says, "No post rider from the East arrived yesterday.
No post rider from the South has as yet appeared
and the post rider from Winchester and Mt. Sterling
has not been here for three weeks." Truly a vexa-
tious situation for an editor who had to depend upon
such sources for news items for his paper.

On March 15 the cabinet-making shop of Porter
Clay, a brother of Henry Clay, was destroyed by fire
and "considerable damage was done before it was
extinguished." On March 22 the Gazette announced
that "the shareholders in the Kentucky Vineyard Company yesterday held a meeting at the house of Captain

[1] Interview with Asa Farrow, Draper MSS. 13CC1.

Postlethwait, where a sample of Kentucky wine was exhibited, which was supposed only to want age to make it equal to any. The company will dine together this day, when they will drink their own wine." In the same issue of the Gazette also was published a letter addressed to Governor Claiborne of the Mississippi territory, brought by Lieut. Wilkinson and written by James Wilkinson, dated February 17. This letter revealed the opening of the Port of New Orleans, but with a six per cent duty on all kinds of produce. John Bobb advertises "for several able bodied men who are willing to work in a brick yard," and Benjamin Lloyd announces "tight barrels, hogsheads and double barrels for sale at Upper end of Main street."

On March 29, the Kentucky Vineyard Company held a meeting at Postlethwait's tavern and elected John Bradford, William Macbean, James Maccoun, Benjamin Stout, Samuel Brown, George Anderson, John A. Seitz, Thomas Hart, Jr., Henry Marshall, Robert Patterson, Walker Baylor and Andrew McCalla as directors. The Gazette says: "Mr. Du Four presented the company with two casks of wine, one of Maderia grape, and one of Cape of Good Hope grapes. Several foreigners present pronounce these as good as European wines, although they were made from cuttings secured in New York and Philadelphia in the year 1798."

On April 18, 1803, the trustees held their meeting at Brent's tavern and voted to reserve one room over the market house for their own use, and on the same date authorized the Lexington library to build another room "provided they would pay the expense of same." On May 3, 1803, James Morrison advertised "for sale the mill and distillery which adjoins Lexington on a lot of 13 4-5 acres. Mill house 30 by 40 feet and two story high. See John Cocke on the premises."

William Leavy advertised a "large assortment of Books, writing paper, quills, and wafers," and on May 17, the Gazette says, "A gentleman from Lexington has just returned from Natchez and advises Kentucky

products are now bringing the following prices: Flour
$4.50 per barrel, bacon per hundredweight $8, lard
per hundredweight $8, pork per barrel $80, whiskey
50 cents per gallon. In the same issue appears announcement of a stage coach line established to run
from Richmond, Virginia, to Frankfort, Kentucky.
Hugh Crawford advertises "he will do blue dying at
the 'Sign of the Golden Boot,' where he also makes
boots and shoes." William Berry advertises he is
now building a powder mill on South fork of Elkhorn,
five miles from Lexington, "where he intends selling
powder at two shillings per pound." On May 18,
1803, the clerk of the Board of Trustees was directed
to supply the clerk of the county court with "a copy
of the town plat by making a true copy from the one
in the trustees' book."

During the same month, we find the county court
fixed the tavern rates for this year as follows: "Breakfast, hot, 1 shilling, 3 pense; cold, one shilling; Dinner,
hot, one shilling six pense; supper, hot, one shilling,
three pense; whiskey, 1-2 pint four pense; brandy,
1-2 pint six pense; French brandy, one shilling per
half pint; Rum, one shilling same; Maderia wine per
bottle, 9 shillings; and all other wines, per bottle, six
shillings." Lodging for the night was fixed at 6
shillings, oats per gallon four shillings, corn per gallon
four shillings, Hay and stabling for 24 hours, 9 shillings; pasture four shillings, "cyder" per quart six
shillings, and "strong beer per quart six shillings."[1]

At the same term of court, the judges fixed the
width of the roads leading out of Lexington and in
this county to be as follows:

Limestone Road (Lexington to
    Bourbon line) ....40 feet wide
Strode's road (from where it turned
    out of Limestone to county line) 30 feet wide
Russell's road (from Lexington to
    Bourbon Line) .... 30 feet wide

1 County Court Order Book No. 1, page 30.

Georgetown Road (Lexington to
    Scott Line) ....30 feet wide
Leestown Road (Lexington to Scott
    county Line) ....30 feet wide
Bethel Road (Leestown Road to
    Scott Line past meeting house)...30 feet wide
McBride's Mill road (Bethel road to
    Woodford) ....20 feet wide
Frankfort Road (Lexington to
    Woodford Line) ....40 feet wide
Scott's road (Lexington to Woodford
    Line) ....30 feet wide
Curd's Road (Lexington to Jessa-
    mine Line) ....30 feet wide
Hickman's road (Lexington to
    Jessamine) ....40 feet wide
Tate's creek (Lexington to
    Kentucky River) ....30 feet wide
Boonesborough (Lexington to Clark
    county line) ....40 feet wide
Winchester Road (Boonesborough
    road to Clark County Line)...........20 feet wide
Cleveland Road (Boonesborough to
    Roger's Mill) ....20 feet wide
Todd's mill road (Strode's road to
    Jessamine) ....20 feet wide
Hornback Mill Road (Scott road
    to Jessamine Line) ....20 feet wide
Parker's Mill Road (Scott's road
    to Jessamine) ....20 feet wide
Bethel meeting house road (to
    Georgetown Pike from Bethel
    meeting house, as far as the
    Scott county line, partly marked
    but not cut) ....20 feet wide

On May 31, 1803, William West advertises he
has "received a large assortment of dry goods,
queen and hardware, teas, wines, seasoning, fish, sal-
mon, shad and herrings, anvils, Ketland's pistol and
gun locks, Crawley steel, Blistered steel, and stockings
of all kinds." On June 4, Andrew McCalla was
elected Trustee in the room of John M. Boggs, and on

the 7th the Gazette announced the wedding (on May 26) of Mr. James Haggin of Mercer County to Miss Henrietta Humphreys of Fayette County, and Mr. John Goodlet of Scott County to Miss Rebecca Patterson, daughter of Colonel Robert Patterson of Fayette county. Seitz and Lauman announce receipt of a large assortment of queen, hard and china wares, books, ink, quills, and wafers. John Caldwell states he "will do red and blue dying on High street at 'The Sign of the Spinning Wheel' and goods returned promptly." James M. Bradford announces "the publication by him of a work, 'Notes on the Navigation of the Mississippi', with nine plates showing the most difficult passages in the River," a book that is now something of a rarity. On June 27, 1803, the Gazette published a letter complaining of the quality of Kentucky flour received at New Orleans port, and suggested that future sales depended upon improvement. On June 29, the Trustees "Ordered—the Market House to be extended on northeast side, as far as Short street, as soon as convenient," and also "granted in-lot No. 14 to the heirs of Nathaniel Shaw, per Benedict Vanpradelles, attorney." This lot is now 427 West Main street. On July 3, 1803, the county court employed Lloyd Holmes, 'taylor,' to do some work, but the record does not disclose its character, and on same date granted a license to preach to Jacob Creath, a Baptist Preacher. William Tod was "granted permission to build a cotton spinning factory on Water street," (now Vine street) where the Curd Hotel afterward stood, and today occupied by a produce house, just east of Mill street.

John Bradford resigned as town trustee and Thomas Whitney was elected in his place. William Todd, Jr., was chosen clerk of the Board of Trustees, and Nathaniel Prentiss elected Clerk of the Market House. William Scott was "granted permission by the county court to build a water mill on Town Fork of Elkhorn below Lexington." William McDaniel was licensed to "keep a tavern at his home in the county," and Robert Stewart was "presented his credentials and was licensed to perform the marriage ceremony." He later wrote the early history of the Presbyterian denomination in Kentucky, of which only mutilated portions can be found. At same term of court William Thompson, George Shinglebower and George Weigart were licensed to keep taverns in the Town of Lexington. The Trustees employed "Jacob Irvine, saddler, to repair and mend the harness belonging to the town." Edward West was "allowed one pound ten shillings for making the seal of the town." The accounts of John Fisher, bricklayer; Aaron Woodruff, shoemaker, and Caleb Williams, shoemaker, were ordered paid. The store of Trotter and Scott was robbed of nine beaver skins, the property of Elisha Winter and valued at $36.00. Maccoun and Tilford moved their store to the house "formerly occupied by Samuel and George Trotter, where they have received a large cargo of new merchandise, suitable to the present and approaching season." At their next meeting, the Trustees appointed a committee "to have the earth taken off the surface of Short street, between Tibbatt's and Tyree's, and off surface of Upper street, between Jordan's and Sumption's shop, for purpose of leveling the ground for the Market House."

John Fowler was chosen congressional Representative without opposition, and William Russell, James Hughes, James True and Henry Clay were elected state Representatives.

On August 16, 1803, "a banquet was given at Postlethwait's tavern in celebration of the purchase of Louisiana, with John Bradford, Chairman, and James Hughes, Vice-Chairman. A large and enthusiastic audience responded to the numerous and well-worded toast." J. Kennedy, manager, "announces prices on the Lexington and Olympian Spring stage coach at 21 shillings from Lexington, 15 shillings from Winchester, and 9 shillings from Mt. Sterling."

In the issue of the Gazette for August 23, attention is called "to the numerous burglaries having taken place in Lexington within the past few nights. Mr. Keiser, Mr. Downing and Mr. Hise were visited by the midnight prowler" but their losses were not given. Others who were robbed were Captain Rose, of $60, and Mr. Young, of $25. On same date the Gazette published amounts of Kentucky products exported from the Blue Grass between January 1 and March 31: Flour, 4,597 barrels; Cider, 2,249 barrels; flax, 3,700 pounds; lard, 12,045 pounds; distilled spirits, 5,507 gallons, and 101 hogsheads of tobacco.

Alexander Frazier announced "he has commenced business on his own account on Main street, two doors above Bradford's printing office, where he will make and repair watches and clocks."

On August 30, 1803, the Gazette published this notice: "We are authorized to say that proposals will be issued in a few days for the publication by subscription of the 'Political, Commercial and General Reflection on the late cession of Louisiana to the United States,' by Allen Bowie Magruder. Price to subscribers fifty cents, 1-2 at time of the subscription and balance at delivery of work. Will be put to press as soon as 250 subscribers are secured." No doubt these original subscribers would be gratified if they could know the value today of this little brochure in the book marts. Even copies in damaged condition bring prices beyond the fondest dreams of the author or printer. On October 10, 1803, James Looney was granted license to keep a tavern in Lexington and David Reed, saddler, was employed by the trustees "to repair all the town property"— evidently referring to the harness of the ox team used on the streets. Robert Russell and George Hamilton were granted permission by the County Court "to erect mills on North Elkhorn creek." The trustees also ordered paid the accounts of Drs. Frederick Ridgely and James Fishback.

On October 4, 1803, the Gazette says: "A gentleman of this town has received a newspaper from Liverpool, announcing the arrival at that port of the Brig "Deane" under Captain William Deane, with a cargo from Alleghany River, which passed down the Ohio and Mississippi rivers, three thousand miles within land, being the first vessel to make such a trip." On October 10, the Trustees "ordered paid, the accounts of Thomas Ochletree for three months as watchman, amounting to ten pounds, and the account of John Newell, for same service amounting to five pounds, eight shillings." John Kennedy advertises the beginning of a "Stage coach service to Frankfort, every Monday and Friday, leaving Lexington at day break, from Mr. Bradley's Inn. Passengers 9 shillings each, and allowed ten pounds of baggage. 1 1-2 cents per pound extra."

On October 18, 1803, the Gazette announces "A sufficient number of subscribers to Mr. Magruder's book 'Reflections on Cession of Louisiana to United States' have been now received and printing will start at once and deliveries will be made in November." In same issue, Mr. A. B. Magruder announces "he intends publishing the History of Indian Wars in the Western Country of North America and desires those acquainted with the relative forces to communicate them as soon as possible." The Gazette refers to the large sale of the Kentucky Almanac printed by John Bradford for the year of 1803, which issue contained, in addition to the usual information found in a publication of this kind, a poem on page 31:

A RHAPSODY ON WHISKEY.

"Great Spirit hail! confusion's angry sire,
And like the parent Bacchus, born of fire,
The jail's decoy, the greedy merchant's lure:
Disease of money, but reflections cure.
We owe, great dram? the trembling hand to thee:
The head-strong purpose, and the feeble knee,
The loss of honor, and the cause of wrong,
The brain enchanted, and the fault'ring tongue.

Whil'st fancy flies before thee unconfined,
Thou leav'st disabled prudence far behind;
In thy pursuit our field are left forlorn,
Whilst giant weeds oppress the pigmy corn.
Thou throw'st a mist before the farmer's eyes;
Thy plough grows idle, and the harvest dies.
By thee refresh's, no cruel norths we fear;
It's always warm and calm when thou art near,
On the bare earth, for thee, exposed we lie,
And brave the malice of a frowning sky.
Twere good we ne'er should meet, or never part;
Ever abscond, or even tend our call,
Leave us our sense entire, or none at all."

The October term of the County Court seems to have been devoted to having premises cleaned and "hitching posts repaired." John Robinson, "weaver," was granted authority to apprentice two lads, and Alexander Hall was "allowed three shillings for one wolf scalp."

Joseph Charless advertised in the Gazette on November 1, offering to buy rags at three cents per pound, or 18 shillings per hundred. Also, George A. Weber, "Baker and brewer, will buy good barley, if delivered at his brew house." On November 8, 1803, John Jordan, Jr., postmaster "offers $200 reward for the apprehension of the man who stopped and robbed the post rider, about 9 o'clock last night three miles this side of Paris." John Pope, "attorney at Law, advertises the removal of his office to Lexington," and John Foley, advertises "he is making gun powder at South Elkhorn at two shillings per pound if 25 pounds are taken." Brown and West announce "Patent stills for sale, which any carpenter can build, and all disagreeable odors and taste eliminated." On November 23, 1803, the County Court ordered to be "purchased twelve thousand shingles from Archibald Allen and Joseph Bryant, at twenty-four shillings per thousand, for delivery at the court house."

At the December meeting of the town trustees, an order directed "Nathaniel Prentiss to secure and keep as standard, a set of weights and measures for use in the Market House, on account of the confusion growing out of lack of uniformity in present weights." The trustees also directed that the following supplies be purchased: "For the Market house, 17 perch of stone from Jacob Springle; for hire of negro man, belonging to Robert Frazier; for sixty loads of stone, from John Robert Shaw; Rafters and lathes, from Ludwell Carey; six thousand four hundred shingles, from Jarett Ficklin."

The Gazette for this date, also contains the advertisement of John Robert Shaw, who "returned thanks for those who have favored him and he is now offering to quarry and will sell crushed stone at very reasonable rates:

"John Robert Shaw, who now excells,
In blowing rocks and digging wells,
Can water find—by the new art;
As well the fresh—so well the salt.

Since conjurors became so wise,
In telling where salt water lies;
In hope I shall not be forsook,
I've tried the art of Mr. Cook.

And to my friends I do declare,
A witch I never was before;
Before my master doth get rich,
Come unto me, the art I'll teach.

No stipend of my friends I take,
I'll shew them all for friendship's sake;
Then all that wish to dig salt wells,
May easy learn that Shaw excells."

On the same date, Patrick McCullough announces he is declining the mercantile business, desires to close all accounts and has deposited his books with Lewis Saunders and Company for the purpose of collecting what is due him. On December 13, 1803, Mr. Andrew Holmes, merchant, died, and the trustees attended the funeral services. William Smith "of New Jersey, opens

a music school and will publish a book of sacred
music suitable to all occasions." On December 26,
1803, the firm of Trotter and Scott agree to dissolve,
the first-named continuing the business "at the old
stand."

On December 31, an election was held for trustees
to govern the affairs of the town for the year of 1804,
and resulted in the choice of the following:

Alexander Parker	76
John Jordan, Jr.	74
Thomas Whitney	57
Engleheart Yeiser	54
David Stout	45
Arch. McIlvane, Sr.	42
Mathew Elder	40
Total	388

Daniel Bradford, son of John Bradford, was the
Master of the Masonic Lodge for this year, and was
chosen for this same position for a number of succeeding years. He was captain of the Lexington
Light Infantry in 1812, professor at Transylvania at
1813, Mayor of Lexington in 1841, and died in 1851
much lamented by a rare circle of friends.

At the year's last meeting of the county court it
was ordered that the county be divided into three
districts—

First district, Limestone road to Scott's (Versailles)
pike.
Second district, Limestone road to Tate's creek
pike.
Third district, Tate's creek pike to Scott's road.

All were to extend to the county boundaries.

The Gazette, in its final issue for this year, published a long speech from Mr. Breckinridge advocating
the carrying into effect the Treaty with France,
alongside a copy of the report made by Capain John
Rogers regarding the destruction of the United States

ship in the harbor of Tripoli. Some alarming reports were in circulation in Kentucky that Spain was opposing the transfer of Louisiana territory to the United States, and that an armed force would be needed to effect possession. As result of this rumor, the yearly muster of the Militia of this county was attended by all members and also a large number of volunteers.

The editor of the Gazette does not mention in his columns the New Light Schism from the Presbyterian Church organized this year, nor the extraordinary rain of reddish hue, which many thought was a "shower of blood," that fell in several parts of Kentucky.

EVENTS OF 1804.

THE new year was ushered in with the unual comments by the Gazette about "the unusual weather" and delay to the mails. The new trustees were presented to Thomas Lewis, who administered the oath of office, and their first meeting was devoted to procuring a "new supply of candles and glass lanterns to be hung in the market house."

County court orders for the January term mention Robert Kay and Joseph McChord as doing single and double weaving, Robert Holmes a wheel and chair maker, Archibald McIlvane a cabinet maker, and Peter Paul a stone cutter. Henry Hite was granted license to keep a tavern at the intersection of Frankfort and Georgetown pikes. Jeremiah Murphy and George Weber were licensed to keep taverns in Lexington, as was Francis Crikle, whose Inn was at the corner of Main Cross and Short streets. A new store, owned by D. C. Dean, was "opened opposite the market house."

The editor of the Gazette, under the heading "The Laborer is worthy of his hire," called attention to the cash expenses of his establishment at $50 per week, exclusive of the paper. "This commodity has to be purchased during the winter when the mills are running in order to assure a supply for the entire year. Subscriptions now at $2.00 if paid in advance before March 1st, otherwise $2.50 per year."

George Norton advertises "a large assortment of nails of all sizes" and Jacob Todhunter announces he "has an opening for an apprentice to learn the tanning business." On January 17, 1804, the Gazette says: "The Eastern mail due yesterday did not arrive, neither did the Southern Mail due on the 10th inst. The failure of these mails at this particular moment, as expectation is on tiptoe for interesting information from Louisiana Territory, and from England, is unfortunate. Should anything important arrive either this evening or on Thursday, no time shall be lost in laying it before our readers in a Gazette Extra. Owing to the indisposition of one of our carriers, some of our subscribers in town were not served last Thursday. Those who did not receive that issue can secure same by calling at office."

On January 24, 1804, the Gazette says: "Two mails are now due from the East, and as result, we have no late news for our readers." John McCall, at Cross Plains, advertises "his flour mill is now equipped with a screen, fan and good pair of French burrs." George Pozyer announces "he will attempt a trip to New Orleans, and will transact business for others." This week one hundred and forty-three shares of the Kentucky Insurance Company were sold by order of the court, and brought the sum of $105. per share.

The Gazette announces the "death of Mrs. Polly Bright, wife of Nicholas Bright, the Boot and Shoe manufacturer, on February 14th," and in same issue Robert Holmes advertises for "hog bristles for his brush factory located at corner of Main Cross and Short streets, where he also makes Windsor chairs and spinning wheels."

On February 21, the Gazette editor advises: "William Smith, lately from New Jersey, has deposited with him the manuscript for a book of Sacred Music entitled 'The Gamut'." John Lowry advertises "he intends starting East with a fresh supply of furrs on March 15th, and desires all that owe him to come forward and settle." John Baptiste Kalb died on February 18, and James Morrison, "Agent for the United States," states that "James Coleman will expose for sale, all the public boats now on the Kentucky, Ohio, or Salt Rivers." "The Lottery" is advertised, with John Pope, Thomas Wallace, George Trotter, Jr., Daniel Bradford, James Fishback, Andrew McCalla and Thomas Bradley as managers, the proceeds to go towards building a house for the Kentucky Medical Society. William Todd and John Pope advertise they are lawyers and can draw up all kinds of papers. Dr. Frederick Ridgely announces "his removal to Woodford county," while Brown and West claim "they have taken out patents on wooden stills, which we think will be more satisfactory than metal ones." Hugh Crawford advertises "he does blue, red, green, yellow and brown dying, at the 'Sign of the Golden Boot,' at the old court house at Main and Cross streets." Walker Baylor and Son advertise "they will buy tobacco if delivered at their warehouse on the Kentucky River, or at their store opposite the Market house." John Foley announces "he has on hand gunpowder at his mill at South Elkhorn, five miles from Lexington, or at Lewis Saunder's store in Lexington." Edward Turner of Lexington was this month appointed Registrar of the Land Office in the Mississippi territory for Adams county, west of the Pearl River.

On March 6, 1804, the Gazette states that "a number of Shawnee Indians have arrived in Lexington for the purpose of placing their children in schools." In the same issue is announced the execution of James May and John Sutton "known better as 'little Harp,' in the Mississippi territory on January 8th." William Jordan, attorney; John Keiser, tavern keeper, and George Esmond, bricklayer, are mentioned in the county court orders for the March term of court.

In the issue of April 10, 1804, the Gazette published a letter signed by Commodore Bainbridge, announcing capture of the ship 'Philadelphia' at Tripoli, on November 1, 1803. Banks and Ownings advise "they have received from Philadelphia, a large assortment of merchandise which is for sale in the house lately occupied by John Jordan." The Gazette also announces the wedding of John Walker Baylor of Lexington and Miss Sophia Weidner of Pittsburg. D. C. Dean says, "Have moved my store from opposite the market house to the dwelling formerly occupied by Buckner Thruston, opposite the new building for the Kentucky Insurance Company, on Main street east of Upper."

On April 24, 1804, John Bradford advertised in the Gazette:

"For lease 21 years—the lot on Main street now used as printing office, 50 by 212 feet back to Water street. Brick building 50 by 25 feet, two stories high, with an addition 50 by 17 which is one story high, all brick. On ground floor are five rooms with fire places, front room 22 by 22 feet. Next room is 22 by 17 feet, back room is 17 by 17 feet, another ditto, 17 by 15 feet, and another 17 by 11 feet. On second floor are four rooms, one 26 by 9 in which the stairs land, and one 15 by 9 feet. A brick spring house 20 by 10 feet in floor of which rises 36-inch stream of very cold water. Hewn log stable 20 by 12 feet and frame carriage house. In back yard a spring of cold water exclusive of those named in spring house. About half of lot was originally wet but has been reclaimed by 500 loads of dirt."

On May 1, 1804, the Gazette announced, "The Go By, the first sea vessel built at Frankfort, has been captured at sea by an English frigate. It was built by John Instone." A pamphlet of 20 pages was written regarding this capture, which shows that the vessel was owned by Jones, Postlethwait and Saunderson, had sailed from Santo Domingo to Curacoa, and was captured by some French war vessel, and shortly afterwards was taken from this vessel by H. M. Ships of War, 'Diana,' T. J. Mailing, Commander, and, 'Pelican' John Marshall, Commander, and by them taken to Jamaica. No copy of this pamphlet is known to exist in or around Lexington. It is certainly an interesting exhibit of the enterprise of the merchants of Central Kentucky.

Mrs. White "from London, has Millinery (scoop and bonnets) made and umbrellas covered, veils, fur-bows, caps and feathers," the Gazette says.

On May 8, the Gazette announced "the marriage on the 5th inst." of "Robert Wickliffe, attorney of

Bardstown, to Miss Margretta Howard of Lexington."
On the same date the Gazette says "Kentucky products
are now bringing at New Orleans: Bacon, 8 cents per
pound; buttter, 25 cents per pound; corn meal, $2.00
per barrel; flour, $4.00 per barrel; tobacco, $6.00 per
hundred; hemp, the same, and lime 50 cents per
bushel." William Morton and Samuel Postlethwait
dissolve partnership with the latter continuing the
tanning business. On May 15, 1804, the Gazette advertises: "Just published and for sale at this office—
The Ghost of Ostrahan, a remarkable occurence which
recently took place in the Island of Barbadoes." Charles
Wilkins says he is "in the brick house opposite the
court house lately occupied by Parker and Grey,
with an assortment of dry goods, hard, queen and
china ware, and has employment for four good rope
makers." Waldermar Mentelle advises "he has just
received a physiognotrace completed on a new construction by which perfect profile likeness can be taken
in a few seconds."

The death of Robert Megowan after a long illness,
is announced.

James January, attorney, and John Downing, tavern
keeper are mentioned in court orders for this month.
Thomas Hart, Jr., advertises "For sale, a farm near
Lexington, and will accept in payment, 20,000 gallons
of whiskey to be delivered in four annual install-
ments." John Caldwell advises "he is carrying on the
wheelright business, and does blue dying on High
street, at the 'Sign of the Spinning Wheel,' where goods
may be left." Daniel Bradford announces he "has
just published and has for sale at the office of the
Gazette 'Notes on the Navigation of the Mississippi'."
The Gazette also announces "the death of John Harrison on May 26th, long a citizen of this town." John
Jones advertises "His tavern is now the Green Tree"
and on June 5, John Postlethwait announces "he has
leased his tavern to Joshua Wilson, late of Bairdstown." On June 19, 1804, the wedding of John Clifford,

of Philadelphia, to Molly Morton, daughter of William Morton, is mentioned.

The trustees of the town at their June meeting "announced the bridge at Main and Mill street is now adjudged a nuisance and is ordered to be removed and the ground leveled." On July 3, 1804, Will Morton advises he has sold his tanyard but name of purchaser is not disclosed. Porter Clay, cabinet maker, and Robert Bradley, tavern keeper, "at the sign of the Traveler's hall," are referred to in the county court orders during the July term. On July 10, the Gazette carries the advertisement of Banks and Owings, apprising the public of "the importation from Philadelphia of a large assortment of dry goods, hard, queen, china and iron wares, Deckart Rifles, gun and pistol locks, groceries, etc., and many other articles too numerous and tedious to mention." Drs. Fishback and Steele announce their partnership for the practice of medicine and surgery. Caleb Williams, boot and shoemaker, says he is removing his shop next door to Walker Baylor, "who is opposite the Market House on Main street."

On July 4, 1804, the annual "celebration of Independence Day was held. The entertainment was lead by the uniform companies under Captains Bodley and Keifer, and, after the parade, marched out to Maxwell's springs, where an elegant repast was served. John Bradford was president, with John Maxwell and Thomas Irvin as vice presidents. There was seventeen toasts and six volunteer toasts, all of which were drunk to the discharge of salutes by the companies. Allen B. Magruder's toast, 'May the Wings of Liberty never loose a feather' was vigorously cheered."

In his "Voyage to the West of the Alleghany mountains," Michaux says: "In 1804 the articles manufactured in Lexington are very passable and the speculators are ever paid to make rapid fortunes, notwithstanding the extreme scarcity of hands. This scarcity proceeds from the inhabitants giving so decided a preference to agriculture, that there are very few of

them who put their children to any trade, wanting
them in the fields. At Charleston and Savannah cabinet makers, carpenters, masons, tinners, tailors and
shoemakers earn $2.00 per day, and it costs $6.00 per
week to live. At New York and Philadelphia he gets
$1.00 per day and spends $4.00 per week living, while
at Marietta, Nashville and Lexington, these workmen
earn from $1 to $1.50 per day and can subsist for a
week on one day's labor."

On June 12, 1804, the Gazette has an advertise-
ment of "Robert Bradley's tavern on the highest point
of the public square, with new dining room 54 by 32
feet." Samuel VanPelt continues "making pumps."
On July 31st the Gazette announces "the death of
General Alexander Hamilton, killed in duel with
Colonel Burr, on the 11th inst." In the issue dated
August 7, 1804, the Gazette chronicles "the death in
New Orleans on 4th inst, after a short illness, of Mr.
John A. Seitz, a native of Germany and citizen of this
place." On August 14, Nicholas Bright, the boot and
shoe maker, died, and so far as has been learned left
no confirmation of the tradition that he was associated
with the development of right and left shoes.

On August 28, 1804, John Jones announces "he has
worked over the Green Tree Tavern," and on September 4 Andrew McCalla advertises "he has patented
an apple pearing and cutting machine, and warns
all from using the same." On September 11, 1804,
the Gazette published this notice: "On Saturday night
at 11:30 P. M. fire broke out in the shop of Fishel and
Gallatin, coppersmiths on Main street. Fire engine
of the Lexington Fire company was out of repair, and
has been for nearly twelve months, nor has the
company had a meeting in twice that time. The
Union Company has only 53 members, each of whom
has only two buckets." There is a tradition that considerable rivalry existed among the members of the
different fire companies. Under the laws of the town
every owner of a house valued at from $300 to $1,000
was required to provide himself with one bucket to

be kept in a convenient and proper place, and "shall possess and keep in readiness additional buckets according to higher valuation of his property—two buckets for each house valued at from $1,000 to $1,500, three buckets where house was valued at from $1,500 to $2,000, four buckets where house was valued at from $2,000 o $3,000, and five buckets where house was valued above $3,000. Whenever an alarm of fire was sounded it was the duty of every resident of the town to assemble at the place of the fire, with his buckets, and there place himself ready to obey the orders of the General of the Union Fire Company." Additional legislation later provided that in the event of a citizen being incapacitated from attending the fire in person, he should station himself in his doorway and deliver his buckets to the first person who should pass. The number of the buckets were fixed by the Assessor, whose duty it was to see that each house had the requisite number and that they were all in good order. "No explanation was offered as to what was expected to happen should the first person passing the house of the incapacitated householder have his own buckets with him. The spectacle of a fat and prominent citizen running to a fire with five or more buckets on his arms should have been a sight long to be remembered."

In the issue of the Gazette dated September 18, 1804, an item mentioned that "M. Chateau, with a number of Indians from Osage Territory, passed through Lexington enroute eastward." On September 25 the Gazette advertised that "Thomas Dudley, Jr., and Daniel Shortridge say they will start from the Falls of the Ohio by boat to Missouri, with a new barge of forty tons burden, and will freight her back at $5.50 per hundred pounds." On October 9, the Gazette announced: "Died on Saturday last (October 6th) Mrs. Francis Scott, consort of General Charles

Scott, of Woodford County." Richard Ashton and
John W. Stout dissolved their partnership, with the
latter continuing the business.   On October 16, the
Gazette published notice of the "appointment of Harry
Toulmin as Judge of the Mississippi Territory, and,
to reside on the Tombigbee." Wyatt and Redd announce they have "lately secured a smith from Philadelphia to make coaches." Frederick Hise, "on Main
street, next door to Mr. Cross, advertises sugar, tea,
coffee, wines, and salt fish." The wedding of Alfred
Grayson, Esq., of Washington, Kentucky, to Miss
Letitia Breckinridge, daughter of John Breckinridge is
announced on Ocober 28. John Delisle advertises in
the Gazette for December 25, that "he makes surgeon's instruments, elecctrifying machines, machines
for cutting watch wheels, at Mr. Prentiss next door to
the prison."

The year 1804 will be remembered as the inauguration of the "Friends of Humanity." This formidable
movement, under the Baptist preachers Holmes, Barrow,
Sutton and Tarrant, with others and their congregations, declared for the abolishment of slavery, alleging
that no fellowship should be had with those who owned
slaves. They usually were styled "Emancipators" but
called themselves "Friends of Humanity," and their
efforts displayed so much fiery zeal that at last they
attracted sufficient attention to compel the church
associations to pass resolutions condemning the "practice of ministers meddling with the slave question, or
other political subjects." In 1807 these Emancipators
withdrew from the General Baptist Association and
formed the "Licking-Locust" association, but the movement finally lost impetus and gradually died away,
leaving the slavery question to be decided by the
War of 1861-1865.

Judge George M. Bibb was elected Master of the
Masonic Lodge this year, and was Grand Master for

Kentucky 1804-1807. Innes B. Brent, an old member of Lexington Lodge, became the first master of No. 9, chartered at Henderson on September 18, 1804.

This year also brought the election of Christopher Greenup, who had kept a store at corner of Main and Mill streets in Lexington some years before, as Governor of Kentucky with John Caldwell as Lieutenant Governor. Thomas Jefferson was re-elected President of the United States, and the next spring (1805) appointed John Breckinridge of Lexington, the Attorney-General of the United States.

EVENTS OF 1805.

THE Town of Lexington experienced some severe weather with the beginning of the year of 1805, and in the issue of the Gazette dated January 1, the editor says, "The cold weather still continues. By yesterday's post we received Philadelphia papers up to the 13th ulto., but Washington City papers only to the 7th ulto. Our accounts from Europe are twenty days later than before received. London dates only to the 13th of October. By them it appears the War between England and Spain had actually commenced, although no declaration had been made, and the British had captured some Spanish Money ships with twenty millions on board. The British also made successful attacks on the French fleet at Boulongue."

The first bank building in Kentucky erected for that purpose was completed this month, at corner of alleyway on north side of Main street between Upper and Limestone, afterwards occupied by Thompson and Boyd as harness shop. The election for trustees to govern the town of Lexington for the year of 1805 resulted in the following:

John Jordan, Jr.	64
Thomas Whitney	61
David Stout	54
Alexander Parker	51
Thomas Bodley	34
John Bradford	34
Mathew Elder	33

The Gazette also announced, "Died—on Monday last (31st) Mr. Patrick McCullough, an early adventurer and long a resident of this town," and "Mrs. Jane Maxwell, mother of John Maxwell, died on December 27th, and on 28th ulto. Miss Mahala Ayers, daughter of Mr. Samuel Ayers."

Mr. John J. Du Four advertised "Potatoes for sale at the Kentucky Vineyard, on Kentucky River," alongside of which appears the notice that "Mr

George Bibb has removed his law office to Lexington."
The newspaper published the wholesale prices Kentucky products were bringing in the New Orleans port as follows:

> Bacon—14 cents per pound
> Cotton—17 cents per pound
> Flour—$6 per hundred
> Hams—25 cents per pound
> Tobacco—$5 per hundred pounds.

In this same issue appears a letter of one column length regarding the rumor that some white Indians speaking the Welsh language lived at the head of the Missouri. The author of this letter, the Honorable Harry Toulmin merely was repeating the story told by Mr. John Childs of an interview with Maurice Griffith, who claimed to have made the trip up that river about forty years previous.

Charles Wilkins advertises "he has opened his store in the brick house, opposite the court house, lately occupied by Parker and Gray, with dry goods, hardware, Crawley steel, and Dorsey's best iron. He can use four or five good journeymen rope makers." Brown, Hart and Company advertise "for twelve negroes to work in the Salt Petre works in Madison County," and Thomas Wallace announces "receipt of a shipment of merchandise from Philadelphia, at his store opposite the court house." On January 7, the Gazette says, "No mail from Eastward yesterday. On Friday morning at 8 o'clock, the mercury stood at four degrees below zero. On Saturday morning at same hour it stood at 30 degrees above." The Kentucky Insurance Company declared a half-yearly dividend of $8 per share, and a card was published from the Governor of Kentucky, calling to the attention of the citizens that the time for redeeming their lands, sold for the direct land tax, would shortly expire. On same date James Morrison published a notice calling attention of citizens to the fact "that they have paid taxes only upon those lands which are in the counties in which they reside." Allen B. Magruder requests "all those who have any information regarding the different christian sects in the western country, please to communicate with him." The approaching coronation in France is mentioned by the Gazette and Abraham S. Barton, clerk of the Kentucky Insurance Company, heralds "payment of the recently declared dividend." Elijah W. Craig says he has leased "the house occupiel by William West, and has opened a large assortment of good hardware, and all kinds of wines, brandies, and Jamaica spirits."

The town trustees received a petition from the Union Fire Company "that the town employ a chimney sweep," but no action seems to have been taken upon this request. This month witnessed the arrival in Lexington of James and Thomas Prentice from New England, who set up a woolen mill and paper mills where Tarr's distillery afterwards was located (now covered by the Louisville & Nashville Railroad yards). They called their settlement for employees "Manchester" and gave the main street of the settlement the same name. Christopher Keiser advertises "for three apprentices to learn the blacksmith's trade." The Gazette announces "Died—on Saturday morning (13th) Mr. Alex. Adams, aged 85 years, one of the first settlers in this town." The newspaper says, "We are now two mails in arrears from Eastward, owing to bad weather. We are informed thirteen boats have been lost in the Ohio River near Limestone, account of their damage by ice." James Welch and Maxfield Ludlow, commissioners, advertise Dayton, Ohio, town lots and give the terms upon which they may be secured. John Bradford is appointed by the county court to adjust the estate of Patrick Mc-Cullough, and William Macbean opens "his vendue store, where he will sell all kinds of produce, merchandise and shares in the Kentucky Insurance Company."

Elisha I. Winter advertises "For sale, 1,300 acres of land on the Tate's creek pike, as I intend leaving the state." On January 22, 1805, Major John P. Wagnon "opens a hotel in the large two-story brick house, just above the building intended for the Kentucky Insurance company, on Main street." On January 22, the Gazette says: "The Mail due yesterday has not arrived. The weather continues bad. The mercury in Fahrenheit's thermometer stood yesterday morning at zero and this morning at 2 below. On Friday last (19th) it fell 46 degrees in seven hours." In same issue, "The death of Peter January, senior, is announced." A one-column article, signed "Dr. Waterhouse," upon the "Pernicious effects of smoking cigars," is published alongside the card from Robert Bradley, denying there is any small-pox in Traveler's Hall. Lawson McCullough advertises "for a runaway apprentice, named William Vaughn, for which one pense reward is offered, and who had been learning the tailor's trade." Hugh Diffen advertises "he has again taken possession of his old stand at Millersburg where he will entertain man or beast."

On January 29, 1805, the Gazette announces "the marriage on the 15th inst. of Dr. Elisha Warfield of this town to Miss Maria Barr;" also the death "on 26th inst. of Mrs. Ann Stark, consort of John Stark." This same issue contains a long list of owners of lands in various parts of Kentucky, to be sold "under their failure to pay the direct land tax."

Another traveler visited Lexington this year and left record of his experiences, to be found in the Journal of Josiah Espy, which was published in Philadelphia in the latter part of the same fall:

"Lexington is the largest and most wealthy town in Kentucky, or indeed west of the Alleghany mountains. The main street of Lexington has all the appearance of Market street in Philadelphia on a busy day. . . . I suppose it contains 500 dwelling houses, many of them elegant and three stories high. About 30 brick buildings were then raising and I have little doubt but that in a few years it will rival not only in wealth, but in population the most populous inland town of the United States. The country around Lexington for many miles in every direction is equal in beauty and fertility to any the imagination can paint and is already in a hgh state of cultivation. It has, however, one fault to a Pennsylvanian, an intolerable one—it is badly watered."

On February 5, 1805, the editor of the Gazette admits "having some pressing demands, and is under the necessity of calling on those indebted to him. No mail yesterday from East of Chillicothe, consequently, no late news. Upwards of two hundred crafts of various sizes have passed the mouth of the Kentucky in the cakes of ice, some of them having persons on board frozen to death." The marriage of Major George Trotter to Miss Eliza Pope is published, alongside a card from Richard O'Brien, consul at Algiers, giving details of "the ship action in front of that place."

On March 7, 1805, the Trustees, in order to improve the attendance of the members at their meetings, adopted the suggestion of John Bradford requiring "any member of the Board, as much as 15 minutes late, to be fined one bottle of wine." This manoeuvre was evidently successful as subsequent meetings show a full roll-call. Drs. Barry and Boswell announce they have opened an office in Paris, "in the brick house opposite the court house formerly occupied by Dr. Warfield." A long list of Madison and Lincoln county land owners is shown in the delinquent tax list sales. The editor of the Gazette says that "the post rider who arrived yesterday brought nothing farther from the Eastward than Chillicothe. We are at a loss to account for such repeated failures as have taken place during the past winter. The subject demands enquiry by the proper authority." Hart and Bartlett announce "they have purchased of Thomas Dye Owings, 200 tons of castings which they will sell cheap." On March 12, 1805, Thomas Wallace announces he "has imported from Philadelphia another assortment of merchandise, which he will exchange for cash, hemp or tobacco." On same date the Gazette says "the eastern mail due yesterday has not arrived when this paper was put to press." The Gazette says that "on 12 o'clock this day, Mr. Jordan's ship, 'General Scott,' built at General Scott's landing, was launched on the Kentucky river. Several ladies and gentlemen from Lexington left to see the launch." Another item states that "a number of citizens, with several magistrates and the sheriff, visited a house in which a wheel of fortune has been operating for several days. It was removed to the court house yard and burned. About $4,000 has been taken by its proprietor in the short time the wheel had been in town." Alexander Parker sold his interest in the store to his partner, Joseph Gray, and Lewis Saunders advertised "he will buy cheeses, tallow and whiskey, if delivered at Biddle's old stand, opposite the nail factory." This is the first and only time the name of Biddle appears in the Gazette or court records.

On same date, George Anderson "at stone house near the market house, announces his return from Philadelphia, with an assortment of Ostrich feathers, silver ornaments, ladies long silk gloves, silk, cotton, and morrocco suspenders, damask table linens, mill, pit, cross cut, veneering and hand saws, books, writing paper, ink, quills, and wafers." On March 19, 1805, William M. Nash "announces he has removed to his new frame house on Limestone, above Wilson's tavern, and wants two smart lads to learn the saddle business." James Johnson and company advertise "a paper mill is now conducted by two European master workers, Cross and Warnick, and they now manufacture all kinds of paper. Over two hundred reams of wrapping paper now completed." On March 26, 1805, the Gazette says, "The large ships which have been detained at Louisville for twelve months account of insufficient water to pass over the falls, has departed." Doctor Michael Schaag "advises he has found a cure for madness caused by bites of dogs, and will instruct

one or two medical students." Leavy and Gatewood
form a partnership and "announce receipt of a considerable quantity of merchandise from Philadelphia,
amongst which are some pocket pistols." Lawson
McCullough on March 26th, publishes the name of an
individual who purchased a suit of clothes and failed
to pay the entire amount. His advertisement contains
details and itemizes a list of the materials consisting
of buttons, threads, twist and other items, used in
making the suit. On April 2, 1805, the shareholders
of the Kentucky Insurance Company elected William
Morton president, Alexander Parker, Thomas Hart,
Jr., John Jordan, Jr., and James Morrison as directors,
and Thomas Lewis, Thomas Wallace and John Bradford as auditors. In the same issue the Gazette says:
"There is a report that General James Wilkinson has
been appointed Governor of Upper Louisiana," and
that "an unknown ship of 400 tons is lying at Limestone waiting high water to proceed down the River."
Drs. Elisha Warfield, Samuel Brown, James Fishback
and R. W. Downing publish an endorsement of Olympian Springs, in Montgomery county, "now owned by
Thomas Hart, with commodious rooms, accommodat-
ing servants, level roads, music, dancing, bathing,
swimming, riding, hunting, etc." John A. Cope advertises he has "removed from Adair county to Lexington where I propose to practice law." John Lowry
turns his hat making business over to Hiram Shaw,
and at the same time Cuthbert Banks and Thomas
Dye Owings dissolve their parnership. George M.
Bibb offers "for sale the house and lot where I now
live." On April 9, 1805, the Gazette carries the items:
"Married—On Thursday last (4th) Ebenezer Sharp,
professor of languages at Transylvania, to Miss Eliza
Lake, both of this town" and "on 9th March, Samuel
Postlethwait, merchant, formerly of this town, to Miss
Anne Dunbar, at Natchez," also "Notice is received of
the death of Alexander Macgregor, of this town." In
the same issue, editorials announce appointment of
George M. Bibb as circuit judge in place of Buckner

Thruston, resigned. J. Lyle, at Lyle's Dale, opens a
school for young ladies. Godfrey Bender, on High
street, advertises "for two apprentices to learn the
tobacconist trade and has for sale manufactured chewing tobacco, segars, Rappe, French Rappe and snuff."
The farm of George Maxwell, deceased, "2 1-2 miles on
Tate's creek pike" is advertised for sale by John
Maxwell. On April 16, 1805, Thomas Lewis, attorney,
is married to Miss Lucinda Barlow of Scott county.
In this same issue, the Gazette refers to a squirrel
hunt "held in Madison county and 8,857 skins were
counted at close of the day." William Macbean "will
Auction a fine coachee and harness," and on April
23, the Gazette carries the advertisement of John
Ogilby for "a lost saddle from Bradley's stable, with
name of the maker 'John Bryan' saddler of Alexandria,
Va., under the skirts. This saddle had deep skirts
inlaid with leopard skin and stitched with silver cord.
The surcingle and girts were of yellow worsted cloth
webb. Leopard housing edged with bear skin, stitched
stirrup leathers and plated irons, plated bit and
boadoon bridle." The Eagle tavern now advertises
"it is in the commodious building lately occupied by
the Bank, and nearly opposite the court house, and is
constantly supplied with genuine liquors. Has extensive bedding and is attended with care." F. D. T.
Calais, tobacco manufacturer, "in the house adjoining
the jail desires to purchase tobacco" and John Downing
"opens a house of entertainment in the commodious
frame house on Main street, nearly opposite the court
house, named 'The Sign of the Buffalo,' where good food
and good cheer may be had." Victor Ardaillon "lately
arrived with an assortment of jewelry and will be found
in Mr. Wilson's tavern, where he will always be ready
to serve his friends. He will make but a short stay."
On May 7, 1805, "Julia Logan respectfully informs
the ladies of Kentucky she has commenced business
near Mr. Lowry's hat manufactory in Lexington, in
the millinery line and has for sale fashionable silk,
sattin, straw, and chip hats, nonnetts, scoop, etc."

David Logan announces "he is making and repairing umbrellas." On May 14 Peter F. Roberts, "on Main street opposite the Bank, needs five negro boys, 12 to 15 years of age, to work in his tobacco factory."

The Gazette published a letter from a Lexingon business man who was on a visit to New Orleans, quoting the prices the following Kentucky products were bringing at that port, and for which he said there was a ready market:

Potatoes—$4 per bushel
Beef—$8 per barrel
Flour—$8 per barrel
Corn—75 cents per bushel
Butter—25 cents per pound
Hams—15 cents per pound
Whiskey—50 cents per gallon

At the May meeting of the trustees, they voted the first tax levied on shows "Theatrical performances, puppet shows, tumbling acts, rope or wire dancing, balancing of any description, or any show whatsoever, whether fictitious or real, for money, shall pay from 10 to 200 dollars—permit limited to one week." At this same meeting Thomas Ardon "was licensed to shew lyon at $5 per week."

On May 21, 1805, the firm of Krickel and Boyd dissolved and in the issue for the 28th the Gazette notes: "Sailed from lower landing at Louisville on Monday last, the brig 'Kentucky,' William Cranston, master. She had been chartered by John W. Hunt and Company, and ladened with corn, kiln dried corn meal, staves etc., and destined for Charleston, S. C.."

In the same issue we find, "On Tuesday last (May 22nd) Aaron Burr, Esq., late Vice-President arrived. On Thursday he attended a concert and on Friday left town for New Orleans." A very meagre statement considering the subsequent happenings.

On June 4, 1805, Frederick Hise advertised in the Gazette that he had "received a considerable shipment of wet goods, candies, looking glasses in marble and gilt frames, large and small waiters, all of which are displayed at his store opposite the market house." Samuel and George Trotter "advise the receipt of sixteen tons of Dorsey's and Bermer best bar iron from Juniatta furnaces, and window glass from New Geneava." On June 18th, announcement is made "of the opening of the books for subscriptions for opening a canal at Falls of the Ohio, with John Jordan, Jr., Alexander Parker and John Bradford as commissioners to receive subscriptions." In the same issue the Gazette tells about "a party of discoverers under Captains Lewis and Clark, which left the mouth of the Missouri on 19 May 1804, and when the express had left them the party had fortified themselves for the winter 1600 miles above the mouth of the Missouri at Fort Mandane. The entire party is in good health excepting Charles Floyd who died from cramps 20th August."

James Condon, tailor, advertises "he is now in the house lately occupied by Mr. Woodruff, on Cross and Water streets," and Mrs. Condon informs the ladies she is "just from Baltimore with the newest fashions and solicits their patronage." Francis Downing and Company advise "they are prepared to do house painting, sign painting, papering, gilding and repairing old looking glasses, also take shaded and cut profile likenesses with the physiagnotrace. Four apprentices will be taken, if they call at an early date."

On July 2, 1805, the following notice appeared in the Gazette: "Yesterday a dividend of $4.00 was made on each share of the Kentucky Insurance Company stock. During the past six months the Company sustained considerable loss by insurance, which accounts for the small dividends." It was signed, "John L. Martin, Secretary." In the same issue the fact was noted that "By act of Congress on 3rd of May last, all foreign coins, excepting Spanish dollars, and part of dollars, ceased to be legal tender for payment of debts in the United States, as the Act of Congress, making French, Spanish and Portuguese gold coins and French crowns tender, expired on that date." Notwithstanding this ruling, it was over twenty years before foreign coins ceased to be offered to our merchants. On July 9, 1805, the editor of the Gazette comments, "The editor was never more in want of money than at present." He adds: "The mercury stood at 5 P. M. Saturday at 92 degrees and at same hour yesterday was 94 degrees."

John Keiser advertised "At the Sign of the White Horse, for men who understand building boats for the New Orleans trade and who can float coal down the River." Wyatt and Redd, "on Main street, opposite Wilson's tavern, needs three or four apprentices to learn the coach making business." On July 30, 1805, Dr. Alexander Patrick, opens a "supply of medicines at house of Mr. Bodley, where he offers his services in practicing medicine and surgery." In this same issue, the Gazette announces:

> "The printers and book sellers of the Western county will hold a meeting in Lexington on the 1st Wednesday in October next, the object of which is to take such necessary measures as may be thought advisable to form an association among the printers and booksellers, similar to the literary fair in the Atlantic states, thereby to facilitate the publications and interchange of works of merit."

A house and lot on Water street with frontage of 16 feet and depth of 32 feet, adjoining William Tod and William Leavy, "in front of which is an excellent spring," is advertised for sale. On August 6th, John Lowry advertises "he has beaver fur for sale at his hat making store at Corner of Main and Cross streets."

Allen B. McGruder's appointment by the Secretary of the Treasury as advocate of the United States for settlement of Land Claims in Lower Louisiana is announced, with a salary of $1,500 per year. In the same issue the Editor refers to the "many inquiries

made to him regarding the possible meeting of the
British and French fleets," but admits no Eastern
newspapers have been received giving any information
on this subject. Lawson McCullough moves his tailor
shop from High street "to the new frame house at
Main and Mill streets, adjoining Lewis Saunder's
store, and nearly opposite Thomas Hart's store."

On August 13, 1805, the Gazette announced "the
wedding on 6th inst. of John Tilford, merchant, to
Miss Polly Trotter, daughter of George Trotter." On
same date a letter is published, signed by Captain
Meriwether Lewis, addressed to the President of the
United States regarding the incidents encountered by
his exploring party up to April 7, 1805. George A.
Webber announces "he has just completed the erection
of 'warm and cold' baths for the commodation of the
citizens of Lexington, on Water street, between Mill
and Upper."

The Gazette also published the result of the elec-
tion held during this month for seats in the General
Assembly: For State Senator, Edmund Bullock; for
Representatives, William Russell, Henry Clay and
Gwinn R. Tompkins.

Richard Ashton, coachmaker, "on Main street, opposite the store of Robert Holmes, desires one or two
good apprentices who can come well recommended."

In a news item in the issue of the Gazette dated
August 20, 1805, appears a story of "the Blacks of
the Isle of St. Domingo, massacring or expelling the
whites, and have declared themselves free." No further comment is made on this historical incident,
several victims of which afterwards made their homes
in Lexington.

In the same issue the Gazette pays this brief
tribute: "Died—On 18th inst. John Strode senior, of
Strode's station. He was celebrated as honest a man
as ever God made." Also, it advises that "Colonel
Aaron Burr arrived in town last evening from Ohio.
We understand he will remain a day or two and

spend some time at Olympian Springs." Allen B. Magruder states "he is going to Louisiana and will leave all loaned papers in the care of Mr. John Bradford, where the owners can claim them promptly. He expects to secure the Indian side of his History of the Indian Wars, while on this trip to the southward." George Poyzer "offers his assistance to merchants as he has opened a commission house at Nashville and will act as agent." William Babb was elected Master of the Masonic Lodge for this year, and on August 27, 1805, the Gazette says, "William Boston, apprentice to Mr. Hanson, roofer, fell off Castleman's roof and instantly expired."

William Todd, clerk, announces that "the Trustees of the town of Lexington, on August 28th, appointed John Bradford, John Jordan, Jr., Thomas Bodley, and Thomas Whitney, committee to pave Main street sidewalks, between Main Cross and Mulberry streets, which the owners fail to have done before September 15th."

In the Gazette issued September 3, 1805, the editor is advised of "the appointments of John Breckinridge, Attorney General of the United States, and John Coburn as Judge of the Territory of New Orleans." Woodson Wrenn opens some "new Merchandise at William Morton's new brick house on Main street," and "John Jordan, Jr., advises he is winding up the accounts of Seitz and Lauman, and also, those of John A. Seitz, and will all that owe these firms please come forward and settle." Lewis Saunders "moves to a new brick house adjoining where he formerly kept," and Abraham S. Barton and Company move into "the house vacated by Lewis Saunders, where they have opened a new lot of dry goods, hard ware, cabinet maker's tools, saddlers tools, Ketland gun locks, Fuller's shears, desk and bureau mountings, silver rim castors, brass andirons, shovels and tongs.

mantle lamps, Crawley Steel, laces, umbrellas, straw
bonnets and school books."

The following week the Gazette announced, "On
Saturday last (7th inst.) William Creighton, Secretary
of State for Ohio, was married to Miss Eliza Meade,
daughter of Colonel David Meade, of Jessamine
county." The Gazette also comments on "a display of
'Kitefoot' tobacco,[1] received by Daniel Bradford, from
a friend at Baltimore with a letter describing how same
is grown and cured."

George Anderson, advises "he has received by
barge 'Ann,' James Riddle, master, from New Orleans,
twenty boxes bright Havvannah sugar, six boxes of
brown Havvannah sugar, seven barrel of loaf sugar,
99 dozen long cork bottles of claret and three tons of
campeachy logwood."

On September 17, 1805, "a dancing school is opened
in the three story brick building, next door to the
Post office, the terms being $6.00 per quarter." Follow-
ing this is a long letter from some anonymous writer
regarding the society and manners at Olympian Springs.
The Treaty between General Wm. Henry Harrison
and the Indians made at Vincennes, is published in
this same issue; also, the announcement of the "arrival of General Moreau and lady at New York, on
ship New York, Captain George, 48 days from Cadiz."
Cornelius Coyle, tailor, advertises "for a runaway apprentice named James Watson, for whom one pense
reward will be paid." On September 24, "Francis
Downing of this town was married to Miss Peggy
Gardner, daughter of Captain John Gardner of this
county."

The muster of the Fayette county militia was held
at the farm of Colonel Abraham Bowman on the 19th
and continued for two days, but no record has been
found of the number in attendance. A small item
reveals "the discharge of all sailors of the United
States Navy, held prisoners by the Bey of Tripoli,"

[1] So called account resemblance of stems to a Kite's foot.

but makes no comment about this national disgrace.

The Gazette on September 24th, says, "Joseph Green begs leave to acquaint the public that with the assistance of a gentleman from London he has commenced making patent pianofortes with additional keys, quality, touch and tone. Pianos constructed in the usual way are not calculated to resist the effects of changeable climate and he has manufactured his up solid of construction, upon such secure plan as to remove doubts of their durability. Orders can be placed at the manufactory on Main street where a specimen can be seen."

Mr. Nugent "opens his dancing school at Mr. Bradley's New Rooms," and on October 1 the Gazette changes its day of publication to Saturday, "on account of the alteration of time of arrival and departure of the mails."

On October 7, 1805, the Gazette publishes "a copy of the Act of the Kentucky Legislature incorporating 'The Indiana Canal Company,'" and announces "on 5th inst. the marriage of Mr. John Starks to Miss Elizabeth Price, daughter of Byrd Price, both of this county." In the next issue, the Gazette moved its printing date back to Thursday, and announced "the arrival at Philadelphia of the U. S. Frigate President, with Captain Bainbridge and a number of American prisoners from Tripoli. Yellow fever is raging at Philadelphia and New York." A notice is carried of the meeting of the "Booksellers and Printers of the Western country," which was held in Lexington on October 2, 1805, with John Bradford as president and T. Anderson secretary. On October 10, 1805, there appears an advertisement "for a good stage-driver to handle stage from Limestone to Frankfort, once each week, and only sober men need apply." In the same issue the death is announced "of Patrick Gullion, a citizen of this town whose age is not known but supposed to be upwards of 100 years, as he was a very old man when he came to Lexington, twenty years ago."

Colonel Joseph Crockett, United States Marshall for Kentucky, published a card "explaining the direct land tax."

On October 17, 1805, the Gazette carries an advertisement of "John Jones, cotton manufacturer on Water street, for ten apprentices." John Bryan, saddler, cap and harness maker, opens a store on Main street, "where he makes ladies saddles, hog skin, buckskin and plush seats. Gentlemen's saddles made of English trees and leathers." Jacob Lauderman "informs his friends he continues in the tobacco business on Main street, opposite Wilson's tavern, where he manufactures twenty to thirty thousand pounds per year into chewing, pig-tail twists and smoking tobacco of different kinds, cut and in papers, segars, Scotch and Rappee snuff. He desires to purchase two or three hogsheads of Kitefoot tobacco." The trustees of Transylvania publish a card regarding the prosperous condition of the Seminary, which is signed by James Trotter, chairman, and W. L. McCalla, clerk. James Hughes, attorney at law, "advertises his office for rent," and John Coburn says he has "laid out a town, one mile above Limestone creek, on banks of the Ohio, where lots can be had on reasonable terms."

On October 30, 1805, the Gazette announced "the death of Reverend James Waddell, of Albemarle County, Virginia, much lamented." The visit of Lord Nelson to London is also noted with comment regarding the fevers raging in London and New York.

On November 11, 1805, the Board of Trustees published an order "prohibiting the sale of spiritous liquors, beers or cider, by retail, in the Market House, or on the lot on which it stands." This order was signed by John Bradford, chairman, and William Todd, clerk. Dr. Frederick Ridgely advertises 1,000 acres of good Military land in Ohio for sale, and "will accept young negroes, horses, hemp, tobacco, or bacon in payment." Woodson Wrenn, "merchant of this town, was married to Miss Polly Grant, daughter of Colonel John Grant, of Boone County." Samuel Redd, of Lexing-

ton, is married to Miss Dorothy Bullock." James
Hawthorne, "tailor and ladies habit maker, commences
business in the brick house, opposite Charless' Printing office, on Main street." On November 21, 1805,
the Gazette begins the publication of "Travels to the
westward of the Alleghany mountains, in the states
of Ohio, Kentucky and Tennessee, by F. A. Michaux,
M. D., which has been translated by B. Lambart." On
same date, the Gazette announces the arrival in Lexington of "twenty-four Indians, from several nations,
who were present at the Treaty of St. Louis,
who are on their way to visit the President at Washington." The Gazette also says, "The mails now
arrive from Eastward every Wednesday and Saturday
at 9 A. M., and depart every Sunday and Thursday
at 2 P. M. From Versailles and Frankfort, the mails
arrive every Sunday and Thursday at 2 P. M., and
depart Wednesday and Saturday at 10 A. M. Mails
from Virginia, North and South Carolina, East Tennessee, Richmond, Ky., and Barboursville, every Thursday at 5 P. M., and departs every Sunday at 6 A. M.
Winchester, Mt. Sterling and Upper Blue Licks arrive every Thursday at 5 P. M. and departs Friday at
8 A. M." On November 28, 1805, Elisha I. Winter, Jr.,
advertises he "intends leaving the State and desires
to sell land at Tate's creek, 15 miles from Lexington,
1,000 acres on which is a merchant store and grist
mill, overshot and double geared, French burrs and
Laurel hill stone house, 50 by 40 feet, four stories, a
saw mill and distillery, with two stills of 250 gallons
capacity."

Under same date the Gazette publishes the petition to the Kentucky Legislature regarding the Ohio
River canal to be built around the falls of the Ohio,
signed by John Bradford, Alexander Parker, Adam
Steele, John Jordon, Jr., William Trigg, Martin D.
Hardin, John Rowan, Peter Ormsby, George Wilson,
and James Hunter as managers.

Loftus Noel, "tailor, opens a shop at the house
lately occupied by Major Morrison on Short street,"

and George Shindlebower, "barber, hair dresser and peruke maker, opens a shop one door below Mr. Wilson's tavern on Mulberry street, where he is prepared to thatch the crowns and smooth the chins of all those who needs his services, having engaged an assistant from Europe." Mr. Delisle, "from Paris in France, offers for sale an electric machine for a complete course of natural philosophy. He also makes machines for cutting watch dials, also darts and broad and small swords."

The suit that has been pending for several years with the Transylvania Seminary as plaintiff and the Surveyors of the State as defendants was at length decided by the Court of Appeals, in favor of the Plaintiff, which was to receive one-sixth part of the fees from each principal surveyor; Samuel Blair, Treasurer of the University, issued "warning to all such to come forward and settle." The Gazette also refers to the new "city ordinance" regarding the quota of fire buckets "each resident must have on hand at all times," but does not disclose the number required.

Woodson Wrenn "removes his store to George Teagarden's old stand on Main street, next door to Samuel and George Trotter's store."

On December 5, 1805, the Gazette publishes a copy of the petition signed by citizens of the Town of Lexington addressed to the President, Directors and Governors of the Bank of the United States, to establish a branch of such bank in Lexington. John L. Martin announces that he is "closing out the estate of Gabriel Madison, deceased," and Porter Clay, cabinet maker, moved his shop to his new brick house built for that purpose, immediately back of the Bank, and fronting the houses of John Jones and Mr. Pew." Thomas January and Henry Purviance, "doing business as Thomas January and Company, open an assortment of Dry Goods, in the Brick house opposite Trotter's store," and Maccoun and Tilford "move their store to the new brick house opposite the Market House."

On December 19, 1805, the Gazette announces "the death on 16th inst. of Mr. William W. Downing, of inflamation of the brain. He was long a resident of this place." Thomas Hickey, tailor, "on Main Cross street, opposite Mr. Bain's new brick house, offers his services and flatters himself upon his experience in the principal cities of Europe and lately in Philadelphia, where he has a fashionable correspondent who will keep him supplies with the latest fashions."

On December 26, 1805, John Wigglesworth, "just arrived from London with an assortment of the most fashionable goods, opens a store opposite the Insurance office, offering all kinds of dry goods, laces, silks, tools, books, etc." Mr. and Mrs. Green announce they "will open a school for young ladies on January 6th, at $8.00 per quarter. Mr. Green still makes pianos at $180.00 each."

The town of Lexington grew considerably during this year and "new brick" houses are mentioned in the various advertisements. Colonel Thomas Hart, in writing to Samuel Brown at New Orleans, says "we have had a greater emigration from Virginia and Carolinas than were experienced in two years before, and I think our numbers will double before the next census will be taken."

The Gazette closed the year with but little comment on the "lack of news," and makes no reference to European affairs, as had been its custom during the preceding months. Forced to depend upon Eastern newspapers for the principal news, the non-receipt of the mails caused the editor of the Gazette to publish poetry, jokes and other insignificant items from almanacs, along with Acts of Congress and the Kentucky Assembly, many long political cards and religious arguments. Seldom did local items appear, however. Evidently "what every one knew was not news." With our modern facilities for gathering and spreading news it is difficult to comprehend just how primitive were the resources of the pioneer editor. The only personal contact he had with the outside world was through travelers passing through Lexington, and, the packhorse drivers and wagoners coming from Limestone with shipments to merchants of Lexington. These were expected to pick up all bits of news and pass them along to all who would listen, and of course this kind of news lost nothing in the re-telling.

There is a tradition that many of the post riders and pack horse drivers would do but little talking upon their arrival at a village until they had been "fortified" by a salvo of their favorite drinks. These were usually strong enough to loosen the tightest tongues. The merchants of Lexington who made the "trip to the Eastern settlements" always returned with bundles of Philadelphia and Baltimore papers many of which were months old, but all of which were welcome and were passed from hand to hand until they became unreadable. The receipt of any very recently dated newspaper, with items of unusual interest such as War or Peace, usually was broadcast by some stertorian voiced citizen, who mounted a table or chair in a tavern "tap" room where all had the benefit of the news without interfering with the urge to "wet his whistle." The news was read, explained, discussed and then carried to the homes to be re-distributed among "those so unfortunate as not to have been present at the reading." Another source of information was supplied by the custom of many of the Taverns to keep files of out-of-town newspapers on tables in their tap rooms, where the customers could read at their leisure.

EVENTS OF 1806.

WHEN 1806 arrived the Town of Lexington was approaching the zenith of its manufacturing prosperity. The capital of the Blue Grass country had enjoyed remarkable trade to the South and West, and it was natural there should spring up those local establishments for the manufacture of such easily made goods as the excessive cost of transportation from the sea coast made attractive. "Any article that could be made locally, with raw products and the local labor, and then sold at all, could bring its producer enormous profit, as he was saving the cost of transportation, which in many cases, ranged as high as 33 1-3 percent." The prosperity of the early adventures in manufacturing caused others to seek additional products to be made into commercial articles.

One favorite method of securing cheap labor was through the apprenticeship of orphan boys, and during this period the order books of the Fayette County court contain many orders placing such boys under the guardianship of various individuals, "to be taught the trade and mystery," of all the well-known trades. The frequency with which these boys "eloped" may not be a good indorsement of the treatment they received. During the years of 1805 and 1806 the following are named in court orders, as receiving boys to learn a trade: Robert Kay, printer; James McChord, weaver; Robert Holmes, chairmaker; Beriah Baines, locksmith; Peter Paul, stonecutter; Jeremiah Murphy, Francis Crickle, and George A. Webber, inn-keepers; George Heytel, tanner; John Fisher, bricklayer; John McCall, saw miller; George Esmond, bricklayer; Christopher Smedley, tavern keeper; James McIsaac, cartright; William Scott, fuller; Alexander Frazier, silversmith; Anthony Blest, inn keeper and Hugh Crawford, tavern keeper at the old court house. Trades and professions named in the court orders for the January term of 1806 court were: Alfred W. Grayson, attorney; William Satterwhite and William Thompson, hotel keepers; James Dunning, nailer; John Cross and Mordecai Harris, tavern keepers; Isaac Reid, shoemaker; John Caldwell, spinning wheel maker; Francis Preston, blacksmith; William Nash, saddler, and Francis Downing, painter.

The firms mentioned in the court orders were Owen and Clovis, Allen and Boggs, Ayers and Fisher, Metcalf and Barr, Coons and Hite, Hughes and Weathers, Keiser and Patterson, Banks and Ownings, Ashby and January, Jenkins and Rogers, Stephens and Winslow, and Ball and Rogers.

Nothing has been found in any of the local records regarding the industry conducted by stock-buyers and drovers. F. A. Michaux, writing in 1802, mentions "the great droves of cattle and horses being sent to the Southern states at that time." Cumming, who traveled in Maryland during 1807, wrote that he had passed "a drove of one hundred and thirty cows and oxen, which one Johnston was driving from the neighborhood of Lexington in Kentucky, to Baltimore." Cumming says that Johnston had six assistants to help him drive his stock.[1] "The drover could not have been the producer in this trade, because the delivery of this produce to the markets required more time than the ordinary farmer could spare from home." The Wilderness road had been used by these drovers until the newer routes through the present state of West Virginia were opened. Originally called the "Wilderness Road to Kentucky," it was referred to as the "Great Road" in Virginia and later became known as the "Great Wagon Road" and afterwards as "the Stage road." One account says "It has been estimated that over 70,000 people passed over Cumberland Gap before the trail there was wide enough for wagons."

Following the hunters carrying their supplies came the pack horses in single file, and these made the trail wide enough for the creaking wheels and

[1] See also Thwaite's Early Western Travels, No. 4, p. 228.

struggling teams in later years. Frequently called "the Kentucky Road," it was used by a majority of those coming into Kentucky until the Ohio river route began to be protected and the road was opened through the Kanawa valley district.

There is a tradition that considerable opposition arose as to making the "Wilderness Road" wide enough for wagons, the "pack horse men" claiming it would put them and the horse-breeders out of business. Many of the first wagons were made entirely of wood. The wheels were only huge cross-sections of hickory, gum or white oak sawed round. The camping places were well marked, and the one essential feature was plenty of water. The wagoneers usually slept under the wagons in order to avoid being trampled by the horses during the night. The packhorse drivers, and later the wagoneers, were accused of every crime or depredation that occurred in any community, but their principal endeavors seem to have been confined to "lifting" a fat hen now and then or "borrowing" some orchard fruit, or a few fence rails with which to build a fire. The one individual who never lacked for a job was the man who could successfully pack a horse so the load would stay, or who could get the load in a wagon distributed so it would not be overbalanced on the rough roads. The diamond hitch was unknown then, and before the wagons came into use on this trail, huge baskets, wallets or large sacks were assembled for the horses and the loads were evenly packed in these. Horses were generally led in divisions of ten to fifteen, each horse carrying 200 pounds and going in single file. They usually proceeded at a walk, led by one man with another driver following the last horse.

Just when the stock drovers began business in this vicinity would be difficult to determine. Some stock was driven over the mountains even before the Indian depredations had entirely ceased.

Effort to improve the "Wilderness Trail" began in 1792, and it was after 1797 that the name "wagon road" was given to it. After 1802 three other roads were built and opened across the mountains. Through the western part of Kentucky and by way of Nashville, using the trail that was afterwards the road from Limestone to Nashville, drovers were able to drive all over Mississippi and Alabama. In later years, this business reached large proportions and continued so until after the War Between the States.

The commodity produced in the South and mostly desired by our settlers was cotton. This was brought overland to Lexington, much of it being referred to as "Cumberland River" cotton. In the hands of our grandmothers this staple was made into jeans, so long famous as a Kentucky product. Within the last few years this industry has taken a new lease on life and mills are springing up in several localities in Kentucky to meet modern demands.

With its growing manufacturing interests Lexington entered the year of 1806 as the premier production center of the West. "All trails and roads lead to Lexington," and there was a constant stream of visitors. Advertisements from other towns began to appear in the Gazette, one of which was "Samuel January's house of entertainment at Maysville, at the Sign of the Square and Compass."

This year began with considerable excitement in the columns of the Gazette as to who, and who was not, interested in the Indiana Canal. Many cards appeared over various signatures in the Gazette for and against this project, and finally John Brown, late Senator from Kentucky, wrote a card in which he admitted he was interested in this canal on account of its advantages, and this seems to have caused the subject to be dropped, as no further reference to it is found.

The affairs of the town for this year had been placed in the hands of a new Board of Trustees. As

a result of the election held late in December the
following were chosen:

John Springle	65
Edward West	56
John Jordan, Jr.	52
Thomas Bodley	49
Mathew Elder	42
John Bradford	35
Thomas Whitney	35

Whitney declined to serve and another election was
held which resulted in selection of George Trotter, Jr.,
to fill the vacancy.

The first meeting of the board resulted in considerable discussion as to the condition of the streets
and "Pavements," and frequent mention is found in
their minutes about the mud, with suggestions for
cleaning the streets. The record fails to show what
action was taken.

On January 6, 1806, the Gazette says "Joseph
Harbeson, just from Philadelphia, at the Sign of the
Still, advertises for two apprentices in the copper and
tin business," and in the same issue the editor says
"The Gazette will be issued hereafter on Thursday
at the price of two dollars per annum. Although the
Editor has not been much in the habit of dunning, yet
he would assure his patrons his wants have been and
are now great and numerous. Last evening the Post
arrrived bringing two mails, due last Saturday. He
had been detained by high water." John Bradford
advertises "for rent, the brick house at corner of Short
and Mill streets, opposite the Presbyterian meeting
house."

In the issue of January 9, 1806, the Gazette published the dispatch of Admiral Collingwood, dated
November 6, 1805, which announced the death of
Admiral Lord Nelson and described the action at
Trafalgar of October 19, 1805. He gives many details
of this famous action, but does not say "England
expects every man to do his duty." He does say

that "few signals were necessary as we had previously determined our mode of attack." The only other European news was a description of the advance of the wings of Napoleon's army against the Austrians at Ulm.

In the same issue E. W. Craig announces "the removal of his store to the White House on corner opposite Mr. Leavy's store." Maccoun and Tilford state "they have dissolved partnership" and John Johnston says he had "just arrived from Philadelphia and will do plaistering and stucco work. His daughter is prepared to make and have for sale split straw Dunstable and Leghorn bonnets, flowers and wreathes of the newest fashions, at Main and Cross streets, the fourth house above the first square." John Bobb announces a raise in the price of common brick, and Robert Bradley advertises "Traveler's Hall for sale." On January 16, 1806, "Abner Legrand informs his friends he has just returned from Philadelphia where he selected a large and excellent assortment of merchandise, which he is now opening in the house formerly occupied by Maccoun and Tilford." And in same issue is a small notice "requesting all citizens interested in securing another bank in Lexington to meet at the house of William Satterwhite to discuss the propriety of such petition."

The Gazette, also announced "the death on 11th inst. of Mrs. Edward Payne, consort of Edward Payne, Esq. She was in her 78th year and had been married 56 years." Abraham S. Drake, 'Taylor', late from Philadelphia, advertises he has commenced business in the house formerly occupied by Holmes, the taylor, on Main street opposite Benjamin Stout, the saddler." Daniel Halstead and Company "open a store on Main street, in the house of Mrs. Parker, lately occupied by John Bryan, the saddler, where a wide assortment of merchandise including dress goods and a few leghorn hats, two horses and a light spring wagon with harness, also will be sold."

John Grant, painter, glazier and paper hanger, "moves his shop to Main street, in the house opposite George Young, shoemaker." The Gazette published the first number of the "Journal of Dr. Cowdrey," one of the naval prisoners just released after captivity by the Bey of Tripoli. This journal ran through many of the succeeding issues, and gave a vivid description of the treatment accorded the unfortunate seamen. On January 23, 1806, the Gazette deplores the receipt of "no mail from the Eastern states since Saturday week. We know the delay is not due to impassable roads, because we have talked to a gentleman who had just traveled the post road. The southern mail has been so long deranged that we never calculate on receiving any information in it. Mail from Charleston, S. C., are two months on the way."

At another meeting of the trustees held on January 18, 1806, it was voted "that it is expedient and advisable for the interests of the Town of Lexington as well as the general welfare, that a bank of the United States be established in Lexington." In the issue of January 23, the Gazette states that "the Indians are gathering in force and threatening Detroit. All the people near that station are much alarmed."

Luke Usher from Baltimore informs the public "that he has removed his factory to Lexington, at the Sign of the Umbrella, next door to Traveler's Hall, where he will keep a supply of umbrellas and parasols finished in the neatest manner. Merchants and travelers may be supplied with umbrellas at this factory on more advantageous terms than by importing them. Also, has for sale an assortment of Medicines amongst which is 226 pounds of salts glauber, 121 pounds of cream tartar, 86 pounds flour of sulphur, 14 pounds camphor, 38 pounds senne alex and three pounds of opium." This advertisement marks the introduction to Lexington of the man who built the first Theatre and for many years controlled the theatrical destinies of Lexington, Frankfort and Louisville. He conducted a hotel, at which all traveling companies were cared for, operated a brewery, served several terms as a member of the Board of Trustees and died in 1827 while acting as steward for Transylvania Seminary.

John Rogers, on David's fork of Elkhorn, "advertises two grist mills with French Burrs for sale, also one distillery." On January 30, 1806, the Gazette says "Yesterday two Indians, a Chickasaw and a Choctaw, fought and one stabbed the other. Dr. Fishback dressed same but the father of the injured man removed the dressing and used his own treatment." Succeeding issues do not divulge the success of this nursing.

Two very long cards appeared in this issue of the Gazette protesting against the establishment of a branch bank in Lexington. Also, John Robert Shaw breaks into poetry again and says—

"In Lexington, my friends may find
Me working at my trade,
At raising stones to suit your mind
And digging with my spade.

N. B.—I shall refuse to work in flint rock, as
I have been blown up three times."

On February 6, 1806, the Gazette announces. "The Independent Gazeteer, having suspended, the Gazette proposes to issue twice each week. Price $3.50 per annum, if paid in advance."

Thomas and Robert Barr advise that they have just received from Philadelphia and are now opening an assortment of merchandise at E. W. Craig's old stand. Woodson Wrenn closed his store and entered "the tobacco business, manufacturing all kinds of twists and smoking tobaccoes." The marriage of John Bell to Miss Rachael Stout on February 18 is announced, also, the news that "The General Scott, W. Fletcher, master, of 260 tons burden, built on the Kentucky River by John Jordan, Jr., and now owned by Hart and Bartlett, passed the Falls of the Ohio on the 11th inst."

The Legislature of Kentucky passed an Act authorizing the Presbyterian congregation to sell their property on Short, Mill, Main and Cheapside, which they advertise as "divided into four lots on Short street, each 25 feet wide and 74 feet deep; two lots on Mill street, each 20 foot front and 50 feet deep, and two lots on Cheapside, each 20 by 50 feet, with benefit of an alley six feet wide running parallel with present alley betwixt four first and four last-mentioned lots."

In the issue of the Gazette dated February 19, 1806, proposals for bids were advertised "for a new brick meeting house at Bryan's station" and signed by Asa Thompson, William Dudley, John Mason, John C. Richardson, Hezekiah Harrison, John Darnaby and Leonard Young, as committee. Benjamin Grimes made deed of assignment to Evan Francis on February 22, 1806, and on same date Mr. Nugent Gardiner was married to Miss Polly Vanpelt.

On March 1, the Gazette announces "the marriage of Dr. Walter Warfield to Mrs. Margaret Wilson." Leavy and Gatewood advertise that "in addition to their large stock of general merchandise, they also handle Mann's lick salt, for cash only." This issue contains the final chapter of the interesting journal of Dr. Cowdrey "of the captivity of American seamen in Tripoli." Joseph Grey "removes his store to where Hart and Bartlett formerly were" and on March 8, 1806, Mentelle and Downing dissolve their partnership with the last-named continuing the business, "which is located opposite Pope's law office, where new chair making patterns can be found." In same issue the Gazette says, "Died—Yesterday, Captain David Robinson in his 77th year. He was an early adventurer in this country and shared the dangers and hardships of the first settlers." James Condon, "Tailor, moves his business to his new brick house on Mill street, next door to Colonel Thomas Hart," and William Wright says "he is blacksmithing two miles from Lexington, on Bryan's station pike." Richardson Allen purchased "the interest of Samuel Plumber and Nancy his wife, formerly wife of William McCracken, deceased, in both real and personal estate." Mrs. John Pope, consort of John Pope, Esquire, died.

In the next issue of the Gazette is to be found "the attempt to assasinate Thomas Paine, at his home near New Rochelle, New York." Wilkins and Tannehill "open their store in the place formerly occupied by John Jordan, Jr., near the court house, where they have for sale a large assortment of wines, liquors, teas, coffee and groceries." David Logan announces "he proposes to establish a linen and worsted tape manufactory, and will use machines." George Leiby advertises "a two-story brick house, an oil mill and brick yard on Mulberry street, all for sale."

On March 22, 1806, announcement is made "that the copartnership of Simon and Hyman Gratz expired by limitation on February 3rd, 1806. All those indebted to this firm will please settle at once. In the future the business will be Simon Gratz and Company."

The Gazette publishes the following prices of Kentucky produce on the New Orleans markets:

> Brick—$120 per thousand
> Butter—18 cents per pound
> Cotton— 2 cents per pound
> Corn meal—$3 per barrel
> Flour—$7 per barrel
> Hemp—$7 per hundredweight
> Pork—$12 per barrel
> Tobacco—$5.50 per hundredweight
> Whiskey—50 cents per gallon.

On March 26, 1806, Henry D. Elbert advertises he has "opened a coach and sign painting business on Main street, opposite Wilson's tavern." The wedding of John A. Grimes to Miss Lucy S. Broadus, of Jessamine county, is announced. Caleb Williams "desires the services of good journeymen boot makers at his factory on Cross street." The death of Miss Elizabeth McCalla, daughter of Andrew McCalla, is announced in this issue.

On April 5, 1806, the Gazette published notice of the death in England of Mr. Pitt and Lord Cornwallis, and also, a description of the naval engagement between the French and British off St. Domingo "which took place on February 8th, the result of which leaves the trade undisturbed."

On April 9, 1806, the shareholders of the Kentucky Insurance Company elected William Morton president, and John Jordan, Jr., John W. Hunt, William Leavy and William Macbean as directors. "Dutch thread and Tanner's oil, also a few rifles by Wolf at Pittsburg" are advertised by John Jordan. On April 10, the Gazette advises "Died, Mrs. Margaret Downing, consort of Dr. Richard W. Downing." On April 16, 1806, Charles Humphrey and Company "open an assortment of machinery in the brick house lately occupied by Thomas Wallace, opposite the ruins of the court house."

On the same date, the deaths of Miss Maria Blythe, daughter of Reverend James Blythe, and of Thomas Lewis West, son of Edward West, are announced.

On April 19, 1806, George Trotter and John Tilford, Jr., announce "they have formed a partnership and have received a fine assortment of goods from Philadelphia, now being opened at their new store," and in this same issue the Gazette publishes an account of the capture of the Cape of Good Hope by the British.

On May 6, 1806, Julia Logan, "milliner, has received a fine assortment of patterns of the present new fashioned bonnets now being worn in Philadelphia," and says she is opening a shop next door to Dr. Warfield on Main street. J. and D. Maccoun announce "receipt of merchandise from Philadelphia, consisting of stationery, bar iron, books and medicines." On May 13, 1806, the Gazette publishes thirty-two laws, contained in the "By-laws and Ordinances governing the Police of the Town of Lexington," as passed by the trustees at their last meeting. It also has an editorial giving account of three British ships seizing and killing officers and men on ships entering and leaving New York harbour. Joseph Charless appeared before the county court and was relieved of his taxes for the year of 1805 on his book store as "not coming under mercantile store."[1]

In the issue of May 20, 1806, Waldemard Mentelle advertises "paint, gild, mend and make looking glasses, and sells gilt frames and earthenware." On May 27th, the Gazette calls attention to "the ravages of the cut worm, called Army worm, which has entirely destroyed many fields of wheat, rye and corn." On May 31, 1806, the Gazette announces "the death on yesterday of Captain Henry Marshall, one of the early, settlers of this town." The mails are late again— "No mails from New Orleans. There are now five mails due from that interesting quarter."

On June 7, 1806, the Gazette published a Russian description of the Battle of Austerlitz, and in same issue announced the marriage of "Benjamin Park, delegate to Congress from the Indian Territory, to Miss Eliza Barton of this city." The mails have arrived— "Three of the many New Orleans mails overdue are now lying at Frankfort, and will reach the city in a day of two." The cut worm "still is committing many depredations and meadows are left without a sprig of grass standing. Corn is being replanted by our farmers."

George A. Webber advertises his "bath house on Vine street, for the accommodation of genteel guests." On June 14th, the Gazette says, "On next Monday, there will be an eclipse of the sun, large and visable, commencing at 9:14 A. M., and closing at 11:40 A. M." Next to this item William Morton advertises "Coniac brandy that has been in my cellar four years." On June 24, 1806, the Gazette publishes notice of "the fire to Hart and Dodge's rope walk on High street, with a loss of over $7,000." Another item says: "One

[1] Fayette County Court Order Book No. 1, page 379.

hundred citizens met at John Keiser's tavern and voted to ask the Trustees to pass an ordinance requiring all house proprietors to keep from one to four buckets. This action caused the Trustees to hold a meeting and repass their former ordinance, "That houses of over $3,000 value—to keep four buckets; house of $2,000 to $3,000 value—to keep three buckets, and others two buckets. In case of alarm of fire, the householders will repair to same with their buckets."

On July 1, 1806, the newspaper announced "the death of Mrs. Mary Nicholas, wife of the late Colonel George Nicholas." Jesse Bledsoe advised that he is "now practicing law in the office formerly occupied by James Hughes" and on the 5th of July Frederick Hise says he "has opened a new and large shipment of merchandise, suitable to the present and approaching season, opposite the Market House." This same issue contains an account of the Independence day celebration at Maxwell's springs, at which General Charles Scott was president and Generals Robert Todd and William Russell were vice-presidents. "After this meeting, the militia marched to the center of town, and, after firing seventeen salutes, accompanied by toasts, they separated to prepare for the Ball held that night at Bradley's ball rooms," citing an excellent example as to how Independence Day should be celebrated.

Elijah Craig endorses "a carding machine at Georgetown, which will well card 100 pounds per day." On July 8, 1806, the Gazette published an extract from a letter received by a "gentleman in Lexington, from his correspondent at New Orleans," This letter says "two hundred and thirty-seven flat boats and sixty-three ships are unloading cargoes from up the River. Four ships have arrived in port with negroes. Flour is down to $5.00 per barrel, tobacco $5.00 per hundredweight and other commodities in like proportion." Francis Carson, the Water street blacksmith, died on this date, and in next issue his widow, Ann Carson, advertises the shop for sale "for cash only." An item stated that "Edward West's shop was robbed last night of several silver watches." In this issue the Gazette began the publication of a serial titled, "The Kentucky Spanish Association, Blount's conspiracy and Mirando's Expedition," which consumed four and one-half columns.

The Town of Lexington was honored by a visitor[1] who spent several days in Lexington this year, and who published his impressions in his "Travels in America in 1806," as follows:

"Lexington was visited in July 1806.—The Town is composed of upwards of 300 houses. They are principally of brick in a handsome manner—with some pretentions to European elegance. Public buildings consist of a University, Court House, Market House, Bank and four churches, if they may be so called, Lutheran, Presbyterian and two sects of Methodists. The inhabitants shew demonstrations of civilization but at particular times, on Sunday and market days, they give loose to their dispositions and exhibit many traits that should exclusively belong to untutored savages. Their churches have never been finished.— The University is not calculated to lodge the scholars. They amount to 100 and are boarded in the town at 16 pounds per annum.—Public amusements consists of concerts and balls, which are well attended.—The ladies express in their appearance and manner a vast superiority over the men. They are in general better educated and by leading a temperate life of serene repose they preserve a tranquil and healthy appearance.

"A small party of rich citizens are endeavoring to withdraw themselves from the multitude.—There are six or eight families of these better sort who live in a handsome manner, keep livery servants and admit no person to their table of vulgar manner or suspicious character.

"The principal business of the town and State is conducted by the heads of these houses emancipated

[1] Abstracts from Thos. Ashe, page 191-200.

from the vulgar bondage of the common people. That business consists of ordering immense quantities of goods from Philadelphia and Baltimore, and in bartering the same through the State for produce, which they forward to Frankfort and Louisville by land and from these towns to New Orleans by water.—The goods are all British of every kind and the produce taken in exchange consists of flour, corn, hemp, flax, cotton, tobacco, ginseng, etc., and of live hogs, pork, ham and bacon.—The merchants of Lexington not only supply their own state, but that of Tennessee, which lies to the south of them, and part of the Indian territory that lies to the north.

"The market is abundantly supplied with every article of provision found in the first markets of Europe, excepting fish. The highest Tavern charge is 1-2 dollar per day lodging and three repasts, each of which consists of a profusion of meat and game with vegetables of various sorts. Inferior taverns find accommodation at $2.00 per week. There was a time when the reputation (of this town) was so great that a constant stream of immigrants from east deposited here riches and people of numerous providence. This spirit of immigration still prevailing, but many have gone to North, West and South.

"Flour sells for $3.00 per barrel, and corn for one shilling per bushel."

On July 12, 1806, John Bryan "announces he has added fire buckets to his stock of harness and has some new saddles." The marriage of Samuel Long to Miss Harriet Prentiss is published and on the same date items reveal the deaths of Mrs. Robert Barr and Jacob Dischman.

On July 26, 1806, the Gazette expands its chronic complaint, "The mails due this morning have not arrived. The Postmaster knows nothing of any change of time of arrival. The inconvenience to which the Citizens are subjected by the irregularity calls for remedy. It is therefore proposed that they meet at 6 P. M. this evening at the house of Mr. Wilson, in order to take such measures as may appear to them best for ensuring in the future the regular intercourse with other parts of the United States through the medium of the Post Office establishment." It says in this issue "The prospects of the corn crop appear to be very gloomy by reason of the long drouth."

On July 29, 1806, John Wigglesworth advertises he "will depart for Europe on August 25th and will go by way of Philadelphia, and will execute any commission while in Europe for a small fee." The same issue of the Gazette belatedly comments: "The stages from Washington to Frankfort are now timed so they arrive on Sunday and Monday, and have been for several months." The editor sarcastically suggests that "they be timed to arrive twice on each arrival date." Lewis Saunders advertises he has "fifteen tons of Kentucky-made castings for sale, for cash or produce."

On August 2 the Gazette says, "We were blest last evening with a refreshing shower for the first time during the summer. Should it continue seasonable the farmers may raise sufficient grain for home consumption, but it is feared nothing will be raised for export." Dodge, Hart and Company advertise "for hemp to be delivered at their new factory on High street between Upper and Mill streets, and D. S. Norton announced he had erected "a wool carding machine in Lexington which will pick, break and card wool at 10c per pound. Endorsed by Soubray and Montgomery, John Adams, Josiah Brady and Pat. Barr."

Up to this period of the growth of the Town of Lexington, there had been no distinct grocery stores, but such commodities were sold along with general merchandise. During August of this year, David Williamson first began to advertise himself as a "Grocer" and was followed the next year by several others.

On August 7, 1806, Benjamin Howard was elected to Congress without opposition, and Henry Clay, John Pope and William Russell were chosen to represent

Fayette county in the State legislature. Charles Caldwell advertises, "Lost a drab surtout coat, lined with yellow flannel and a silk velvet collar, for which a reward will be paid." Bast and Young, coppersmiths and tin smiths, have received from Baltimore a large assortment of copper and tin, stills, vats and brew kettles. They also, have stores at Danville and Shelbyville, in addition to their store on Main street opposite Logan's cuttlery shop, which they operate under the name of Alte and Company."

On August 25, 1806, the Gazette says, "J. R. Shaw was blown up while at the bottom of a well of Lewis Saunders's place two miles from Lexington." Notwithstanding his frightful injuries, he recovered sufficiently to write and publish his "Life and Adventures" this same year. On September 1, 1806, the marriage of John Lowry, hat maker, to Miss Flora Clark is chronicled, and William Dorsey, "cooper—three doors above Mr. Ayers, and opposite Mr. Rankin's on Main street, offers to make new whiskey barrels." In the issue dated September 11, 1806, the Gazette discloses, "Colonel Burr, late vice president of the United States, reached town this morning" a very brief notice of what was afterwards the sensation of that period. James Robert, "Gold and silver smith commences business in house lately occupied by Mrs. Boggs, nearly opposite Daniel Bradford's printing office on Main street." Dr. Barry announces he will "practice medicine in the shop formerly kept by Major Boyd and afterwards as a post office." On September 25, the Gazette announces the marriage on the 18th "of William Todd to Miss Polly Legrand of this county." Barry and Garrett apprized the community of "the receipt of a large assortment of merchandise from Philadelphia, which they are now opening at their new store." Also, a notice disclosed that "Mr. Throckmorton proposes to erect a steam mill in the city, and invites all interested to meet him at Wilson's tavern."

On October 6, 1806, the Gazette announces "the arrival at St. Louis, of Captains Lewis and Clark, who have been on a discovery tour to the westward." Richard Willis advertises he is "now selling 'Willis' new fashioned shoes." Daniel Briner, "tobacconist, lately from Philadelphia, has opened his shop on High street, near Major Morrison's and Edward West." On the 27th, the Gazette announces "The death of Miss Jane, sister of James and Thomas Hawthorn."

In the issue of October 30, the editor says: "Public curiosity is still on tiptoe relative to the subject of Colonel Burr's visits to the Western country. He is still in this town where he has been for some time, yet all his transactions are enveloped in mystery. Various are the conjunctures on the subject. That some grand object is in contemplation we have no doubt, and we are disposed to think that object not unfavorable to the interests of the Nation. At present, it would be improper to publish our opinions, but if our suspicions are well founded, a few months will probably lay his plans before the Public." The editor may have thought it improper to publish his opinion at that time, but in a few months he did not hesitate to express himself freely.

On the same date, David Williamson advertised "his store for groceries on Mill street, next door but one to Mr. Craig's, and nearly opposite Mr. Gray's store." Samuel Scott sought "fullers to work at his mills, four miles below Lexington, where steady work can be had."

On November 10, 1806, the Gazette says, "On Wednesday 5th inst., J. H. Daviess rose at Frankfort and presented the Court with an affidavit in reference to Colonel Burr. Public opinion in Frankfort appears much in favor of Colonel Burr." In the issue dated November 13, the Gazette revealed that "the Grand Jury for examining the writ against Colonel Burr dismissed same account of the failure of witnesses to attend." On the 17th, the Gazette announced that

"Captain Lewis, of the Oregon-Missouri exploring party, passed through Frankfort last week on return to the City of Washington, and was accompanied by a chief of the Mandan tribe." In same issue there is published the opinion of Judge Harry Innes, in the Case of the United States vs. Aaron Burr, and a list of witnesses, among whom were John Jordan, Jr., Thomas Bodley and Jesse Bledsoe, from Fayette county.

William Macbean purchased the property on Tate's creek, fifteen miles from Lexington, of Elisha I. Winters, who "is now operating the Winter mills." Abner Legrand "opens a new store in the house lately occupied by Jordan and Brother, where he will sell bar iron, castings, window glass and hollowware, from Pittsburg." Francis Krickle and John Shields dissolve their partnership in "a tavern on Main street" and on November 24th, John Robert Shaw publishes a card telling of his remarkable recovery from his injuries, "thanks to the unremitting, skillful and assiduous attention of my surgeons, Doctors Fishback, Dudley and Warfield."[1]

At an election held on November 27, 1806, George M. Bibb was elected Representative in place of Henry Clay. On December 15, 1806, the Gazette noted that "the Honorable John Breckinridge, Attorney General, died suddenly yesterday at 8 A. M., of an affection of the stomach. His body will be interred at one P. M. this day."

On December 18 the Gazette announces "William T. Barry, was elected Representative in the Kentucky Legislature in place of George M. Bibb, resigned, and Ninian Edwards was appointed the fourth judge of the Court of Appeals, in place of Colonel Thomas Todd, who was appointed Chief Justice."

The Gazette has a small advertisement of Reverend John Lyle, but makes no comment on the Female

---

[1] See also, Life of John Robert Shaw, page 200.

Academy established by this preacher at Paris, Kentucky, the first of its kind in the west.

On December 25, 1806, the Gazette published a long letter from Allen B. Magruder, of Opelousa, Louisiana, giving the difference between Spanish and the United States control. The Gazette closed the year with the usual complaint regarding the severe weather and the very unsatisfactory condition of the mail service, and published extracts from "The National Aegis" and the "Boston Repository" giving an exposition of the Burr Conspiracy.

THE FIRST DIRECTORY.

DURING the year of 1806, Lexington received its first printed Directory, published by Joseph Charless, the Irishman. Fleeing from the Emerald Isle, because of his activities in the political riots of 1798, he settled in Philadelphia, and after a stay of a few years came to Lexington and started a newspaper with Francis Peniston as his partner. This directory was published as a part of his Almanac for that year, and the only copies now known are to be found bound in a volume of Almanacs in the Louisville Public Library and in records of the Wisconsin Historical Society.

This was not the first directory for the pioneer metropolis. During the year 1801, some unknown party wrote a pen and ink directory for Lexington, and additional copies were to be had by making a copy from the original. One such copy was owned by the late Colonel W. R. Milward but was borrowed, and the copy together with the borrower, "went west." To this day its presence remains a mystery.

The copy of the Charless directory for the year 1806, found in the Louisville Library is evidently not complete. The center business street of Lexington during that period was Upper street, yet this copy fails to show a single person living on this street or any business house, and furthermore, only five lawyers are shown. It is hardly possible that Lexington ever had so few of that profession. The names of other Lawyers are to be found in the records of the circuit court, and while they may have resided in the county they would undoubtedly have had offices in the town.

This directory says on the title page:

"Lexington has 104 brick buildings, 10 stone houses and 187 frame and log houses. A Court House, Jail, Market House and four places of public worship; a handsome lodge for free masons; an Insurance office;

the Transylvania University—this seminary has five professors, and is governed by a Board of Trustees; a public library, containing several hundred volumes of the most valuable books, stands on a corner of the public square. Messrs. Todd and Jones, two ingenious mechanics, have erected machinery for carding, roving and spinning cotton—Mr. Todd's containing 288 spindles, Mr. Jones 154. Extensive works are now erecting by Mr. Todd for carding and spinning hemp, by machinery. Mr. Hunt's duck factory keeps 40 or 50 hands employed."

The 1806 directory in full follows:

MAIN STREET

Names	Occupations
Anthony Blest,	Innkeeper,
Neriah Barnes,	Innkeeper,
——— Dalton,	Taylor,
Benjamin Futhy,	Blacksmith,
Wm. Palmeter,	Stone-quarrier,
J. R. Shaw,	Stone-cutter,
James Looney,	Stone-mason,
Thomas Looney,	Post and Rail maker,
Raney Bell,	
Solomon Buzzard,	Butcher,
John Haggart,	Post and Rail maker,
George Coons,	Brewer,
Joseph Beatty,	Post and Rail maker,
Wm. J. Duty	School master,
James Teague,	Foreman for Wm. Morton,
John Morton,	Sheriff,
William Shellers,	Shoe maker,
Samuel Calvert,	Hatter,
Leaven Young,	Shoemaker,
Mrs. Hargy,	
John Cocke,	Baker,
R. W. Downing,	Physician,
Joseph Charless,	Printer and Bookseller,
William Essex,	Bookbinder,
John Adams,	Hatter,
George Adams,	Hatter,
Jacob Keiser,	Butcher,

Names	Occupations
William Huston,	Saddler,
George Norton,	Nailer,
Christopher Smedley,	Taylor,
Patterson Bain,	Hatter,
Thomas Anderson,	Printer,
Isaac Holmes,	Chairmaker,
John M. Boggs,	Taylor,
Fishel and Gallatin,	Copper and tinsmiths,
Michael Schaag,	Physician,
D. White,	Milliner,
Mrs. Parker,	
Lewis Saunders,	Merchant,
James Weir,	Merchant,
Mrs. Barton,	Milliner,
Hart & Bartlett,	Merchants,
Samuel Downing,	Merchant,
J. Maccoun & Tilford	Merchants,
George Anderson,	Merchant,
E. Yeiser,	Tanner & Currier,
Mrs. Clark,	
Henry Marshall,	Innkeeper,
Daniel Bradford,	Printer,
John Bradford	
S. D. J. Calais & Company	Tobacconist,
Christopher Coyle,	Taylor,
J. Biddle,	Grocer,
Wm. Leavy,	Merchant,
Brown & Warfield,	Physicians,
Samuel & George Trotter,	Merchants,
Julia Logan,	Milliner,
E. W. Craig,	Merchant,
C. Williams,	Shoemaker,
R. Miller,	Merchant,
C. Trotter,	Merchant,
John Cross,	Baker,
F. Hice,	Toyman,
John Downing,	Innkeeper,
Thomas Wallace,	Merchant,
Joseph Hudson,	Merchant,
Alexander Parker,	Merchant,
Charles Wilkins,	Merchant,
John Jordan, Jr.	Shipping Merchant,

Names	Occupations
Brooks & Crysdale,	Merchant,
Wm. Satterwhite,	Innkeeper,
Robert Frazier,	Silversmith,
William Morton,	Director-Ky Insurance Company,
Alexander Frazier,	Silversmith,
William Tyree,	Taylor,
L. Lindle,	Baker,
William Edwards,	Innkeeper,
James Boyd,	Deputy Postmaster,
L. L. Holmes,	Taylor,
Thomas Whitney,	Cabinet maker,
Isaac Reid,	Shoemaker,
M. Rule,	Stonemason,
——— Tracy,	Stocking weaver,
Wm. Patrick,	Physician,
P. J. Roberts,	Tobacconist,
Benjamin Stout,	Saddler,
C. Keiser,	Blacksmith,
Joseph Wilson,	Innkeeper,
John Martin,	
John Postlethwait,	Cashier of the Bank,
Jacob Lauderman,	Tobacconist,
Mrs. Holmes,	
Mr. Beck,	Portrait painter,
John Anderson,	Carpenter,
Maddox Fisher,	Bricklayer,
Benjamin Wexell,	Taylor,
——— Bishop,	Teacher,
Benjamin Parish,	Cabinet maker,
Samuel Ayers,	Silversmith,
Henry Marquit,	Tanner & Currier,
——— Dunn,	Plaisterer,
Ebeneezer Sharp,	Teacher,
Rev. Adam Rankin,	
Mrs. Lake,	
Andrew Biggs,	Shoemaker,
William Dorsey,	Cooper,
Benjamin Lloyd,	Cooper,
John Fisher,	Brickmaker,
——— Grant,	Painter and Glazier,
Samuel Vanpelt,	Pumpmaker,

Names	Occupations
George Newman,	Laborer,
John Wyatt,	Coachmaker,
John Hymer,	Blacksmith,
Mrs. M'Gowan,	
William Fisher,	Bricklayer,
Thomas Fisher,	Bricklayer,

MAIN CROSS STREET.

Thomas January,	
John Arthur,	
John Stout,	Coachmaker,
Thomas Ockletree,	
Joseph Day,	Bricklayer,
John Eads,	Blacksmith,
John Loman,	Rope-maker,
Robert Chipley,	Shoemaker,
George Doxen,	Shoemaker,
Peter Crouse,	Blacksmith,
Mathew Elder,	Bricklayer,
John Elder,	Bricklayer,
Mrs. Starks,	
Richard Ashton,	Coachmaker,
Mrs. Reynolds,	Schoolmistress,
Mathias Shryock,	House-carpenter,
Nathaniel Morrison,	House-carpenter,
Robert Holmes,	Chair maker,
Hugh Crawford,	Shoemaker and Blue dyer,
James Goodman,	Stocking weaver,
Nathaniel Lowry,	Hatter,
Hiram Shaw,	Hatter,
James Lemon,	Tailor,
David Logan,	Umbrella & Chip Bonnet Mfgr.
Aaron Woodruff,	Shoemaker,
James Rose,	Shoemaker,
William Porter,	Tanner & Currier,
Francis Krickle,	Saddler,
George Shindlebower,	Barber,
Jacob Boshart,	Skin dresser,
Frederick Shevil,	Cooper,
George A. Webber,	Baker,

MILL STREET

Names	Occupations
Thomas Hart, Jr.,	Merchant,
Henry Clay,	Attorney at Law,
Sam'l. Wilkinson,	Whitesmith,
Thomas Hart, Sen.	
Mary Findley,	Seamstress,
Porter Clay,	Cabinet maker,
George Trotter, Jr.,	Merchant,
Mentelle & Downing,	Painters,
Mordaccai Harris,	Shop keeper,
Jacob Clair,	Saddler,
Elijah Oliver,	Shoemaker.

WATER STREET.

J. Condon,	Tailor,
John Jones,	Cotton spinner,
William Todd,	Cotton spinner,
John Williams,	Cotton spinner,
George Young,	Shoemaker,
—— Fleming,	Shoemaker,
—— Hanson,	Carpenter.

HIGH STREET.

Robert Price,	Boarding house keeper,
Joseph Hostutter,	Butcher,
Robert Bell,	Weaver,
John Hamilton,	Rope Maker,
John Hull,	Butcher,
Thomas Vaughn,	Blacksmith,
Elisha Gordon,	Tanner,
Peter January,	
Adam Weigart,	Carpenter,
David Woodruff,	Shoemaker,
Charles Vigus,	Shoemaker,
William Douds,	Well Digger,
Adam Hutts,	
John Tompkins,	Merchant,
John Stilfield,	Wagonmaker,
George Weary,	House joiner,
Benedict Vanpradeles,	
Samuel Deweese,	Cooper,
John Caldwell,	Wheelright,

Names	Occupations
Archibald McCullough,	Blacksmith,
John Fisher,	Shop Joiner,
William T. Banton,	
George Brownlee,	Reedmaker,
Melchoir Myers,	Butcher,
George Young, Jr.,	Shoemaker,
John Jones,	Cotton spinner,
Godfrey Bender,	Tobacconist,
Edward West,	Silversmith,
Elisha Allen,	Tailor,
Lawson McCullough,	Tailor,
David Dodge,	Rope maker,
John Leiby,	Brickmaker,
Robert Campbell,	Potter,
George Sowerbright,	
David Williams,	School master,
Thomas Bodley,	Circuit Clerk,
Robert McCormick,	Shoemaker,
Archibald Campbell,	
Asa Farra,	Post and Rail maker,
Ebeneezer Farra,	
Henry Lonkard,	Carpenter,

MULBERRY STREET.

William Bobbs,	Brickmaker,
George Adams,	
—— Hawkins,	Laborer,
David Stout,	House Carpenter,
Robert Grinstead,	Bricklayer,
—— Monks,	Nailor,
John Sprinkle,	Bricklayer,
Fielding L. Turner,	Attorney at Law,
Samuel Beel,	Laborer,
John Downing,	House carpenter,
Simon Hickey,	Blacksmith,
Allen Davis,	Bricklayer,
James Wilson,	Carpenter,
James Shohoney,	Carpenter,
Patrick Gullion,	
Martha Johnston,	School mistress,
Mrs. Nicholas,	
—— Wilson,	Cabinet Maker,

Names	Occupations
—— Ruths,	Innkeeper,
Jeremiah Murphy,	Innkeeper,
Warner Hawkins,	Stone mason,
William Nash,	Saddler,
Thomas Reid,	Tinner,
William Reid,	Chairmaker,
Mrs. Kelly,	
Mrs. Barr,	
George Sowerbright,	Laborer.

SHORT STREET.

James Eads,	
Mrs. Parker,	
William Bartlow,	
John T. Miller,	Coppersmith,
Oliver Keene,	
James Morrison,	
Chester Shaw,	Innkeeper,
Mrs. Wilson,	
John Pope,	Attorney at Law,
James Fishback,	Physician,
John Keiser,	Inn Keeper,
Andrew McCalla,	Apothecary,
Thomas Tibbats,	Baker,
Robert Bradley,	Inn Keeper,
George Staley,	
John Jones,	Inn Keeper,
John P. Wagnon,	Inn Keeper,
Nathaniel Prentiss,	Jailor,
James Blythe,	Teacher,
Buckner Thurston,	Attorney at Law,
—— Warfield,	Physician,
John Brown,	Nailor,
James January,	Attorney at Law,
Mrs. M'Daniel,	Seamstress,
Henry Colehouse,	Nailor,
Robert Russell,	Stone cutter,
Joseph Wingate,	Blacksmith,
William Emmens,	
John Sloan,	Tallow candler,
Peter Paul,	Stone cutter.

An analysis of this directory shows that Lexington had 21 merchants, 14 inn keepers, 11 tailors, 5 saddlers, 10 blacksmiths, 4 nail makers, 2 stone quarriers, 4 tobacconists, 1 brewer, 7 hatters, 3 schoolmasters, 5 teachers, 4 bakers, 5 tanners, 3 milliners, 1 plaisterer, 16 shoemakers, 6 physicians, 4 stonemasons, 3 printers, 3 post and rail makers, 1 bookbinder, 5 butchers, 3 chairmakers, 3 copper and tinsmiths, 5 lawyers, 3 cotton spinners, 2 stocking weavers, 4 cabinet makers, 4 silversmiths, 1 toyman, 1 grocer, 4 coopers, 9 brick-layers, 10 carpenters, 3 coach makers, 3 rope makers, 2 barbers, 2 painters and glaziers, 3 brickmakers, 1 skin dresser, 1 portrait painter, 1 pump maker, 1 umbrella maker, 1 blue dyer, 1 chip bonnet maker, 1 whitesmith, 1 weaver, 2 well diggers, 2 breeches makers, 3 wagon makers, 1 house joiner, 1 stone cutter, 1 tallow candler, 1 reed maker, 1 potter and 1 apothecary.

The only preacher named is the Reverend Adam Rankin, who is shown as living on Main street. He controlled the property now on the north side of Main street east of Walnut. No other directory for Lexington has been found until the 1818 directory was published, followed by the McCabe's directory of 1838.

Joseph Charless did not tarry long in Lexington, but departed for the new town of St. Louis, where he became the editor of the Missouri Gazette, the first newspaper published west of the Mississippi River, the initial number of which appeared on July 12, 1808. Francis Peniston, who had been the partner of Joseph Charless, had removed to Lexington from Bairdstown, and shortly after the departure of Charless for St. Louis, returned to that town.

THE IMPRESSIONS OF A VISITOR.

IN addition to the Charless directory and the sketch of Lexington by Thomas Ashe, the most elaborate and thorough description of the capital of the Blue Grass for the year of 1806 is to be found in "Sketches of a Tour to the Western Country, through the States of Ohio and Kentucky," by Fortesque Cuming, which was published in Pittsburg in 1810. He approached Lexington by way of the Russell Cave pike, through Bourbon County, and when crossing North Elkhorn creek met General William Russell, who was returning homeward from the trial of Aaron Burr at Richmond, Virginia. Cuming says:

"The country had insensibly assumed the appearance of an approach to a city—the roads very wide and fine, with grazing parks, meadows and every spot in sight cultivated. Soon after parting with the General, we were gratified with a view of Lexington, about half a mile distant, from an eminence on the road. On entering the town we were struck with the fine roomy scale on which everything appeared to be planned. Spacious streets and large houses chiefly of brick, which since the year 1795 have rapidly taken the place of the original wooden ones, several of which yet remain.

"We turned up the Main street, which is about 80 feet wide, compactly built, well paved and having a footway twelve feet wide on each side. Passing several very handsome brick houses of two or three stories, numerous stores well filled with merchandise of every description, and the market place and court house, we dismounted at Wilson's Inn[1] and entered the travellers' room, which had several strangers in it. Shortly after, the supper bell ringing, we obeyed the summons and were ushered into a room about forty feet long, where at the head of the table, laid out with neatness, plenty and variety, sat our well-dressed

[1] Afterwards Phoenix Hotel.

hostess, who did the honours of it with much ease and propriety. We retired early, and next morning before breakfast went to the market, which is held every Wednesday and Saturday. We were surprised at the number of horses belonging to the neighborhood farmers, which were fastened around on the outside, and on entering the market place we were equally astonished at the profusion and variety of most of the necessities and many of the luxuries of life. There was not, however, such a display of flesh meat as is seen in Pittsburg, which might be owing to the warmth of the climate at that season. Prices were nearly similar to those at Pittsburg—beef 4c per pound, bacon 8, butter 12 1-2, lamb 25c a quarter, corn meal 42c per bushel and everything else in proportion. Vegetables were in great abundance and very cheap, and were sold mostly by negro men and women— indeed, that race were the most predominant both as to sellers and buyers. Our beds had been very good, and our breakfast and dinner today were correspondent to our supper last night—displaying a variety neatly and handsomely served up, with excellent attendance.

"I employed the forenoon in running over and viewing the town. It contains three hundred and sixty-six dwelling houses, besides barns, stables and other outhouses. The streets cross each other at right angles, and are from fifty to eighty feet wide. A rivulet which turns some mills below the town runs through the middle or water street, but it is covered by an arch, and levelled over it the length of the street. It falls into Elkhorn a few miles to the N. W. There are societies of Presbyterians, Seceeders, Episcopalians, Anabaptists and Roman Catholics, each of whom has a church, no way remarkable excepting the Episcopalians', which is very neat and convenient. There is also a society of Methodists, which has not yet any regular place of worship. The court house now finishing is a good, plain brick building of three stories, with a cupola rising from the middle of the square roof, containing a bell and a town clock.

The cupola is supported by four large brick columns in the center of the house rising from the foundation through the hall of justice, and in my opinion adding nothing to its beauty or convenience. The whole building when finished will cost about fifteen thousand dollars. The Masonick hall is a neat building of brick, as is also the bank, where going for change for a Philadelphia bank note I received in specie one per-cent advance, which they allow on the notes of the Atlantic Cities for the convenience of remitting. There is a public library and a university, called Transylvania, which is incorporated and is under the government of twenty-one trustees and the direction of a president, the Reverend James Blythe, who is professor of natural philosophy, mathematicks, geography and English grammar. There are four professors besides—The Reverend Robert H. Bishop, professor of Moral Philosophy, belles letters, logick, and history; Mr. Ebeneezer Sharp, professor of Medicine, etc., and Henry Clay, Esq., professor of Law. The funds of the University arise from the price of tuition (which is lower than in any other seminary of learning in the United States) and from eight to ten thousand acres of first rate land, granted to it by the State of Virginia, five thousand of which are in the neighborhood of Lexington, and three thousand near Louisville at the Falls of the Ohio. The legislature of Kentucky have also granted it six thousand acres of valuable land, south of the Green River. Its yearly income from the lands now amounts to about $2,000, which will be soon increased. There are no fewer than three creditable boarding schools for female education, in which there are at present above one hundred pupils. An extract from Mrs. Beck's card, will convey some idea of the progress of polite education in this country:

"'Boarders instructed in the following branches at the rate of two hundred dollars per annum, viz: Reading, Spelling, Writing, Arithmetic, Grammar, epistolary correspondence, elocution and rhetorick; Geography with the use of maps, globes and the armillary sphere; astronomy, with the advantage of an orrery; ancient and modern history, chronology, mythology and natural history, natural and moral philosophy; music, vocal and instrumental; drawing and painting and embroidery of all kinds; artificial flowers, and any other fashionable fancy work, plain sewing, marking and netting, etc.'

"The card indicates a regular course of education, as it proceeds through the successful branches, all of which cannot be studied by an individual at the same time. Mrs. Beck is an English lady, and is in high reputation as an instructress. She is now absent, having taken advantage of a vacation to visit the Olympian Springs, about fifty miles from Lexington, much resorted to on account of the salubrous effects. There is no regular academy for males, but there are several day schools. The number of inhabitants in Lexington in 1806 was 1,655 free white inhabitants and 1,165 slaves, in all 2,820. The whole number may now be safely estimated at 3,000.

"There are three nail manufacturers, which make about sixty tons of nails per annum, and there are ten blacksmiths' shops, which find constant employment for a considerable number of hands. There are two copper and tin manufactories, one of whose manufactures was to the amount of $10,000 yearly; the other is on a smaller scale. There are four jewelers and silversmiths, whose business is very profitable. Seven saddler shops employ thirty hands, the proceeds of whose labor is annually from twenty-five to thirty thousand dollars. There are four cabinet makers' shops where household furniture is manufactured in as handsome style as in any part of the country, and where high finish which is given to the native walnut and cherry timber precluded the regret that mahogany is not to be had but at an immense cost. Three tan yards and five currying shops manufacture about 30,000 dollars worth of leather every year.

"There is an excellent umbrella manufactory; one brush, one reed, four chair and two tobacco manufactories, which make chewing tobacco, snuff and cigars. Three blue dyers, five hatters, who employ upwards of fifty hands and manufacture about $30,000 worth of fur and wool hats annually. Ten tailors, who employ forty-seven journeymen and apprentices. Fifteen shoe and boot makers, who employ about sixty hands and manufacture to the amount of about $30,000 yearly, and two stocking weavers. Two brew houses make as good beer as can be got in the United States. A carding machine for wool is a great convenience to the manufacturers of that article. There is one manufacturer of bailing cloth for cotton wool, who employs thirty-eight hands and makes thirty-six thousand yards, and two cotton spinning machines, worked by horses, yield a handsome profit to the proprietors. An oil mill, worked by horses, makes fifteen hundred gallons of oil per year. Seven distilleries make near 7,000 gallons of spirits yearly. Four rope walks employ about sixty hands and make about three hundred tons of cordage annually, the tar for which is made on the banks of the Sandy River and is brought to Lexington at from 18 to 25 cents per gallon. There are two apothecaries' shops, and five regular physicians. Twenty two stores retail upwards of three hundred thousand dollars worth of imported foreign merchandise annually; and there is one book and stationery store on a very large scale, and two printing offices, where gazettes are printed weekly. In the neighborhood are six powder mills, that make about 20,000 pounds of powder yearly. There are seven brick yards which employ sixty hands and make annually 2,500,000, and there are fifty brick layers and as many attendants, who have built between thirty and forty good brick houses each of the last years. The Presbyterian society is now finishing a church which will cost $8,000. Manufacturers are progressing in several parts of the state. Having been informed Mr. Prentice from New England, who is keeper of the county gaol, had collected much local information respecting Lexington, with an intention of publishing an account of its settlement, progress and present state, I called upon him and he very politely communicated to me everything I interrogated him on; as to his book however, it will be given to the public on some future day. I will not anticipate it, but merely mention one circumstance as a proof how much luxury has progressed here. Last year there were in Lexington thirty-nine two wheeled carriages, such as gigs, and one horse chaises, valued at $5,570, and twenty-one four wheel ones, coaches, chariots, etc., valued at $8,900; since then four elegant ones have been added to the number. This may convey some idea of the taste for shew and expense which pervades this country. There are now here 1,500 good and valuable horses and 700 milk cows.

"The Police of Lexington seems to be well regulated as one proof of which there is an established night watch.

"The copper coinage of the United States is of no use in Kentucky—the smallest circulation coin being a silver 1-16 of a dollar. There are four billiard tables in Lexington, and cards are a good deal played at taverns, where it is more customary to meet for that purpose than at private houses. There is a coffee-house here, where is a reading room for the benefit of subscribers and strangers in which are forty-two files of different newspapers, from various parts of the United States. It is supported by subscribers, who pay six dollars each annually, of which there are now sixty. In the same house is a billiard table, and chess and backgammon tables, and the guests may be accommodated with wine, porter, beer, spirituous liquors, cordials and confectionery. It is kept by Mr. Terasse, formerly of St. Bartholomew. He had been unfortunate in mercantile business in the West Indies, and coming to this country and failing in the recovery of some property he had shipped to New York, he had no other resources left to gain a provision for his family, but the teaching of the French language and dancing in Lexington. The trustees of Transylvania College (or University, as the people of Lexington proudly call it) employed him in the former, but had it not been for the latter, he might have starved. And here it may not be impertinent to remark, that in most parts of the United States teachers of dancing meet with more encouragement than professors of any species of literature, or science. Disgusted at length with the little encouragement he received, he bethought himself of his present business, in which he has become useful to the town and seems to be reaping a plentiful harvest for his ingenuity. He has opened a little public garden behind his home, which he called Vauxhall. It has a most luxurious grape harbor, and two or three summer houses, formed also of grape vines, all of which are illuminated with variegated lamps on every Wednesday evening, when the musick of two or three decent performers sometime excites parties to dance on a small boarded platform in the middle of the arbor. It is becoming a place of fashionable resort."

PIONEER PREACHERS AND PULPITS.

PREACHERS were slow settling in Kentucky, but a few missionaries came through "the Gap," on their own account, to proclaim the "riches of the life hereafter."

Many of the churches were started by a few faithful adherents gathering together, meeting around in the various cabins until they were strong enough to organize a congregation and secure a permanent place of worship. Some of the itinerant preachers who visited these meetings mention the cordial reception and avid interest with which they were received by the pioneers. "The field was ready for the reapers," and Lexington was not long in acquiring a house of worship, but many a sabbath day passed before regular serices were held each Sunday. This is not hard to explain. The settlers were few in numbers and were divided by their denominational beliefs, and as a result all had to wait growth sufficient to support a church.

The thought of having a church for the Town of Lexington seems to have been in the minds of the settlers, as we find in the minutes of the trustees, under date of December 20, 1781: "Ordered—That 13 poles square be left for a house of worship and a graveyard to include the old burying ground." No immediate action seems to have been taken on this offer and not until November 12, 1788 were the trustees, "Resolved, that one-half of the grounds appropriated for use of a house of public worship be granted to the people called Regular Baptists, to be laid off on the northwest side extending from Main street to Short street, and they shall erect thereon a house of public worship within the term of four years." This property is now occupied by the First Baptist Church. A similar resolution was introduced at the same time "Authorizing the southeast half of the same lot to the people called Prisbeterians."

The minute book of the trustees shows in-lot No. 45 was set aside "for a clergyman." In 1788, William McCall conveyed this particular lot to Michael Rybolt. It had frequently been published that this lot was given to William McConnell, "clergyman," but inspection of other records shows he drew in-lot No. 44. A record found in the suit of John Hull vs. the Trustees of Lexington[1] is for a lot on High street—In-lot No. 79, between Spring and Patterson—"which had been issued to the Reverend Adam Rankin as the first minister of the Gospel to settle in Lexington."

In all probability, services by the Presbyterian missionaries were held in various cabins before 1784, but no record has been found giving their names or the dates they were in Lexington. Services were held at McConnell's station, one mile below Lexington.

The subject of the graveyard lot came up at a meeting of the trustees held on May 26, 1789 and again on May 7, 1791 when a motion was made to complete the deed but it failed to pass. This subject was evidently introduced for the benefit of the Presbyterians, but they had secured a lot at the southeast corner of what is now Walnut and Short, until recently occupied by Morton Junior High School, where a one story log cabin had been raised and called Mt. Zion, probably the first attempt to establish a regular house of worship for the Presbyterian congregation in Fayette county. It stood 12 feet back from Walnut street and 15 feet south of the Masonic Lodge line.

During the summer of 1784 a call was extended to the Reverend Adam Rankin, then living in Augusta County, Virginia, who accepted and arrived in Lexington about October 1, 1784, to take charge of the Mt. Zion congregation. He also, preached at Pisgah, and at McConnell's station. "With his arrival there promptly began an acrimonious discussion because of his views on Psalmody. Upon this subject there was

---

[1] Deed Book "Z", page 375—Fayette County Court.

a serious and much debated difference amongst his
congregation as many of the pioneer Presbyterians
would never sing Watt's version of the Psalms, and
they made the metrical versions of Rouse a test of
fellowship." This difference "rapidly became insur-
mountable and the membership split, and those who adhered to the ideas of Mr. Rankin secured possession
of the church," forcing their opponents to go elsewhere. The latter group perfected an organization
and appealed to the town trustees, who applied to and
received authority from the Virginia Assembly in
1789 to sell the western portion of the public square,
now bounded by Main, Short, Mill and Cheapside. In
the minutes of the trustees, under date of January 1,
1790, "said Robert Megowan as commissioner for said
church informs them they have already contracted for
the building a house of public worship and are under
engagement to have the timbers on the ground by the
5th." This congregation met with financial difficulties,
and, in 1792, leased the Main street portion of this
lot to Thomas Hart, Jr., and John C. Bartlett in a
lease signed by John Maxwell, John McDowell,
Alexander Parker, Thomas Wallace and George Trotter,
Sen., as trustees for the church, evidently an attempt
to raise funds to complete the construction of the
Church on the Short street side of this lot, facing the
corner now occupied by the Security Trust Company.

Through the efforts of Robert Megowan, Robert
Patterson, James Trotter and Robert Steele the building was completed and several years later a balcony
was added for the colored members. The first pastor
of this church was the Reverend William Calhoun,
according to a petition found in the Wisconsin Historical Society.[1]

"We, the subscriber members of the Lexington Presbyterian Congregation, do oblige our-
selves to pay yearly the several sums to our
name annexed unto Mr. William Calhoun, or

[1] Draper MSS. 3MM45.

to such persons or person as may be appointed to collect the same, for the whole of his labors as a minister of the Gospel among us.

"Witness our hands this 11th day of September, 1793—

Robert Patterson	Henry Marshall
James Trotter	Samuel McMillan
Samuel Blair	J. Morahan
John McConnell	Robert Barr
William Ward	John Little
James Walker	Geo. Anderson
Sam'l Holliday	John Van Pelt
Mary McConnell	Mary Stevenson
Jane Willeys	Thomas Hutson
Robert Campbell	Robert Wallace
John McDowell	Joseph Walker"
James McDowell	

Mr. Calhoun later became minister to the congregations at Ash Ridge, on the Russell Cave pike, and Salem and Cherry Grove in Scott County. In 1797 he returned to Virginia.

In February 1796, Mr. Calhoun was succeeded in Lexington by the Reverend James Welch, who preached three Sundays each month to the Lexington Church and on the fourth Sunday occupied the pulpit at Georgetown. On this Sunday his place was frequently filled by the Reverend James Blythe, acting president of Transylvania University. Dr. Welch accepted the chair of languages at Transylvania in 1799, but continued as pastor until October, 1804, when he resigned to devote his entire time to teaching.

During his pastorate his compensation was not sufficient to supply the needs of his family and he practiced medicine, in which profession he was a graduate. His second wife was the widowed daughter of Robert Patterson, whom he married after his removal to Dayton, Ohio. He died at VeVay, Ind., in November 1826.

After the resignation of Dr. Welch, the Reverend Robert Stuart and the Reverend John Lyle preached to this congregation until the arrival of the Reverend Robert Cunningham from Georgia in 1807. About this time the members numbered about forty and with the arrival of Mr. Cunningham the congregation began the erection of a new building on the southwest corner of Broadway and Second, which was completed in the latter part of 1808, and the building at Short and Mill streets was sold under authority granted by the Kentucky Legislature, in an act passed in 1805. In later years this congregation became the First Presbyterian Church.

Mr. Rankin and his adherents continued at Mt. Zion until May 1793, but no services were held during 1792. Later, this church became connected with the Associated Reform Church. After a tempestuous career, during which many charges were preferred against him, Mr. Rankin announced he was "going where the Lord directed him" and departed from Lexington, but news was received of his death a short time later while at Philadelphia. His widow died at the home of her son, John M. Rankin at Columbia, Tennessee, on July 27, 1836. The Lexington Intelligencer in announcing her death says, "She was a resident of this place 43 years." This congregation withered away, but later some of the members became the nucleus of the present Second Presbyterian Church.

The Synod of Kentucky held a session in Lexington on October 14, 1802, being then composed of the Presbyteries of West Lexington, Transylvania and Washington, with the first named consisting of all the territory between the Kentucky and Licking rivers. The preachers listed were James Crawford, Samuel Shannon, Isaac Taul, Robert Marshall, James Blythe, James Welch, Joseph P. Howe, Samuel Rannals, John Lyle, Barton W. Stone and William Robinson.

The Synod reports for the years of 1803 and 1804 were very discouraging. This denomination lost many members by the constant emigration to the new territory north of the Ohio, where cheap land, free from

law suits induced many to remove as soon as the
Indian troubles ceased and crops could be attended in
safety.

The Methodist Episcopal denomination began its
efforts to establish societies in Central Kentucky in
1786, when James Haw and Benjamin Ogden were
appointed missionaries by Bishop Francis Asbury, at
a conference held at Baltimore the same year. In
1787, the Kentucky Territory was divided into two
circuits, the Cumberland embracing the Southern Kentucky and middle Tennessee area, and the Kentucky
Circuit comprising all the balance of this State.
In 1788, the Baltimore conference divided the Kentucky Circuit into the Lexington and Danville circuits
and placed Francis Poythress and James Haw in charge
with Henry Birchett as assistant. The Lexington
circuit included all of the territory from the Kentucky
to the Licking river, with a portion of Harrison county.

In the latter part of 1788, Thomas Williamson,
Peter Massie and Benjamin Snelling were sent to the
Blue Grass. In 1789 James Haw took charge of the
Lexington circuit with Wilson Lee and Stephen Brooks
as assistants.. Barnabas McHenry worked with them
for some months and then passed to the Danville cir-
cuit. Benjamin Snelling returned to Virginia and
Peter Massie departed for Tennessee.

On May 13, 1790 the Reverend Bishop Francis
Asbury rode into Lexington, guarded by Hope Hull
and sixteen men with thirteen guns[1], to attend the
Conference to be held at Masterson's station, located
five miles northwest of Lexington on what is now
the Spurr Pike, and included in the area belonging
to the United States Narcotic farm. This meeting was
held in a two-story log building and continued for two
days, during which Wilson Lee, Thomas Wilkinson and
Barnabas McHenry were ordained. Bishop Asbury's
diary says: "On May 13, 1790 being court term I preach-

[1] McTyerie's History of Methodism, page 440.

ed in a dwelling house in Lexington. The methodists do but little here, others lead the way." This visit was of great importance to the infant church and "revived the lagging interest." The conference report shows 424 whites and 32 colored members, but those residing in the town of Lexington are not shown separately. There was evidently only a few of these and they met at irregular intervals in different homes, but in 1789 this society purchased a lot containing one small log cabin on southwest corner of Short and Back (now Deweese) streets from Samuel and Esther McMillan of Harrison county. Tradition says Francis Poythress preached the first sermon in this building, but even with a house of worship regular services each Sunday were not held until after 1819.

The duties of the circuits required the absence of the preachers from Lexington most of their time. Riding their indefinite circuits through the Wilderness, they preached the Gospel in cabins, on the sides of the trails, or where ever they could find any one to listen to their messages. Pastors were assigned to this circuit and they alternately occupied the various pulpits until "they married and located," or removed to other circuits. The extent of this circuit prevented their frequent attendance upon the Lexington congregation until the circuits were reduced in size.

John Sewell preached to the Lexington and near by churches assisted by Benjamin Northcutt and John Page, during 1791 until the arrival of John Ray. The conference of the West for the year of 1792 was again held at Masterson's and amongst the assignments was John Ball and Gabriel Woodfield to the Lexington Circuit, but the latter confined his effort to that part of Fayette now included in Jessamine county. The next summer Mr. Ball went to Cumberland and John Metcalf succeeded him. In 1794 Acquilla Sugg was assigned to Lexington, but his health failed and he was relieved by Thomas Scott, until the arrival of Henry Ogburn late in the fall. The next year the Conference met again at Masterson's and

Mr. Sugg was returned to Lexington. In 1796 Rev. Williams Kavanaugh was appointed to Lexington, but after a few months he felt that he could not conscientiously continue in the denomination and resigned. John Watson filled the vacancy until relieved by John Buxton, who remained only one year. The minutes for this conference contain references to "the large migration to Ohio, amongst whom were many Methodists of the Kentucky churches, so great, that many societies were broken up." The Lexington church petitioned to make their church a circuit to itself, and Thomas Wilkerson was put in charge but his health failed and the next year was relieved by Benjamin Lakin, John Watson and Thomas Allen. Miles Harper preached to the Lexington Church in 1801, Lewis Garrett in 1802 aided by Samuel Douthett, "the pathetic preacher", John Sale in 1803 and 1804. In 1805 the Conference was held in Scott County on October 5th and the diary of Bishop Asbury says:

"On the 8th preached to a small gathering in Lexington." In 1806, George Askins was assigned to Lexington and he promptly started agitation for a new building on the old location. He was succeeded by Thomas Wilkerson who completed the new building which was occupied until 1819. In this year the congregation completed a new two story brick building on the north side of Church street between Limestone and Upper which is still standing. This building was used until the congregation removed in 1841 to High street where they still remain.

An interesting account of the Lexington Church which shows its slow growth, is to be found in the following letter written by the Reverend B. T. Kavanaugh of Houston, Texas: "In Fall of 1819, the revival at Ebeneezer church in Clark county carried much influence over Central Kentucky, and affected the Lexington church greatly. Previous to that time there was not a young person in the society, none when I joined there. Old father Chipley, Challen,

Bryan, Gibbons and a few others were the fathers of the church."

There seems to have been a split in this congregation during 1798 or 1799 and one division undertook to build a church on north Broadway about where the Lexington Opera House now stands, but in 1806 reconveyed the property to the original owners and the congregation reunited. The Literature of this Community was enriched by the schism when George Brownlee and John Murphy published "A Defense of the Late Society of Methodists against the charges of the Rev. William Burke" in 1802. One cause for the slow growth of this denomination was their well advertised opposition to Slavery. "Entering the Union as a slave owning State, a large proportion of the population of Kentucky, while admiring the zeal of the preachers and the truths of its doctrines, felt that interference of the church with an institution that was purely civil had led them beyond the provinces of the church." The continued agitation of the question no doubt caused many to seek their religious homes elsewhere.

Tradition has it that there were less than fifty Catholic families in Kentucky in 1787. In that year Bishop Carroll at Baltimore recognized their needs for a spiritual advisor and sent the Reverend Mr. Whelan to take up the work as a missionary. He remained until 1790, but no record has been found to show that he held any services in the Town of Lexington. In January, 1794, the Reverend Stephen T. Badin and Reverend M. Barrieres walked from Limestone into Lexington and took over this work. Father Barrieres passed most of his time in Scott county, residing with the Gaugh family near White Suphur, while Father Badin covered the central part of Kentucky. He was a native of France and had escaped from Bordeaux during the revolution of 1792, landing at Baltimore where he was ordained the following year, the first priest ever ordained in the United

States. Upon his arrival in Kentucky he found no churches and was compelled to hold mass in the homes of his communicants. One of these homes was that of Dennis McCarty, Agent for John Moyland,[1] who had a store on Main street facing the court house, and another, was at the home of Thomas Tibbats, on North Broadway.

Father Badin was a learned, indefatigable worker, and his ready wit made him welcome in the houses of the pioneers. Traversing the Wilderness on horse-back in all kinds of weather, he did much to overcome the prejudices of the pioneers. After four years of labor he received assistance in two new arrivals but in three years both of these gave up their lives in the service, and in 1799, the Reverend Thomas Thayer, a converted Congregational minister, arrived to assist in the work. With but little encouragement they struggled on and were rewarded with a growing list of communicants who determined to have a place of worship. There were probably not five Catholic families in Lexington when Father Badin began his efforts, but the missionary work was not permitted to slacken and success rewarded his efforts. In 1804 a lot was purchased[2] from Samuel Ayers and Jane McNair, executors of estate of John McNair, located on west Main street, part of in-lot No. 18, just east of the present First Baptist Church, on which there was a small one-room log cabin. In this building Father Badin officiated until 1812, when the congregation had grown and their needs required a larger home. In 1810, a mass meeting was held at the court house, and a subscription was started by Captain Nathaniel Hart, and Colonel Joseph Hamilton Daviess, the Grand Master of the Masonic Lodge of Kentucky, both of whom fell in the Indian warfare in the next year. On May

---

1 John Moyland was a brother of Stephen Moyland, colonel on staff of General Washington during the Revolutionary War. Another brother was Archbishop of Cork.
2 Circuit Court Book "B", page 184—Fayette County Clerk's office.

19, 1812, a small brick building was dedicated on East Third street on a lot purchased from Robert Todd for $312.[1] The remainder of the woodland was reserved for a cemetery. This building was used by this congregation until the dedication of St. Peter's on North Limestone on December 3, 1837.

Father Badin was furloughed in 1821 and returned to France, where he wrote and published "The Origin and Progress of the Missions in Kentucky", an interesting and valuable addition to any Kentucky library.

Suffering many privations, these pioneer priests endured the miserably furnished huts, with poor fare; long rides through the snow, rain, heat, or cold, to reach the homes of the parishoners. They spent their lives trying to improve the spiritual conditions, relieve the suffering and console the dying, and their names will be revered in Kentucky as long as Catholic history is read and appreciated.

The Baptist Church probably exceeded all other denominations in numbers for many years after the first settlements. A large increase was secured when Elder Lewis Craig left Spottsylvania county, Virginia, in 1781, with his entire congregation, in a caravan that since has been known as "The Traveling Church." Some of these members stopped near Gilbert's creek in what is now Garrard county, but in the following year many of the families removed to South Elkhorn where they erected a church and employed Mr. Lewis Craig as their pastor. Tradition mentions that a large number of Lexington Baptists attended this church, which was the scene of frequent revivals. One letter written from Lexington August 10, 1801, says: "Last Sunday the Association was held at Higbee's six miles from Lexington, where it is said there were 8 to 10,000 persons."

[1] County Court Book "G", page 464.

Services had been held probably in the cabins of the pioneers in the Town of Lexington, but no records have been found to show this until the arrival in 1787 of Elder John Gano, who had been a Chaplain in the Continental Army throughout the entire war and had endured the hardships of the Valley Forge Winter.[1] He migrated to the Blue Grass and with the assistance of Edward Payne began a movement to erect a home for the Baptists in Lexington.

A small building was constructed on the graveyard lot, and services seem to have been held for a few years but R. H. Bishop says, in his "Outline History of the Church in Kentucky," 1808—"the lot is now occupied as a common burying ground upon which they (the Baptists) have a frame building, which was used for several years as a place of worship. The church, however, appears to have been extinct in 1804-5 and the building allowed to go to decay." The Kentucky Gazette on November 6, 1810, refers to the Burying ground "and the venerable meeting house and demolished walls."

This lot had been deeded to the Baptist congregation by the town trustees September 29, 1789,[2] mentioning the trustees of the Church as Reverend John Gano, Edward Payne, Thomas Lewis, William Payne, William Stone, Jr., and Elisha Winter, "in trust for the sole use of the Baptist Church holding the doctrines and maintaining the disciplin set forth in the Baptist confession of Faith." This deed was filed in April court, 1790. On March 19, 1806, "the surviving trustees hereby appoint James Beatty in the room of Elder John Gano, deceased: Henry Payne in the room of Elder William Payne, who has removed to Mason County, and Lewis E. Turner, in the room of Elisha Winter, who has removed out of the State." In the latter part of 1815 the trustees then remaining met and organized the First Baptist Church with Richard Grey,

[1] Autobiography of Rev. John Gano, published by Southwick and Hardcastle, New York City, 1806.
[2] Fayette County Deed Book "R", page 252.

James Fishback, William Stone, Henry Payne and Lewis E. Turner as trustees and they conveyed the property on April 11, 1818—"the lot for the Baptist Church, the Town Fork Church having relinquished her right, do hereby vest the First Baptist Church of Lexington with the right to use it for the purpose designated."

The Town Fork Baptist Church was located four miles west of Lexington on the Frankfort Pike. It had been organized with ten members in July 1786, with Lewis Craig, John Taylor, Ambrose Dudley and Augustine Eastin as organizers. In 1802, it reported a membership of 120. The Town Fork Church sent messengers each summer to the Elkhorn Baptist Association until the War of 1812, most of them being residents of Lexington, and as the Lexington Church did not appear on the minutes of this association until the year 1818, it seems to confirm the tradition that the Lexington church was inoperative and the Baptists of Lexington attended the Town Fork Church.

This church was upset by a serious dissension caused by "the Emancipators," who claimed no fellowship should be held with slave owners, and, this contention caused a number to secede from the parent church and establish one of their own. This body erected a small building on Mill street, opposite Transylvania,[1] under the leadership of James Fishback, but the effort lasted only a few years and the congregation gradually drifted back to the First Church, while the Reverend James Fishback became a follower of Barton Stone, taking some of his former members with him. In 1817, conciliatory efforts united the members and placed the church upon a more solid foundation, leaving the cause of their separation to be settled by the War between the States.

After the death of the Reverend John Gano in 1804, the services of the Reverend Jacob Creath, Sen., were secured but he soon became involved in a diffi-

---

[1] Then in Gratz Park.

culty with Thomas Lewis, one of his trustees, on account of some slave transaction. "The breach widened, parties were formed and finally the whole Baptist Association became involved in the quarrel. The Church faded under the blight of this fierce contention," but the denomination survived the struggle and continued to grow.

After these two bodies had re-united in 1817, a move was started to erect a new church, and the Kentucky Gazette in issue dated August 27, 1819, says: "The new meeting house of the First Baptist Church will be opened at 11 A. M. next sabbath."

A description of the Town Fork property can be found in District Court Book "C", page 148—January 29, 1800—"a parcel of land included by a post and rail fence around the meeting house and horse yard on the Frankfort road about four miles from Lexington,"

The German Lutherans secured sufficient funds through a lottery in the year 1792 to erect a story and one-half frame building on High street, near the First Methodist Church property, by the efforts of Rev. Benedict Swope, Jacob Keiser, Martin Castle, Casper Carsner and John Smith, and when Mr. Swope removed to Lincoln county they secured the services of the Reverend J. Bailey, as pastor.[1] On August 12, 1799,[2] Edward West and Sarah his wife, "conveyed to Jacob Springer and Melchoir Meyer, surviving trustees of the German Lutheran church, part of out-lot "N", sixty-four feet, bounded by the school house, Robert Campbell's potter shop and Lawson McCullough's house—in trust only for the whole and sole use of a burying ground, graveyard and place of worship to be reserved for such use only and no other purpose." This congregation maintained its organization until the summer of 1818 when a fire destroyed their home and the members scattered. A number of deceased members were buried on the lot at the rear of the

[1] Act of the General Assembly of Kentucky, December 15, 1792.
[2] District Court Book "B", page 465.

present First Methodist Church and in the grove that formerly stood between this church and Mill street. The books of this congregation have long since been given up as lost and it has been impossible to ascertain the date Mr. Bailey began preaching for them. The Kentucky Gazette in an issue dated June 2, 1792, says: "The Reverend Mr. Bailey will preach in Lexington Sunday the 17th." This is the earliest date found.

The "Great Revival" following the Green River and Cane Ridge Meetings increased considerably the religious interest and activity in central Kentucky, and no doubt increased the memberships in all the churches in Lexington. "It is strange that the newspapers of that day published so little about this remarkable occurrence, beyond the power of analysis to explain or the pen to portray.[1] This religious excitement was, no doubt, partly due to the spiritual starvation of the pioneers for over a generation. Many returned "to the Church of their fathers" and others were lead into new movements, indicating a religious unrest. An attempt to establish a new denomination in Lexington is disclosed in a letter found in the Congressional Library at Washington, D. C., written by Colonel Thomas Hart and addressed to the Honorable James Brown at New Orleans, dated Lexington, January 27, 1805:

> "We are endeavoring to establish a new religion similar to the Dunkars and Quakers, not to sue or be sued, but to arbitrate all matters of controversy ourselves in the most amicable manner. I have offered Mr. Clay $20,000 to join and draw up a creed or constitution for us, and that he shall have a certain salary as Arbitrator and $2,000 a year for preaching to us. You will find from the papers that they are likely to accomplish the scheme in Pennsylvania. In Duane's paper is published a dialogue between a lawyer and a parson on

---

1 Shaler's—Kentucky Commonwealth.

the subject that Clay after receiving the paper
from me for perusal, refuses to return it fear-
ing perhaps that it may be made public but
Duane is now publishing a pamphlet on the
subject entitled 'Sampson against the Philis-
tines'. Clay says he is a dam'nd unprincipal
wretch who would wish to see anarchy and
confusion prevail through the Union, but I
differ widely from him, think him a good man
and most heartily wish he could succeed in
his undertaking and I have little doubt but
he will in the State of Pennsylvania."

No other record has been found of this effort and
it evidently ceased with the refusal of the "Commoner."
It is a good illustration of the spiritual unrest of that
period.

Although the first sermon ever preached in Kentucky was at Boonesborough in 1775, by the Reverend
John Lythe, an Episcopalian priest, that denomination
was in no position to follow this effort and care for the
spiritual needs of the pioneers. The readjustment
after the Revolutionary War so weakened this denomination that it was unable to spiritually care for
those members who migrated to the west.

There is a tradition meetings were held by some
of this faith in Lexington during the year 1794 but
no records confirming this report have been found.
During 1796 the communicants living in the town of
Lexington perfected an organization and held some
services in a dilapidated frame building on the corner of Church and Market streets, with the Reverend
James Moore, preaching at frequent intervals. The
building was replaced with a neat brick structure, with
a tower and small bell, the gift of John D. Clifford in
1808. The lot was the gift of William Morton and
Dr. Walter Warfield[1] to the trustees, John Ward, John
D. Clifford, James Prentis, John T. Mason, Jr., and
Robert Wickliffe—"66 feet on Market and 98 feet on

1 Deed Book "M", page 269—Fayette County Clerk's office.

Church, on which stands the Episcopal church." This lot had been purchased in 1804 from Mrs. Keziah Barton and was dedicated "to the use of said Protestant Episcopal Church but to the use of no other sect or denomination of christians and to no other use whatever."

The records in the Bishop's house at Baltimore show the Reverend Samuel Keene, Jr., was selected as missionary to Kentucky but no record has been found to indicate he held any services in Lexington, or even came to Kentucky.

In 1808, steps were taken to organize the parish with Thomas Hart, John Bradford, William Morton, Robert Todd, Walter Warfield, John Postlethwait and John W. Hunt as vestrymen. In 1822, the building was replaced with a larger edifice, better suited to the needs of the growing congregation.

The Reverend James Moore had been officiating as pastor without regular engagement or salary for a number of months, and was succeeded by the Reverend Williams Kavanaugh, who left the ministry of the Methodist Episcopal Church under the advice of Dr. Elisha Warfield, and was ordained a priest of the Episcopal church by Bishop Claggett in Baltimore in 1800. After serving this congregation for several months he accepted a call from the Louisville church and removed to that point. He later went to Henderson where he died in 1806. Four of his sons became ministers in the Methodist Church.

There is a tradition that the new church was furnished by means of a lottery which was conducted under the patronage of William Morton, Walter Warfield, John Wyatt and Daniel Sheely. It was not a complete success and the first two supplied the necessary funds to completely furnish the church, agreeing to be repaid out of the pew rents.

Evidently, all denominations had a hard struggle to get established, as the fewness of their numbers and the lack of religious interest were seriously felt by all for many years. The pay of the preachers was necessarily small, and we know some taught in schools, one practiced medicine, and another, whose beautiful writing can be found on the pages of the deed and will books in the county Clerk's office, increased his income by copying such papers when filed in that office.

Denominational lines in those days do not seem to have been drawn as tightly as at present times. There was a strong inclination to weld some of the congregations evidenced in many of the articles by writers of that period, but only one item indicating action is to be found in the Kentucky Gazette, published September 18, 1804:

> "The Methodists and Presbyterians of Madison county held their meeting to arrange consolidation, but the meeting was broken up by 100 swarms of bees."

This seems to have ended such attempts as the subject is not mentioned again in the newspapers of that period.

For a considerable period after the settlement of Central Kentucky, slaves and free colored people were permitted to unite with the churches of their owners but did not have any vote in the business meetings. Their confessions were received along with their owners, and they received the same baptism. They were frequently disciplined for misbehavior and "for speaking disrespectfully of the church."[1]

Old "Captain" was the founder of the first African Baptist church in Lexington, and died in the summer of 1823 claiming he was past 90 years of age. He was originally the property of Captain Duerett of Caroline County, Virginia, and his wife was owned by a neighbor who desired to emigrate to Kentucky. Captain's owner succeeded in making an exchange of slaves so that Captain and his wife would not be parted and he was brought to Fayette County where

---

1 Bryan Station Baptist Church Record Book, April 1796.

he at once began to preach to a group of slaves in a small cabin near the head of Boone's creek. This church continued for a number of years but the sales of some of the slaves and the removal of some of the owners caused the church to be broken up, and Captain and his wife removed into Lexington, where he located on a small lot belonging to John Maxwell, near the famous spring where the 4th of July was regularly celebrated for a number of years. Mr. Maxwell gave them the use of a small cabin[1] and continued while he lived to protect and comfort them in their efforts to provide religious service for their fellow slaves. Captain's character was good and his labors so successful he "was given the right hand of fellowship" and told to continue his efforts. He had acquired about fifty converts by 1810, all regularly baptized, so they organized a church, but not having any building they met at different places until they were finally granted the use of a small cabin on Winslow street where it is said they attained a membership of over three hundred before his death. This church was the seed from which grew the Pleasant Green Baptist Church.[2]

Captain found much encouragement from members of the white churches as many of them felt the colored members would be more happy and successful in their own church and away from the influence and control of their owners. Captain kept no records of his meetings or of his members and it is only through tradition confirmed by the lawsuit named that the story of his life and efforts have been handed down to us. His endeavor resulted in his race having churches of their own and controlled by themselves.

---

1 Near south end of Lexington Ave. and Euclid Ave.
2 See Welcher Breckinridge vs. Trustees African Baptist Church, Fayette Circuit Court, Box 849.

THE BENCH AND THE BAR.

THE first court held in Lexington used one of the cabins inside the stockade until it was provided with a log building that stood on the north west corner of Broadway and Main, which had been erected with money supplied by the Town Trustees. On March 20, 1780, they voted "the sum of thirty pounds gold, and granted one acre of ground to build a court house, prison and office, provided that court was to be held in Lexington." The jail was a log hut, standing just west of Broadway on north side of Main street. The court house was built of logs, rived with a whipsaw[1] a more detailed description is to be found in an advertisement in the Kentucky Gazette, dated January 16, 1800—

> "For Rent—That excellent stand at the corner of Main and Main Cross streets, Lexington, known by the name of the Old Court House. The House is two stories high with two rooms on each floor, each eighteen foot square, with fire places in each, and two good dry cellars eighteen feet square."

In the issue of the Gazette dated February 16, 1788, a news item and advertisement says—"that a court house committee had been appointed by the court, composed of Edward Payne, Robert Todd, Levi Todd, Thomas Lewis, Robert Johnson, James Trotter and William Campbell to choose the site for the new court house, draft the plans and oversee the erection." Levi Todd, the county clerk, had his office in a one-story stone building, located on the north side of the Richmond pike, just east of the Lexington reservoir. This building burned during the night of January 31, 1803, with the records. A few scraps of paper were carefully preserved, and, under act of the Kentucky Legislature, were copied into eight volumes, and now on file in the vault of the Fayette County Clerk, marked

---

1 Interview with J. Kemper, Draper MSS. 12CC130.

"Burnt Records." Many of the citizens brought deeds and other papers to the clerk's office to be re-entered.

The committee which had been named in the order of Court on February 16, 1788, built a stone court house of eight rooms and a hallway and a four angle roof.[1] It was never very attractive nor satisfactory to those who used it, and evidently considerable difficulty was experienced by Jeremiah Murphy, custodian, in keeping it clean. His salary was 13 pounds per year, which he strongly objected to expending on janitors. During the years of 1804 and 1805 the Gazette frequently referred to the necessity for a new building, and when the time approached for the new Legislature to convene, the Gazette suggested that "efforts should be made to secure a more commodious building." The new Legislature granted authority to hold courts in any building in Lexington and the old Mt. Zion church building at the corner of Walnut and Short streets was used until the new building could be completed. The committee of citizens for the new court house was composed of William Dudley, Hezekiah Harrison, John Parker, John C. Richardson, Leonard Young, Thomas Wallace and Robert S. Russell "authorized to select plans and supervise the construction."

This committee met on February 18, 1806 at Megowan's tavern, opened the bids and accepted the plan of David Sutton, "who was to dispose of the Old court house and to have the new one erected on center of the public ground." Asa Farrar was allowed 15 shillings for fencing the court house yard. The specifications of the new building were—

> "to be 60 by 50 feet, foundation of stone, 3 1-3 feet below the surface and one foot above, and building to be three stories high—first story 14 feet high with walls three brick thick, second story to be 12 feet high and walls 2 1-2 brick thick, and third floor to be ten feet high with walls two brick thick. First floor has

---

[1] On site of present court house.

two offices each 16 feet by 20 feet, arched over
with brick.   Front of house to be of stock
or sand brick, laid with lime and sand mortar.
All the structure to have pavilion roof with
shingles 18 inches long and one inch thick at
lower end.   Court room—the floor for the bar
and the judges seat 20 feet long and two feet
higher than the pavement, with sleepers 3 by
15 inches and 12 inches apart.   Judges seat 3
feet higher than the floor in circular form
with panel work, lawyer's bar, Sheriff's boxes
and a chair for the Judge of the court to be in
neat work.   Lawyers' bar, Judges' seat, two
jury boxes to be bannistered in front; a box
for the accused placed near the center and
back of the lawyers' bar.   The Clerk's table to
be oval and placed between the two jury boxes
and bannistered in; a bench for witnesses to
be placed in front of the lawyers' bar.   Fire
place in each office in same stack of chimneys.
Main floor raised as high as stone work with
clay and rammed hard for the offices and for
that part of the floor which will not be planked,
to be laid in brick or tile.   At the same time
and place will be sold the material of the Old
court House."

This building was faulty in some manner, as the
records of the county court show a considerable sum
of money was spent in 1814, "to keep it in repair."   A
clock was added to the cupola in 1806 but failed to
perform satisfactorily and was replaced in 1814.   In
1823 the first iron fence was placed around the block.[1]

The photographs of this building show it was not
an attractive building but it probably compared favor-
ably with any similar structure of that period west of
the Alleghanies.   It was never admired by visitors
and was much ridiculed by the citizens.   Henry Clay,
in a letter from Washington May 9, 1812, to John W.
Hunt said: "The miserable building put up for a

[1] Kentucky Reporter, February 10, 1823.

Court House in Lexington—the disgrace of the town
and the derision of everybody—ought to admonish us
to proceed with more discretion in our public edifices."

Edward West made the first county seal, for which
he was allowed one pound ten shillings.[1]

A very strong or very large jail was not needed
in Fayette County as "few offenders escaped punish-
ment upon legal technicalities but speedily found himself in the stocks, or at the whipping post, for the
administration of frontier justice had no long code as
their guide, and so only had to consider the needs of
primitive justice." There was a whipping post and
pillory in front of the log jail that stood on Main
street just west of Broadway. Evidently some es-
capes were effected, as the Gazette for January 2,
1790, advertises:

> "TO BE LET—to the lowest bidder at Cap-
> tain Thomas Young's tavern in Lexington, on
> second Tuesday in February next (it being
> court day) at 3 o'clock in the afternoon, the
> building of a STONE JAIL.
>
> Thirty two feet long—twenty feet wide and
> seventeen feet pitch above the lower floor, a
> plan of which will be shown on that day;
> also, the erecting of a pillory and stocks and
> whipping post.
>
> Edward Payne
Levi Todd
Robert Todd
Thomas Lewis
James Trotter."

This stone jail was erected on the west side of
Limestone above Short street, and evidently became
defective in some manner as the Gazette contains frequent advertisements "for escaped prisoners." On
March 25, 1797 another committee was appointed to
"receive bids for a new jail" which was erected near

---

[1] Fayette County Court Order Book "A", page 19.

same location, but even this one was not satisfactory as the Gazette on March 15, 1803 mentions "the unsatisfactory condition of our new jail."

A black locust whipping post, one foot in diameter, ten feet high and 2 1-2 feet in the ground, stood on Main street west of Broadway. This was removed to Broadway just north of Main street, at rear of court house. When the stone court house was built a similar post was erected on northeast corner of the court house yard.[1]

The county court order books contain frequent reference to the "Jail bounds". These marks were placed on the various streets, outside of which prisoners with privileges were not permitted to go. These were usually those confined for debts, and these bounds permitted them to adjust business matters and frequently reside at home. In November 1803 the jail bounds were Mulberry to Water, thence to Mill, thence to Short, thence to Market, thence to Church and back to Mulberry.[2]

Among the court entries for the July term 1798 is a record of the nationality of a number of men who afterwards were prominent in civic affairs: John Arthur and William Ross "from Scotland" were naturalized "they have been two years a resident of the United States and one year a resident of the Commonwealth of Kentucky." Other entries of similar nature for the same term of court mention:

David Reed, from Scotland,
William Reed, from Scotland,
Waldemard Mentelle, from France,
Thomas Whitney, from Ireland,
James H. Stewart, from Ireland,
Cornelius Coyle, from Ireland.

The rush of immgrants from the trans-alleghany states carried with it many who were well prepared

1 Fayette County Order Book "6", page 311.
2 Fayette County Order Book No. 1, pages 85 and 95.

by education and training to be entitled to be called
lawyers, but there was hardly enough practice for all
who located in the Town of Lexington, and a number
soon acquired interests other than "the black letter,"
as we find records to show that some worked as surveyors, some managed their farms, some taught in the
law school, and others had interests in the stores and
participated "in mercantile adventures" down the river.
Among these were Christopher Greenup, afterwards
Governor, who had a store in a stone building located
on the southeast corner of Mill and Main streets;
John Coburn, afterwards United States Judge in Mississippi territory; Charles Humphrey, who had a store
on Cheapside, in addition to a chain of blacksmith
shops, and who wrote several law books; Judge Fielding
L. Turner, who was a partner in several stores, and
at one time conducting an exporting business in New
Orleans; John Cockey Owings, who developed the
Iron Works on Salt creek. All of these names appear
as connected with "trading adventures" at the same
periods their names appear as representing litigants
in the courts.

Many of the pioneer advocates were men of unusual
ability, and "having no precedents as a guide had to
make them." It is regrettable that the exploits of many
of them have escaped the knowledge of the present generation. With only limited libraries and no compiled
reports from other courts, these early lawyers were
dependent upon their knowledge of the common law,
their logical reasoning and their forensic ability to sway
their juries. "Exercising a commanding influence
the short time of seventeen years from the time the
first fort was built converted Kentucky into a state."

The first settler of Lexington who could properly
call himself a lawyer probably was John Todd, who
had been admitted as an attorney in Botetourt County,
Virginia, on May 14, 1771. He was at the "famous
Elm Tree assembly at Boonesborough in 1775,"—after
serving as Aide to General Andrew Lewis in the Battle
of Point Pleasant. He was a member of the first

court organized at Harrodsburg, delegate to the Virginia Assembly from Kentucky, trustee for the Town of Lexington, first colonel of the Fayette county militia, was in command and fell on the battle field at the Blue Licks.

George Nicholas came to Lexington in 1788 and became the first Attorney General for Kentucky. He was first professor of Law in Transylvania Seminary Law department and died in his 55th year at his home now the seat of Sayre College, cutting short a brilliant career.

Buckner Thruston removed to Lexington in 1788, clerk of the first Kentucky Senate, District Judge of Kentucky 1791, U. S. Senator 1805-1809, when he resigned to accept appointment as U. S. Judge for District of Columbia where he served until his death in 1845.

John Breckinridge arrived in Lexington 1793, admitted to the bar in Botetourt County, Virginia, March 1785 and elected to congress the same year from the Albemarle district but resigned and moved to Lexington. U. S. Senator 1801-1805, and then resigned to accept appointment as Attorney General for the United States in cabinet of President Jefferson. He died the next year.

James Brown, brother of Dr. Samuel Brown and of the Honorable John Brown, Captain in expedition against the Indians in 1789, Secretary to Governor Shelby in 1792, removed to New Orleans after cession of Louisiana to United States and several times elected to the United States Senate.

John Pope removed to Lexington November 1805, State representative three times, U. S. Senator 1807-1813, Governor Territory of Arkansas 1829-1833, Congressman 1837-1843. He died July 12, 1845.

William T. Barry came to Kentucky 1796, graduate of William and Mary, also Transylvania University, Commonwealth Attorney for this district, elected to Congress, aide-de-camp to Governor Shelby during the War of 1812, Speaker of Kentucky House of Representatives, U. S. Senator 1814 to 1816, resigned to become Circuit Judge for Lexington 1816-1817, State Senator 1817-1821, Lieutenant Governor 1820, Professor of Law and Politics at Transylvania Law School 1822, Secretary of State 1824, Chief Justice Court of Appeals 1825, Postmaster General in cabinet of President Andrew Jackson 1829 to 1835 when he resigned to accept appointment as Envoy Extraordinary and Minister Plenipotentiary to Spain. He died enroute to take his post. The citizens of Lexington erected a monument to his memory at north-west corner of Main and Upper streets which mysteriously disappeared during the construction of the present court house. His residence still stands on what is now Angliana Avenue.

Christopher Greenup served in Virginia Regiment during early part of Revolutionary War, Member of Virginia Assembly in 1785, clerk of Town Trustees in Lexington, had store at Main and Mill, clerk of District Court at Harrodsburg 1785-1792; Congressman 1792-1797; State Representative 1798; Clerk Kentucky Senate 1799-1802; Judge of Circuit Court 1802; Governor of Kentucky 1804-1808.

Humphrey Marshall, Captain of Virginia Cavalry in Revolutionary War and surveyor; removed to Kentucky in 1780; delegate to Virginia Assembly, state representative four times, United States Senator 1795-1801. He wrote a history of Kentucky in 1812, which in 1824 he re-wrote adding much new material.

James Hughes was the author of the first Kentucky Law Reports, which, in addition to their legal value, add much to the historical information about early Kentucky sites and locations. His copy of the awards of the first Land Court of Kentucky are now in the vault of the Fayette County Court Clerk's office.

George M. Bibb graduated at William and Mary college, and at Hampden-Sidney, removed to Lexington 1793; Circuit Judge in 1805; Member of Court of Appeals 1808, Chief Justice 1809, United States Sena-

tor 1811-1814 and again from 1829 to 1835, then becoming Secretary of the Treasury under President
Tyler.

John Coburn came to Lexington 1784, as partner
in store with George Gordon. Removed to Mason
County 1794, Judge of District Court; Judge Mason
Circuit Court; Judge for Orleans Territory, member
of commission to settle boundary dispute between
Virginia and Kentucky.

Benjamin Howard, member of Kentucky Legisla-
ture in 1800; member Congress 1807-1810; Governor
Louisiana Territory 1810-1812 and Brigadier General
U. S. Army.

Jesse Bledsoe, graduated Transylvania University,
practiced Law in Fayette and Bourbon Counties and
represented both counties in the Kentucky Legislature.
He was secretary of State under Governor Charles
Scott in 1808, United State Senator 1813-1815, Circuit
Judge for Lexington 1822, and professor of Common
Law at Transylvania Law School. He abandoned the
bar for the pulpit during the religious movement under
Barton Stone. He removed to Texas where he died
in 1836.

Joseph Hamilton Daviess came to Kentucky in
1779. He served in the Army in 1792, United States
District Attorney for Kentucky in 1802. He undertook
to secure indictment against Aaron Burr on a charge
of high Misdemeanor, but the grand jury returned
"not a true bill". He was killed while leading a
cavalry charge in the Battle of Tippacanoe in 1811.

Henry Clay began the practice of law in Lexington
in 1798 and was elected to nearly every office within
the gift of his constituents. He was an unsuccessful
candidate for the Presidency in 1832 and 1844 and
left a greater name than either of the victors. "For
fifty years he moulded the composite mind of the
state with such complete mastery as has perhaps
never been equalled in any American state."

An examination of the pleadings of actions brought
in the District Court and the Fayette Circuit Court

show the following appeared representing litigants before the Lexington Bar: James Haggin, Robert Todd, Allen Bowie Macgruder, John A. Cape, Isham Talbott, Thomas Todd, Felix Grundy, William Murray, Jr., William Clarke, Robert Wickliffe, Patterson Bullock, John Boyle, John Rowan, William Jordan, Alexander Marshall, James McChord, William B. Martin, James Fishback, Fielding L. Turner, William Todd, James January, William Stevenson, Alfred W. Grayson, William Warren, Samuel Venable and Edmund Bullock.

The increasing litigation due to "the villianous set of land laws inherited from Virginia" soon crowded the Circuit court and, after 1803, we find additions to the list of lawyers practicing before the Lexington bar. Adam Beatty, Sam. H. Woodson, Wm. McIlheny, Josiah Stoddard, John P. Oldham, John Thompson, Mann Butler, Derrick January, Asa K. Lewis and Benedict VanPradeles. The latter accepted appointment as Registrar of the Land Office in the Territory of Orleans and died January 24, 1809.

The exceptional ability of the Lexington bar at this period gave it a wide preeminence and very few courts could present a similar array of talent and legal acumen.

PIONEER PUPILS AND PEDAGOGUES.

T HERE may have been a school for the children of
the Lexington settlement but no record has been
found for any period until the year 1782 when John
McKinney was installed as instructor in a cabin that
stood on what is now the east side of Cheapside.
"The children used to be in a hurry to get to school
in the morning so they could get a drink from the
spring. They used a horn spoon and the flow of
water was slow, so they could get only a spoonful
at a time."[1] McKinney had been in the Battle of
Point Pleasant (October 1774), where he was seriously
wounded in a personal encounter with an Indian. After
teaching in Lexington for several years, he removed
to Bourbon county, where he died near Clintonville.[2]
One of the pupils of that time says:

> "I was going to McKinney at the time of the
> wild cat scare. He had gone into the school
> very early in the morning before the sun was
> up, probably to write a letter to his friends in
> Virginia, and had left the door half open as he
> went in. When the cat came in, he was sitting
> on the opposite side of the bench writing. He
> saw, as he thought, that the cat was mad and
> threw his ruler at it. It then flew at him.
> McKinney screamed, and when they came in
> from the fort—the old fort—he told them not
> to come near, the cat was mad. He wo'd not
> let them touch it. It scratched and tore him
> very much before he could conquer it, not hav-
> ing the use of his left hand, on which he wore
> a glove. He finally choked it to death. After
> this McKinney taught until the 9th day, when
> he dismissed school. He nearly starved him-
> self and was withal most frightened to death.
> All the scholars that went to the school were
> from the fort. At the time of this incident

[1] J. H. McKinney interview, Draper MSS. 11CC41.
[2] Ware interview, Draper MSS. 11CC166.

there was no other house but the school house
yet built out of the fort. Many of the boys
were sent merely to keep them from wander-
ing about where the Indians would get them."[1]

Another pioneer pedagogue was John Filson, who
wrote the only narrative of the life of Daniel Boone
secured direct from the famous frontier leader. He
produced "The Discovery, Settlement and Present State
of Kentucky," which was printed at Wilmington, Del.,
in 1784, pp. 118; reprinted in Paris, France and Frank-
fort-on-the-Main in 1785; in New York in 1793, and in
London in 1793 and again in 1797, and at least one
other German publication. A copy of the Wilmington
edition with the map laid in and both in good condition, recently sold for a figure far beyond any possible
dream of the author in his lifetime.

Filson's name first appears in the Gazette in the
issue dated January 19, 1788, when a card is published
regarding the proposed seminary in Lexington:

"Tuition five pounds per annum, one-half cash,
one-half produce. Boarding and lodging within
one mile of town at 9 pounds per annum. Those
who wish to secure lodging will apply to Mr.
Barr and Mr. Coburn in Lexington. Begin
sometime in April, and French language with
all sciences and arts will be taught. In the
beginning of April all students will apply for
entrance, as I shall be constantly in Lexington
from that time.
                                          John Filson."

Any information as to the response to this appeal
is entirely lacking. Filson became interested in the
establishment of the town of "Losantiville," now Cincinnati, and left Lexington with Robert Patterson and
Mathias Denman about the close of September 1788,
and in a few days he disappeared and was supposedly
killed by the Indians. Another early teacher was
Thomas Parvin, who had been a typesetter on Brad-

[1] Wymore interview, Draper MSS. 11CC128.

ford's Gazette. He had taught school at Strode's station before coming to Lexington and, after severing his connection with Mr. Bradford, taught for the Town of Lexington.[1] No record has been found indicating any date of his services or the number of children attending. He was succeeded by one ——— Hutchison.

The first mention of a school found in the trustees' minute book is the record of an undated meeting, at which a committee consisting of Robert Patterson, Samuel Blair and Robert Barr "were appointed to lay off part of the public ground set apart for a graveyard, for the purpose of erecting thereon lattin and english school house and make report to the next meeting." This entry follows an item dated March 7, 1788, and precedes a meeting dated November 12, 1788, which contains no reference to this subject.

Isaac Wilson "from Philadelphia college" arrived in 1787, and established the Lexington Grammar school. His advertisement (Gazette January 12, 1788) says: "The Lexington School has opened again. The learned subjects of Latin and Greek and the different branches of science will be taught by Isaac Wilson, formerly professor in Philadelphia College. The expenses of schooling are reasonable as charges are four pounds in cash or produce, boarding to be had at reasonable rates."

A "poor simple looking Simon" is a description of his appearance given by Mrs. Ann Biddle Wilkinson,[2] the wife of James Wilkinson, who had Isaac Wilson as tutor for her two young sons, yet she appeared to be thoroughly satisfied with the progress they made under him.

The only record found of the Scott school is an item in the Gazette of October 1787: "William Scott—schoolmaster—requests all those who owe him for schooling and books to please call and settle."

On October 4, 1788 the Gazette advertised a seminary "for instruction in reading, writing and arithmetic, English grammar, speaking, composition and Geog-

[1] Fielding Bradford interview, Draper MSS. 13CC211.
[2] Penn. Mag. of History and Biography, Vol. LVI, No. 1, 1932-Hay.

raphy was to be opened. Two classes of scholars
are to be taught. First will be taught reading, writing
and arithmetic for eight shillings per quarter, and the
others receive the entire course for ten shillings."

In the Gazette dated October 4, 1788 appears this
advertisement:

> "James Graham notifies the public he will
> open a seminary of learning, and also an office
> at his house where deeds, bonds and other
> agreements will be drawn."

Judging by the frequent advertisements appearing in the Gazette there was no shortage of teachers.
On May 24, 1788, one advertiser claimed "experience
in teaching reading, writing, arithmetic, booking, sur-
veying and navigation, use of globes, etc." Another
teacher advertises on October 11, 1788, "to give instruction in geometry, trigonometry and algebra." The
Gazette for January 8, 1791, advertises:

> "Tis mere necessity that makes it requisite to
> request all those indebited to me for school-
> ing, books, etc., to pay it on or before the
> 20th day of this month. Those readily com-
> plying will much oblige their humble servant.
>   Jacob Lehre."

A night school was operated in connection with
this day school by Mr. Lehre, in addition to which he
served several years as clerk of the Town Trustees
before his removal to Bourbon county where he left
many descendants.

Hugh Wilson operated a school at the corner of
High and Upper streets beginning in January 1791,
which lasted for several years. Thomas Steele had a
night school this same year which also prospered, as
it was still going in 1797. He taught "accounts, navigation and mathematics."

An effort of the town trustees to secure a reliable
teacher for the town school is shown in the issue of
the Gazette, dated April 28, 1792:

"As the time for which the present teacher of
the Lexington school is employed expires on
the last of May next, and as he has informed
the trustees that his health is so far declined
that he cannot continue any longer, therefore-

WANTED.

Teacher to take charge of said school from the
first of June next, who can come well recommended for his abilities as an English teacher,
as also for his morals and no other need apply.
By Order of the Trustees."

Jacob Thomas advertised a music school on December 2, 1792, and Alexander Woodrow a grammar
school March 8, 1794. He also served several years
as surveyor for the Town.

Dates in the Gazette of other "first" advertisements
show schools were conducted by Peter Valentine, a
French school beginning July 1, 1794; "The Music
School," June 13, 1795; Charles Barbier, a French
School, August 8, 1795; Duty's English school, on
Water street near Mill the same year;[1] Chapin's sing-
ing school, May 1797 and Lucy Gray's school for young
ladies, March 29, 1797.

"The Lexington Seminary of Education, for
the benefit of the Societies in this State under
the inspection of the Associated Reform Synod,
of which are at present members John Mason
of New York, Robert Anman of Philadelphia
and Adam Rankin of Lexington, adhering to
the West Minster confession of faith, cate-
cism longer and shorter directory for public
worship, and the form of the Presbyterian
Church, etc.,"

was located on Walnut street between Rankin's Mt.
Zion church and Main street and was under the
management of the local trustees Adam Rankin, John
McChord and David Logan. This deed, recorded in
District Court Book "A", page 346, and dated Sep-

[1] This school seems to have been under Presbyterian control.

tember 10, 1797, represents another effort to teach
"the young mind" denominational tenets along with
the three R's.

R. Gilbert's fencing school was advertised June
6, 1798 and in the issue of Gazette, dated July 11, 1798,
B. Holdish advertises:

> "To the Ladies and Gentlemen of Lexington:
> "I am engaged to return to Pittsburg in a
> few weeks and beg leave to resign my pre-
> tentions to their patronage in favor of W.
> Mentelle, a gentleman since arrived and who
> intends residing in Lexington."

In the Gazette dated July 20, 1798 is advertised:

> "Waldemard Mentelle, encouraged by a num-
> ber of respectable persons, has lately removed
> to the Town of Lexington, where he pro-
> poses, with the assistance of his wife, to teach
> young people of both sexes, French language
> and dancing."

The success of this school enabled the owners to
widen the range of study and they later removed the
school to the north side of the Richmond Road, opposite Ashland where they continued for many years.
No doubt the story of the romantic escape of Mr. and
Mrs. Mentelle from Revolutionary France and their
subsequent experiences among the French settlers at
Gallipolis had much to do with this school being well
advertised.

Other early schools advertised were those of Samuel
Price on March 29, 1798; and of John Hargy and
daughter, who had a school at the former house
of Colonel Robert Patterson, on High street, from
March 28, 1799, until the death of Mr. Hargy June 11,
1802. This school was advertised as "being under
patronage of Reverend Adam Rankin, John McChord
and Archibald McIlvane." This school had been located near the Mt. Zion Church on Walnut street but
was removed to High Street (Gazette, March 1797).
Joshua L. Wilson, July 1799; Charles V. Lourimier, a

dancing school at "Major Morrison's on High street," August 2, 1799; Samuel Munnet, a French school, November 9, 1802; William Smith, December 13, 1803; Mrs. Beck's school for young ladies, February 1, 1805; Ann Welch who began teaching "sewing, knitting and the fine accomplishments" on February 26, 1805, and Mr. and Mrs. Green's academy January 9, 1806.

News items about these schools frequently appear in the Gazette, when commencements were held, and at that time the Principal's address usually had something to say for the benefit of the parents on "the importance of educating children." Many advertisements for teachers made special mention of "sobriety and attention" (Gazette, May 28, 1802). On November 3, 1806 Mr. and Mrs. Lockwood open a boarding school to educate "youngsters," while another teacher claimed "the education of children too important to be tampered with, hence he promised to make all necessary progress."

Many of these schools advertised hours of attendance during the summer months as "6 A. M. to Noon and from 2 P. M. to 6 P. M." Several of them claimed to "prepare for higher schools," evidently referring to Transylvania College.

Transylvania had its beginning with eight thousand acres of escheated land, some of which had been the property of Robert McKenzie, Henry Collins and Alexander McKee, that were set aside by act of the Virginia Assembly in 1780, "to establish a public school, or seminary of learning, under the trusteeship of William Fleming, William Christian, John Todd, Stephen Trigg, Benjamin Logan, John Floyd, John May, Levi Todd, Edmund Taylor, Walker Daniel, John Cowan, George Merriwether and John Cobbs." Seven of these trustees were to meet death at the hands of Indians—John Todd and Stephen Trigg at the Battle of the Blue Licks; John Floyd in Jefferson County; William Christian in Indiana near Louisville; Walker Daniel in Mercer County; John Cowan and John May while riding in boats on the Ohio River, an instance probably without parallel among American colleges.

This school was opened in the house of Mr. David Rice, near Danville in 1785, and in 1788 was removed to Lexington, "tuition five pounds per year, in property, pork, corn, tobacco, etc." The Reverend James Mitchell served as head-master during the term held in 1785 and when the school was removed to Lexington, Mr. Isaac Wilson was elected head at 60 pounds per year. The Reverend James Moore was elected to take charge in 1791. "No suitable house could be had and Mr. Moore subjected himself to the inconvenience of keeping school in his own house," says the trustees' book and they promptly voted him an allowance.

A group of Lexington citizens, realizing the value of the school to the Town of Lexington, had subscribed sufficient funds to purchase Outlot No. 6, now known as Gratz Park, and offered it to the trustees of the school "provided the school is permanently located in the town of Lexington."[1]

A plain two-story brick building of eight rooms and hallway was erected on the north end of this lot, facing Second street, in 1794, and this was the home of the Seminary until 1817, when a larger structure was found necessary and a three-story brick building with a tall cupola was erected in the middle of Gratz Park, with the front on a line with Mechanic street and the home of Mr. Gratz. This building was accidently destroyed by fire in May 1829, by a servant of Cassius M. Clay.

The Reverend James Moore was Principal until 1794. He did much to raise the standard of the Seminary. He had been educated for the Presbyterian ministry, but joined the Episcopalians and became Rector of Christ Church in Lexington. His wife was a daughter of Reverend John Todd, father of the bill before the Virginia Assembly establishing Transylvania Seminary. Mr. Moore was the reputed hero of James Lane Allen's "Flute and Violin."

[1] Minute Book Trustees of Lexington, page 271.

The Reverend Harry Toulmin became Principal in 1794 and this started a sectarian controversy, the Presbyterians withdrawing their patronage and starting a rival academy at Pisgah called "The Kentucky Academy." After much controversy the two schools were merged in 1798 under the name of Transylvania University, and the Reverend James Moore became acting president. On January 8, 1799, the trustees voted to establish a medical department and, also, a law school, with Drs. Samuel Brown and Frederick Ridgely as professors of the first named and the Honorable George Nicholas first professor of the Law school. Medical history of Kentucky will accord Dr. Brown considerable fame for his efforts to spread the practice of inoculation for the small pox. In 1801, James Blythe was made acting President which position he filled until 1816.

The medical school did not have a large number of students at that period and they attended their instructors by visiting from "one doctor's shop to another." Their success after leaving college gave the institution well-deserved fame.

Mr. Nicholas did not long survive the beginning of the law school and was succeeded by the Honorable Henry Clay.

The trustees' minute book of Transylvania presents many interesting items and customs. On June 1, 1789 there was a "committee appointed to draw a scheme for a lottery." At the meeting in October, 1789, "Committee reported upon the success of the lottery." At the January meeting, 1790, "Committee appointed to assist the President in correcting the morals of the students."

Other items mention "kitchen to be erected convenient to the Seminary" and "an agreement with Mrs. Richardson, steward, to diet, wash and mend for the scholars, professors and visitors to the college at 15 pounds per year." Also, "an outdoor leanto with oven, to be built for her use, a new well to be dug and she allowed the right to make a garden and coverlot." (Trustees' book, Jan. 1797). "On account of the excessive cold weather of the past week it will be necessary to erect a stove and pipe in the recitation room at the University" (Trustees' book, March 1, 1797). "No student of Transylvania to take part in any theatrical performance of any kind." (Trustees' book, March 10, 1797). "Religious services to be held daily at sunrise and all students to attend under penalty of confinement to their rooms." (Trustees' book, October, 1798). Other items in this interesting record —"Students will furnish their own bedding, candles and firewood for their apartments." Study hours will be from Sunrise to 8 A. M., 9 to 12 and 2 to 3:30 P. M." "Students shall not play at cards, dice or any unlawful games, nor frequent places of licentious amusements." "Students shall not go to Taverns under any circumstances, either for drinks or free lunch." and "Parents are requested to be very sparing in granting money to their sons."

"No university was ever inaugurated on a broader and more comprehensive scale. Had this system been adhered to Transylvania would today be one of the greatest institutions of learning in the world."

THE TOWN FATHERS.

THE Town of Lexington was governed by a Board of Trustees as provided in the Act of the Virginia Assembly establishing the town. This method of government was continued until Lexington was incorporated in 1832. The first trustees were named in the act, and after that the trustees were chosen by popular vote at elections held the last of each year or, at the beginning of the new year (Gazette, April 30, 1791 and December 10, 1801).

The personnel of the board usually comprised men of varied interests, all were prominent in the affairs of the town, and their actions appear to have been for the best interests of a growing frontier village. Many of the early resolutions of the board seem strange in this day, but the early ordinances show civic concern developed early and the trustees made conscientious efforts to improve the conditions of the Town.

The town had been established by Act of the Virginia Assembly, dated May 6, 1782, which reads in part:

"Whereas, it is represented to this assembly that 640 acres of unapportioned land in the county of Fayette, whereon the court house of said county stands, have been, by the settlers thereon, laid out into lots and streets for a town, and that the said settlers have purchased seventy acres of land contiguous to the said 640 acres, being part of a survey for John Floyd, and whereas, it would tend greatly to the improvement and settling the same if the titles of settlers on the lots were confirmed and a town established thereon,

Be it therefore enacted, that the said 710 acres of land be, and the same is hereby vested in fee simple in John Todd, Robert Patterson, William Mitchell, Andrew Steele, William Henderson, William McConnell and William

Steele, gentleman, trustees, and, established
by the name of Lexington.

Be it further enacted, that the said trustees,
or any four of them shall, and they are hereby
empowered and required, to make conveyance
to those persons who have already settled on
the said lots, as also, to the purchasers of lots
heretofore sold, agreeable to the condition of
the contracts, and may also proceed to lay off
other parts of the said lands as is not yet laid
off and settled into lots and streets, - - . Provided always, that the lots, in said town, which
have been laid off and set apart for erecting
thereon the public buildings of said county,
shall be and remain to and for that use and
purpose and no other whatever."

"that it shall and may be lawful for the
freeholders and free male inhabitants of the
town of Lexington, in the county of Fayette,
and those within one-mile of the court house
in said town aged 21 years, other than free
negroes and mulattoes, who have resided therein for the space of six months and who possess
in their own right within the said town, mov-
able property of the value of 25 pounds, to
elect and choose seven trustees, which election
shall be conducted by the sheriff of said county,
and held at the court house, on the second
Monday in May next, of which previous notice
shall be given at the door of the court house -

The Sheriff shall make a return of the persons elected to the clerk of the court and return a fair copy of the poll, by him taken to
the person having the greatest number of
votes - - .

The said trustees or their successors, or a
majority of them, shall have the power to erect
and repair a market house in said town and to
appoint a clerk of the market, to regulate and
repair the streets and highways; to remove
nuisances and obstructions therein and to im-
pose taxes not exceeding 100 pounds annually on the tithables and property real and
personal, within the said town limits."

This act makes provisions for the election of the trustees and the manner of filling vacancies and also stated the qualifications of the voters. Before notice of the passing of this act had been received, the pioneers had elected on March 21, 1781, Levi Todd, David Mitchell, Robert Patterson, Henry McDonald and Michael Warnock as trustees to control the affairs of the town. This board met and "resolved that the town liad off in in-lots." These in-lots were to contain 1-3 part of an acre each, and they were granted to "each male person above the age of 21 years, each widow, every young man who can make it appear he acts in his own behalf and is not under the immediate control and jurisdiction of some other persons, who at the time of laying them off and distributing them appears to be an actual resident within the place, - - .

"That a number of inlots—not less than thirty— be reserved for public uses and such other purposes as may be hereafter be requisite."

The minute book of the trustees now preserved in the Treasurer's office at the Lexington City Hall, has the act of the Virginia Assembly establishing the town recorded on the first page, then follows the result of the election held for the trustees, then a survey of the town by Robert Todd, dated March 24, 1791 showing a circle one mile from the Court house and containing 2,011 acres.[1] Next is a map of the inlots and outlots, and under date of December 20, 1781 an order directing that "13 poles square be left for a church of public worship."

At the last named meeting the trustees resolved— "each lot holder to build a house, or houses, equal to 18 feet square, with chimney and that James Todd, Charles Williams, George Shepherd, William Howard, Robert Parker, Meason Lunfort and Robert Odd are entitled to Lots."

The only business recorded in the next few meetings was the granting of lots to Benjamin Briggs, Val.

1 See Page 22 for Plat.

Dickinson, William Henderson, William Herrin, Adam
Zumwalt, Joel Collins, James January, James Masterson
and Arch. Dickinson.

One meeting of this board deserves special mention
in view of subsequent happenings.   On August 14,
1782, the board met to appraise the lots issued to James
McConnell, deceased, for the benefit of his heirs, and
to declare forfeited inlot No. 49, that had been issued
to Richard Sharp (now 216 West Main street).   On
the following night Simon Girty and his Indians began
the memorable siege of Bryan's station.   Four days
later one member of the board was a mutilated corpse
on the bloody battle field at the Blue Licks, and another maimed for life.   Following this no meeting was
held by the board until September 30, and the next on
December 12, when Colonel Robert Patterson was
elected chairman and Captain Robert Todd a member
to fill the vacancy caused by the death of Colonel John
Todd.   At this same meeting the board declared forfeited the lots that had been issued in the names of
Elisha Collins, James McGinty and William Mitchell,
and "Resolved—those living on north side of the Town
Branch shall meet on January 2nd at the spring to
assist in walling same."

No other meetings are recorded in the trustees'
book until July 1, 1783, when the trustees "Resolved
—no lots shall be forfeited to the holders thereof, until
12 months after public notice shall be given by advertisement at the court house door."

Below this notice and continued on to the next
page is a list of inlots issued.   No record has been
preserved of any meetings held during the year 1784
but on March 8, 1785 the trustees met and declared
forfeited all lots not built upon.   Evidently some pres-
sure was brought to bear upon them, as they relented
according to the next entry: "Resolved—that it is the
opinion of the said board that the situation of the
holders of the lots forfeited by the above resolution

(from the infant situation of our country, and the difficulty of procuring materials for building) in some measure claim their indulgence."

"Resolved—further, that each lot holder on which time limit has expired for making improvements shall have preference of preemption of such lot, provided the clerk of the trustees on or before the second Wednesday in May be paid the sum of 12 shillings for each lot forfeited." The next meeting recorded in the trustees' book is dated August 9, 1785, when they "Resolved—that Robert Parker retain in his hands of the public money, for transcribing the old book and for furnishing an account book, the sum of six dollars."

This entry indicates another book had been used to record the minutes of the board prior to this date, and the entries had been transcribed into a newer book. This subject came up again five years later when, on March 8, 1790, the minutes show this order:

"Resolved—Robert Patterson, James Parker, Robert Parker and Samuel McMillen do meet and confer on the matter of transcribing the books of the Trustees, and select or throw out such parts as seem erroneous, or useless, and make a report of their proceedings at the next meeting of the Board."

Under this authority the committee evidently did not transcribe any of the minutes for meetings held during the year of 1784, and possibly a number of other meetings.

The next meetings recorded are dated July 3, 1790; September 12, 1790, and February 26, 1791. It would appear, from the entries of meetings held on August 6, 1785 and March 6, 1790, that the minute book of the trustees now preserved in the vault of the City Hall was not the original book used by the trustees. On May 1, 1815, the committee of the trustees for that year, John Fowler, Andrew McCalla and Samuel Ayers, advertised:

"Having understood that one of the record books of the Town was some years ago lost, or mislaid, beg to favor of those that were formerly clerks - - to examined their old records to see if it cannot be found. The present trustees understand it was like a common account book containing about three quires of paper and had been rules for pounds, shillings and pense, in which columns the numbers of the lots were placed, and had a pasteboard cover colored blue or purple, with waves or cracked strokes through the coloring. It was very common, some years ago, for such books to be lent to such persons as wanted to examine into numbers of titles or lots, and which might lie many years unnoticed without some attention. Ten dollars reward will be paid for the return of this book."

On page 16, of the trustees' minute book, dated August 9, 1785, is the first mention of the claim of John Bradford for the town site. The trustees authorized Robert Patterson to employ an attorney to contest this claim, and the suit was tried before the Supreme court for the District of Kentucky sitting at Harrodsburg on June 21st and 22nd, 1786:

"The Trustees of Lexington   plt
    against
John Bradford   dft

Upon caveat for
400 acres of land
in Fayette county.

"This day came the parties aforesaid by their attorneys and the sheriff is ordered to cause to come here immediately twelve good and lawful men who joined to make a jury thereof between the parties, and thereupon came a jury, to wit: Littleberry Mosby, James Moody, Humphrey Marshall, William Gaines, Peter Tardiveau, William Kennedy, Samuel Mc-

Dowell, Robert Johnson, Robert Craddock, John Rogers, James Moore, and James Speed who being elected tried and sworn well and truly to enquire of such facts that may be material and not agreed upon by the parties, on their oath do say that the settlement of the Town of Lexington was made in April 1779. That the town was laid off into lots in April 1779. That the improvements then made and lotts then laid off were upon lands now a part of the Town of Lexington, that the improvements then consisted of a block-house and a dwelling house: That the settlers had begun in April to clear lands and corn planted early in May. The conditions that they settled upon were to lay off a township or village for their own safety. That Colo. Floyd's corner trees has not been found, but that it appears to us from the return of Survey that the dwelling house and part of the Block-house were on Colo. Floyd's land, and the other part of the Block-house and the greater part of the clearing were on vacant lands."

The next entry in this case is to be found on page 503 of the First order book of the Supreme Court as follows:

"Robert Patterson, William Mitchell, Andrew Steele, William Henderson, William McConnell, William Steele, and Robert Todd, trustees for the Town of Lexington.

against

John Bradford

Upon Caveat for
400 acres, etc.
Dfs.

"This day came the parties aforesaid by their attorneys and thereupon all and singular the premises being seen and the court fully under-

stood. It is therefore considered by the Court
that the plaintiffs recover against the said defendant all the land that is comprehended
within the bounds laid out and established for
the said town of Lexington, and it is ordered
that the surveyor of Fayette do survey and
ascertain the quantity of land claimed by said
defendant and which is comprehended within
the bounds of the said town and return a Plat
thereof with a report in this Court. and it is
further considered by the Court that the Plaintiffs recover against the defendant their costs
in this behalf expended."

This seems to have ended the attempt of John
Bradford to claim the site of the town of Lexington.
He was more successful along Cane Run and North
Elkhorn.

The next few meetings of the trustees were con-
sumed with unimportant items but at a meeting held
July 28, 1787, when a full board was present, Robert
Patterson, John Parker, Samuel Blair, John Coburn,
Robert Barr and James Parker:

"Resolved—that a part of inlot No. 43, containing two poles front, on Main street, and six
poles back, adjoining lot No. 44, be granted to
John Bradford, on condition that the printing
press be established in the Town of Lexington,
in consideration of which Mr. Bradford shall
be entitled to the sole use of said lot as long
as the press continues in the Town, with the
right of preemption for the sum of five pounds,
if the press should be removed from the town."
    And further:—
"that said John Bradford, his heirs or as-
signs shall be forever prohibited from erecting
any improvements so as to injure the public
spring."

This entry represents the successful efforts of the
trustees to secure the Kentucky Gazette for the Town
of Lexington. The description of this lot reads—
"where the garrison formerly stood."

At the meeting held on March 7, 1788, the trustees
"Resolved—that such persons whose lots are injured
by the present course of the branch have the liberty
of turning the course of same as near the public
ground as the nature of the situation will admit." They
also ordered all streets to be opened by the first of
August 1788, and further, prohibited any one from
cutting timber from any of the public lots.

It was the custom of the Trustees to meet in
various taverns such as Higbee's, Young's or Megowan's
and at least one meeting was held in the home of
Robert Patterson on West High street. After 1789
the notices usually read "at the court house." On
August 15, 1790 they issued orders—"The public spring
on Main street and the one near the school house, no
longer be used as washing places."

On August 11, 1791 Peter Higbee settled his accounts as Collector of the town taxes, amounting to
99 pounds, 13 shillings. John Keiser was the next
collector and the following year he collected even 100
pounds. James Morrison was elected treasurer for the
board for 1795 and made his report on last day of the
year showing collections totaling 121 pounds, 13 shillings. Evidently these amounts were not sufficient so
the board authorized the Masonic lodge to conduct a
lottery the money from which was to go towards
repairs of the streets, bridges, pavings, sinking wells,
erecting pumps, etc.

Hugh McIlvane was the only member to appear
for a meeting dated June 6, 1796, and he adjourned
same. On July 12, 1797, the board resolved—"that no
person be allowed to fire a gun or pistol within the
limits of the town unless under absolute necessity."

A very irritating event is mentioned in the trustees'
minute book, that caused trouble and complaints against
our city fathers until recently, when we find on May
1, 1797, that the board resolved—

"On account of the town branch having over-
flowed several times, Andrew Holmes is directed to straighten the 'canal' on Water

street, from where it ends to John Cocke's
water mill, and to build a bridge across same
at Lower Street."

This effort to relieve the damages sustained by
the Main street merchants was not successful as further mention of this subject appears at frequent intervals, and on April 9, 1802, the Gazette says:

"The excessive rains on Friday last raised the
water to such extent in the garden of Robert
Bradley on Main street (now 138 West Main)
that it washed down his garden wall which
was of brick, 8 feet high and 100 feet long."

During the years 1798 and 1799 the trustees continued their efforts to have the pavements laid; "repair the canal on Main street, walling and covering
same, and opened a subscription to assist in paying for
same." They also filled up Main street and made it
level as far west as Mill street.

The accounts of the trustees show the Town owned
one yoke of oxen and a plow, and used slaves to work
on the streets. Among the accounts for October 22,
1798, S. Van Pelt was allowed 18 shillings for corn
supplied the oxen; A. Coleman for hire of his slave,
Simon and one unexplained item—"Two gals. whiskey
for two barrels of corn." Stephen Kenyon was paid
"for settling with driver of oxen and for the stone
gutter he built across Main street at Cross street."

After the beginning of the year 1800 the town
appeared to grow more rapidly as the board held more
frequent meetings and the minutes contain many pages
devoted to the opening of new streets, improving pavements, gutters, sinking wells and erecting pumps.

The pioneer method of government by a board of
trustees was changed in 1810, when the Legislature increased the number of board members and the size
of the town funds. In 1832 the Legislature incorporated
the town and under the terms of that act, the citizens
elected a board of councilmen who in turn elected a
mayor.

The minute book of the trustees was rebound several years ago and it is possible some of the pages were bound out of their regular order. The ink on many of the pages has faded badly and it is hoped they will be copied or photostated and thus preserved for future generations, as the earliest written record of the Town Fathers in the interests of the Town of Lexington.

THE MEDICINE MEN.

FOR many months after the erection of the first block house there was no person within many miles who was properly entitled to call himself a doctor. Just who was the first physician to settle in Lexington remains a matter of doubt. Two regularly graduated physicians early appeared in the town of Lexington, but so far as is known did not appear in their medical capacity. William Fleming, a member of the First Land Court spent parts of the winter of 1779-1780 in and around Lexington attending sessions of that court.

James Wilkinson came to Lexington in 1784 and opened a store, but soon became interested in shipping Kentucky products down the river. His career after this episode carried him far beyond the Town of Lexington.

Tradition has Dr. Richard W. Downing arriving in the town of Lexington during 1787, but first record found of him is when he paid taxes in 1791. He resided on the north side of Main street just west of Broadway. He was Surgeon's mate to Colonel Griffith's battalion in the Maryland Line during the Revolutionary war.[1] He died in Lexington August 25, 1812.

Dr. Andrew McKinley, first of record in the Kentucky Gazette advertisement dated August 8, 1789 and in subsequent issues.

Dr. Hugh Sheil employed by James Wilkinson to conduct a store in Lexington (see Wilkinson's letters, in Kentucky Historical Society Register, dated 2 September 1784—31 March 1785 and 16 July 1784). Dr. Sheil also is mentioned in the deposition of Christopher Greenup in suit of John Coburn vs. Mary McConnell.[2] Dr. Sheil's estate was administered by his widow in September 1787. She afterwards married Judge Harry Innes.

1 Register Kentucky State Historical Society, Vol. 6, page 17.
2 Land Trials Book "A", page 82—Fayette Circuit Court.

A Dr. —— Beatty's name appears in the Kentucky Gazette dated November 14, 1788, when he advertises "he is leaving Lexington and desires all that owe him to call and settle."

Dr. Thomas Lloyd's name appears on the tax books for the year of 1789 when he paid taxes on one tithable and three horses. His name does not appear in such record after 1792.

Dr. P. Rootes' name is first found in the Kentucky Gazette dated January 29, 1791, when he advertises "he will write a book on treatment of nervous diseases," etc. No record has been found of such book. He came to Fayette county in 1790 in charge of the slaves of the Meridith family and the library at Winton still has "a complete English Dispensatory" left by him.

Dr. James Welch came to Lexington in 1795 from Virginia to be pastor of the Presbyterian Church at Short and Mill. His subsequent career is told elsewhere in this book.

On May 7, 1791 Dr. Basil Duke received a deed for inlot on southeast corner of Second and Mill streets from the trustees of Lexington, indicating he had been a resident for six months. In June 1796 Dr. Duke and his wife, Charlotte, conveyed this same lot to Dr. Frederick Ridgely. In 1796 Dr. Duke removed to Mason county where he served on a committee with Judge Coburn to receive bids for the erection of Washington Academy.

Dr. John Hole is first mentioned in the issue of the Gazette of July 19, 1792, when he advertised "just received a new line of fresh genuine medicines at my store where I continue to practice physic." His name does not appear in any tax book after 1793.

Dr. Daniel Preston's name is found only in the trustees' book for the town of Lexington, December 26, 1791 (page 37) when he presented his account against the town, amounting to 20 pounds, 13 shillings which was ordered paid.

Dr. Frederick W. Ridgely, born in Maryland, surgeon in Rifle Corps during the Revolutionary War and under General Anthony Wayne in Ohio campaign. In Kentucky Gazette dated December 8, 1792 is found his advertisement announcing the opening of a drug store with Dr. Basil Duke as partner, on Short street opposite court house. This partnership was dissolved in 1797. He married a sister of Peyton Short. In 1799, Dr. Ridgely was elected to one of the chairs in the Transylvania Medical school. He died, aged 68 at Dayton, Ohio, Nov. 21, 1824. Mrs. Short died in Lexington, March 18, 1822.

Dr. James Watkins' name first appears in Kentucky Gazette February 10, 1795, when an advertisement mentions he "was in charge of Dr. Ridgeley's practice for several months during the absence of the latter in the East."

Dr. John Watkins had been in Lexington for some time prior to May 3, 1797, as upon this date Attorney Chas. W. Bird advertised he would settle with those who owed accounts to Dr. Watkins.

Dr. James Collins advertises in Gazette dated November 28, 1795 "just furnished my shop with a new assortment of medicines, where I practice as usual Surgery and Physic."

Dr. Thomas Huff's name is found in the day book of Hunt's store for July 1796, showing he purchased articles for household use.

Dr. John W. Scott's name appears in the same record for October 1796.

Dr. Samuel Brown's name first appears in the Kentucky Gazette dated September 5, 1795, when he advertises "he will practice medicine—opposite Stewart's printing office, and will take one or two students who come well recommended." In 1799 he accepted one of the chairs in Transylvania Medical School. He was the first Kentucky physician to inoculate for the small pox and was also "the founder of the Kappa Lambda Association."

Dr. Walter Warfield, was deeded a lot in Lexington by the town trustees on December 20, 1797, showing he had been a resident at least six months.

Dr. Peter Trisler came to Lexington in 1791 at the head of a Moravian colony who settled along Jessamine creek and the territory south of Lexington. His advertisements appear in the Kentucky Gazette.

Dr. Walter Brashear came to Lexington from Bullitt county and studied under Dr. Ridgely for two years. Married Margaret Barr and after practicing his profession for several years in Lexington, he removed to Louisiana where he later became United States Senator.

Dr. C. Freeman advertised in Gazette dated August 8, 1798 that "he was regularly bred to the Surgery—and lived four years amongst 22 tribes of Indians studying their use of erbs and simples."

Dr. ——— Essex's name first appears in the Gazette dated September 19, 1798, when he advertises "Physician and surgeon—will cure dog bites, jaundice and complaints incident to the human body."

Dr. Joseph Boswell, born in Rockingham County, Virginia in 1778, came to Lexington in 1786, served as surgeon's mate in 4th U. S. Regiment of Infantry in 1799-1800. Married Judith Bell Gist, daughter of Nathaniel Gist and resided on northeast corner of Mill and Short streets. He died in 1833 from treating cholera patients.

Dr. James Fishback is first mentioned in Gazette for September 10, 1802, when he formed a partnership with Dr. Ridgely. He was admitted to the practice of law in 1803, and accepted a chair in the Transylvania Medical school in 1805. In 1819, he was ordained as Minister of the Baptist church and led one division of a split in that denomination. In 1829, he joined the Disciples movement under Barton W. Stone and continued to preach until his death in 1845.

Dr. Alexander Patrick's name first appears in an advertisement dated July 30, 1805: "Have opened a

supply of medicines at house of Mr. Bodley where I
practice Physic and Surgery."

Dr. H. G. Galloway's name first appears in the
Gazette dated January 4, 1803.

Dr. Thomas Davis' name first appears in the Tax
books in 1803.

Dr. William Watts' first appears in Tax books for
the same year.

Dr. Steele's name first appears in the Gazette July
10, 1804, when "he formed partnership with Dr. Fishback to practice surgery."

Dr. ―――― Barry's name for the first time appears
in the Gazette dated September 15, 1806, when he
advertises "will practice medicine at Major Boyd's
room, formerly the Post Office."

Dr. B. W. Dudley's name first appears in the
Gazette for November 20, 1806 when he "formed partnership with Dr. Fishback." Graduate at Transylvania
under Drs. Ridgely and Fishback, he was appointed
to chair of anatomy and surgery of that school and
remained connected with it over forty years. His
reputation rests upon his operations for stone in the
bladder, which he performed 225 times. He was
charged with being behind the plan for removal of the
medical school to Louisville but managed to escape
the odium, although openly accused by other members
of the faculty in a series of pamphlets.

There were probably many more doctors entered
into practice in the town of Lexington, but who, finding considerable competition, closed their "shops" and
passed to the south and west.

The records at Transylvania contain several references to an attempt to organize a Kentucky State
Medical Society. The only item found in the Gazette
is in the issue of February 18, 1804:

"John Pope, Thomas Wallace, George Trotter
Jr., Daniel Bradford, James Fishback, Andrew
McCalla, and Thomas Bradley announce they

are managers for a lottery the proceeds of which will go towards building a house for the Kentucky Medical Society at Lexington."

This effort was successful and the house was completed but evidently used only a few years. No reference to this Society is to be found in the records of the Kentucky State Medical Society, organized at Frankfort in October, 1851.

Of all the diseases "that human flesh is heir to" none is mentioned in the pages of the Gazette, before 1806 so frequently as the dreaded small pox. The disease was very common among the early pioneers, and frequent reference to it is found in the tales of travelers passing through this country. On January 4, 1794 the Gazette says:

> "On Thursday last the inhabitants of this place began the inoculation of the small pox, and have agreed to continue until the 15th, after which they are determined to cease. They have appointed a committee to draw up a remonstrance to the court of Fayette county, requesting that the orders of the court granting liberty to the inhabitants of said county to inoculate, may be rescinded as far as respects the town of Lexington after that date."

Again, in the Gazette dated February 1, 1794, this is found:

> "The small pox has within three weeks proved extremely fatal within this town and its vicinity under inoculation. From the best information we have been able to collect, at least one out of every fifteen that were inoculated have died; it has proved very fatal to young children as very few of that description have recovered."

In May 1801, another scare arose over this disease and the Gazette began a strong educational plan with many articles advocating the practice of inoculation.

Copies of letters from famous medical practitioneers from England and various parts of the United States commending the new practice were published until the Gazette was able to publish "many thousands of our citizens have passed through that disease."

These pioneer medical men of Kentucky left but few written records. Their remarkable achievements in preserving the lives of the settlers would read like romance had there been a channel for the preservation of their deeds. Denied consultation with any one whose opinion was of value, or the use of hospitals and only scant libraries, our medical men were largely dependent upon their courage, skill and ingenuity in the treatment of patients.

Truly, they served life, and the lives of the pioneers are their monuments.

THE POST OFFICE AND POST MEN.

THE confusion incident to the organization of the Federal Government, after the Revolutionary War, caused the postal authorities to neglect the area west of the Alleghany mountains for a number of years. With the unsettled conditions and the dangers incident to the "Wilderness Road" the early settlers of Lexington and the surroundings had to avail themselves of the services of traders and such travelers as journeyed to the eastern settlements to have their letters carried over the mountains "back home." This was, at best, a very uncertain service, but it was all that was available to the pioneers. Some of the wealthy frequently employed messengers to carry correspondence for them. It was much easier to receive letters from the east, than to send an aswer to "the old settlements." Many emigrants from Virginia and Maryland arrived in central Kentucky, with messages, letters and packages from the "folks back east," delivering them in person, if possible, or left at trading places "until called for." On numerous occasions the mail was lost by the death of the carrier from accident or disease.

After the river route became established the mail and eastern newspapers were sent by boats from Pittsburg to Limestone and then forwarded to Lexington along "Smith's Road," by any traveler bound for the town of Lexington.

This very uncertain method of communication existed until July 1787, when John Bradford established "The Kentucke Gazette." He used post riders to deliver the paper to distant points and these men were instructed to bring to his office the various items sent in by the correspondents of the paper, the gossip of the taverns and villages along their routes. These riders made regular trips, carrying message and packages addressed to the residents of Lexington, which were deposited in the office of the Gazette, where Mr.

Bradford maintained a letter box for the convenience of the citizens. On March 6, 1790 he published a list of such letters on hand.

This was the mail service the pioneers of Lexington had until September, 1794, when the Federal Government, recognizing the needs of a growing community, established a post office in Lexington, with Innes Baxter Brent as first postmaster. Born in Prince William county, Virginia, he came to Kentucky early in 1791, and soon afterwards was made a deputy-sheriff and afterwards served as jailor for Fayette county. He kept the post office in the public room of the jail, then located on north side of Main street, about where No. 409 West Main now is. He kept a long box with pigeon holes across the mantle over the fireplace in which the letters and papers were arranged.

The postage was very high in comparison to present day services. For 30 miles and under, 6 cents; over 30 and under 80 miles, ten cents; over 100 miles and under 400 miles, 25 cents. In some cases the sender paid the postage, but usual custom was for the receiver to pay the carrier. In 1806, the postage rate was raised 20 per cent and rates on pamphlets increased to 1 cent per sheet.

During the winter months all mails were very irregular, and frequently no mail was received in Lexington for weeks. The contract for carrying the mails expired January 1, 1798 and no mails were received by the river route until late in March. A small quantity was received from the South, but this route was never popular, on account of the difficulties and constant attacks on the riders. On April 25, 1793, the Gazette announces; "the post rider was ambushed by Indians on Laurel river and killed."

In 1796, post routes were established from Lexington to the various points in Central Kentucky, and mails were dispatched once each week to surrounding towns and Louisville. The riders were welcomed all along the line and carried much gossip by word of mouth. Upon arrival at a village they were immediately surrounded with a host of loafers and admiring friends, who wanted "all the news", together with such embellishments as the riders could add to the facts. By this means, happenings in other communities were broadcast and those living in sparsely settled communities were advised on events, politics, war or pestilence.

Mr. Peter G. Voorhies seems to have served a short time as postmaster, and was succeeded by John Wesley Hunt, who received his appointment from President John Adams, April, 1799. Born in Trenton, New Jersey, his father was post master at that point before the Revolutionary War and was host to the German Commander Colonel Rall, when General Washington and his Continental soldiers captured that post Christmas 1776. During Mr. Hunt's term of office he removed the office to Postlethwait's tavern at Main and Mulberry, where it remained until July 1, 1801, upon which date it was removed to the office of the Kentucky Gazette, on site of what is now 330 West Main street. Andrew McCalla was the assistant under Mr. Hunt during his term of office.

In 1800, a mail route was established from Lexington to Washington, D. C., by way of Wyandotte (now in West Virginia), Owingsville, Mt. Sterling and Winchester. Mail passed over this route every two weeks. Another route was established from Lexington to Robinson's court house (now Nashville, Tenn.) by way of Frankfort, Shelbyville, Bardstown, Russelville on which there were frequent delays. In 1801, the mail which had been arriving via the Wilderness Road was held up at Cheek's cross roads for seven weeks on account of no post rider being willing to make the trip and the Gazette says: "The newspapers all over the land are complaining about the inefficiency of the service."

John Jordan, Jr., an English-born pioneer, was the next postmaster, having been appointed by President

Thomas Jefferson on July 1, 1802 and he held this office until his death September 9, 1813.

After 1808 many changes were made in the methods and facilities for handling the mails and the service became more dependable.

The close of the year of 1806 rings down the curtain upon the first quarter of a century that had passed since that day in 1779 when the settlers drew for lots upon which to build their cabins, and when Fayette county comprised one-third of the State. The little Town of Lexington had made considerable progress in the art of living and in commercial endeavors. With the fields covered with cattle, sheep, and hogs, the absence of the wild game meats were not felt.

Many orchards and vineyards had been planted. Slaves worked gardens, free from the depredation of prowling savages, and supplied turnips, cabbages, beets, peas, juicy corn and fat potatoes to the tables more bountifully than when the fare was limited to deer meat, wild turkeys and corn pone. Tobacco, hemp, barley, oats and wheat were growing on many sloping acres around the town, while corn and rye began the journey through the distilleries to make Kentucky famous.

Transylvania University, the medical school, the Law school and the many private schools brought strangers to popularize the juicy steaks at the Fried Meat Club, or the seductive drinks at Postlethwait's tavern.

"The land shark had not been legislated out of business, and many Blue Grass acres were held with cloudy titles," but the little town of Lexington was far out on the road to a permanent prosperity. The Navigator, published in Pittsburg in 1807, says: "Lexington has about 400 houses, many of them handsome, and about 2,000 people. Thirty mercantile stores, several wholesale, a public academy, two printing offices, a weekly Gazette, one book store (Maccoun,

Tilford & Co.) one book binder. William Essex has one large duck factory and one cotton and muslin factory. There are four rope walks and two nail factories. It is a place of great business."

The zenith of manufacturing prosperity was reached in 1810, and in 1816 the capital invested in factories amounted to $2,337,125. From 1810 to 1820 the roads radiating from Lexington were filled with wagon trains and pack horses, headed to the South and West transporting Lexington's productions. Herds of cattle and horses passed through Cumberland Gap to the East, while droves of mules began the long journey to the cotton fields of Mississippi, Louisiana and South Carolina.

On the horizon of all this prosperity appeared a long dark pall of smoke stretching away until dispelled by the breezes of the Ohio. With the arrival of the first steamboat at the wharfs of Louisville on the first successful up-the-river trip, there began the decline of Lexington's supremacy as a manufacturing center. With the rapid growth of that form of carriage the regular channels of trade were completely changed. The arrival of the first train in Lexington in December 1835 was "too late to prevent the exodus of manufacturers to the river ports, but did prevent Lexington from degenerating into a mere cross roads village."

A century and a half have passed since the first cabin was built in Lexington. Many changes have occurred during these years, and many more will occur in the next decade, but it is hoped these lines will help to keep alive the names and deeds of those pioneers who built for us a community beyond their fondest hopes.

INDEX

INDEX 349

Minute Book of Trustees
309, 311
Mirando's Expedition 245
Mississippi River Naviga-
tion 61, 96, 100, 114
Mitchell, David 5, 8, 11, 14,
19, 23, 24, 38, 309
Mitchell, Hiram 119, 131
Mitchell, Rev. James 304
Mitchell, James 12
Mitchell, William 8, 11,
14, 307, 310, 317
Mitchem, Dudley 99
Mock's Mill 134
Mockquort, Henry 176
Molloy, Anthony 89
Money, Early 37
Money Shipments 182
Monks, Richard 68, 258
Monroe, James 38
Montgomery, Alexander 123
Moody & Downing..........127, 132
Moody, James........139, 183, 312
Moore, Rev. James
283, 284, 304, 305
Moore, John 58
Moore, Moses 51
Moore, William 90, 148
Moore & Beeler 162
Morahan, J. 271
Moravian Settlers 141, 321
Morgan, Charles 77, 78, 97
Morgan's station 92, 93
Morrison, James
89, 102, 103, 106,
110, 112, 113, 118,
127, 128, 131, 139,
153, 162, 191, 203,
213, 218, 259, 315
Morrison, John 6, 7, 8, 12, 14,
18, 19, 23, 79, 95, 105
Morrison, Nathaniel 256
Morrow, James 11, 12, 14,
15, 20, 22, 102
Morrow & McClelland 162
Morton, John 253
Morton Junior High School 269
Morton, Miss Molly 207
Morton, William
46, 58, 63, 71, 75,
76, 78, 90, 117, 140,
186, 206, 207, 218, 224,
242, 243, 255, 283, 284
Morton's store 154

Morton's Tan Yard........68, 207
Mosby, Littlebery 312
Mosby, Captain Robert 49
Moss, Frederick 89
Mount Hope 27, 80
Mount Sterling established
89, 92
Mount Zion Church
269, 301, 302
Moyland, John 76, 89, 93
Muldrow, Hugh 148
Mullanphy, John 146
Munet, Samuel 184, 303
Murphy, Jeremiah 202,
232, 259, 288
Murphy, John 276
Murphy's Tavern 202
Murray, William..............97, 102,
167, 296
Music School 200
Muter, George 147, 148
Myers, Jacob 153
Myers, Melchoir 80, 126,
153, 169, 258

N

Nabb & Company 154
Naff & Polk 175
Nails 165
Nail prices 171
Nail Machine 124, 187
Nail Manufactory..........94, 101,
150, 170, 178
Naming of Lexington 7
Nancarrow, John 92
Napper, John 20, 23
Nash, William N
217, 233, 259
Natchez, Miss. 137
Naturalization of
Foreign born 291
Navigation, Mississippi
River 96
Neal, Archibald 93
Nelson, Admiral Lord 236
Netherland, Benjamin......12, 22
Neutrality Proclamation
97, 109
Newell, John 11, 190, 197
New Fort, Lexington 22
New Light Schism 201
Newman, George 256
New Orleans, Louisiana 56
New Orleans Embargo 184

354   INDEX

Shannon, Hugh 7, 11, 110
Shannon, Rev. Samuel 272
Shannon, William 11, 20
Shannon's Mill 110
Sharp, Ebeneezer....218, 255, 263
Sharp, John 12
Sharp, Richard 310
Shaw, Chester 259
Shaw, Hiram 142, 218, 256
Shaw, John Robert,
    "Life and Adventures" 248
Shaw, John Robert......134, 135,
    150, 199, 239, 248, 250, 253
Shaw, Nathaniel 120, 123,
                134, 179, 194
Shawnee Indian School 204
"Sheaf of Wheat" 34, 149
Sheely, Daniel 284
Sheil, Dr. Hugh 29, 318
Shelby, Isaac 80, 81, 83,
                84, 95, 99
Shelbyville Established 89
Shellers, William 253
Shepherdsville Established....97
Shepperd, George 12, 309
Sheriff's collections 91
Shevil, Frederick 256
Shoe Manufactory....150, 174, 203
Shoemaker—Mulatto 35
Shohoney, James 258
Shooting Match 171
Short, Miss 136
Shortridge, Daniel 209
"Shower of Blood" 201
Shields, John 250
Shingle Prices 198
Shinglebower, George
                195, 229, 256
Shinglebower's Tavern 195
Ship—"Ann" 225
Ship—"General Scott"....217, 239
Ship—"Kentucky" 220
Shipment on River 181
Shipp, Caleb 29
Ships detained by low
    water 217
"Short and Easy Method
    With Deists" 164
Short, Peyton 65, 70,
                77, 78, 136, 320
Short Street fences 73
Shrock, John 144
Shryock, Mathias 256
Sidner, Peter 144

Sidewalks 149
Siers, Daniel 150
"Sign of Boot, Shoe &
    Slipper" 94
"Sign of the Buffalo"....34, 62,
    97, 106, 173, 183, 219
"Sign of the Cross
    Keyes" 35
"Sign of the Golden
    Boot" 192, 204
"Sign of the Spinning
    Wheel" 80, 89, 194, 206
"Sign of the Square &
    Compass" 235
"Sign of the Still" 236
"Sign of the Umbrella" 238
"Sign of the White Horse"..222
Sign Painters 125
Silversmiths............65, 105, 173
Simon & Brown 162
Simmons, M. D. 43
Simpson, Ezekiel 120
Simpson, Joseph 121
Singing School 136
Sinking Creek 112
"Sketches of Tour to
    Western Country" 261
Slaback, Solomon 120
Slate creek Iron works....93, 110
Slater, John 157
Slave Census 155
Slave Churches 285, 286
Slaves, First in Lexington....15
Slaves hired out 92
Slave unrest 162, 180
Slave owners vs.
    Methodists 276
Slave Preacher 285
"Slavery Inconsistent with
    Justice" 164
Sloan, John 259
Sloo, Thomas 76
Small Change 31
Small Pox Epidemic......175, 177
Small Pox, First
    Inoculation 320, 323
Smart, George 102, 107
Smedley, Christopher
                155, 232, 254
Smith, George S. 75
Smith, James & Richard 120
Smith, John, Adventures of 164
Smith, John 66, 103, 104, 281
Smith's Wagon Road 37, 325